The Bible and Social Justice

McMaster Divinity College Press
McMaster New Testament Series

Patterns of Discipleship in the New Testament (1996)

The Road from Damascus: The Impact of Paul's Conversion on His Life, Thought and Ministry (1997)

Life in the Face of Death: The Resurrection Message of the New Testament (1998)

The Challenge of Jesus' Parables (2000)

Into God's Presence: Prayer in the New Testament (2001)

Reading the Gospels Today (2004)

Contours of Christology in the New Testament (2005)

Hearing the Old Testament in the New Testament (2006)

The Messiah in the Old and New Testaments (2007)

Translating the New Testament: Text, Translation, Theology (2009)

Christian Mission: Old Testament Foundations and New Testament Developments (2010)

Empire in the New Testament (2011)

The Church, Then and Now (2012)

Rejection: God's Refugees in Biblical and Contemporary Perspective (2015)

Rediscovering Worship: Past, Present, and Future (2015)

The Bible and Social Justice

*Old Testament and New Testament Foundations
for the Church's Urgent Call*

edited by

Cynthia Long Westfall

and

Bryan R. Dyer

PICKWICK *Publications* · Eugene, Oregon

THE BIBLE AND SOCIAL JUSTICE
Old Testament and New Testament Foundations for the Church's Urgent Call

Pickwick Publications
An Imprint of Wipf and Stock Publishers
199 W. 8th Ave., Suite 3
Eugene, OR 97401

McMaster Divinity College Press
1280 Main St. W.
Hamilton, ON, Canada
L8S 4K1

www.wipfandstock.com

ISBN 13: 978-1-4982-3807-6

Manufactured in the U.S.A.   03/08/2016

Contents

Preface

THE 2012 H. H. Bingham Colloquium in the New Testament and Old Testament foundations at McMaster Divinity College in Hamilton Ontario, Canada was entitled "The Bible and Social Justice." The Colloquium was the sixteenth in a continuing series held here at the College. At the Colloquium, scholars from all over North America shared insights from representative selections across the biblical literature to address this important and controversial biblical theme, insights that demonstrated continuity and diversity in the way social justice was addressed and implemented in Israel and the early church. An interested public attended, heard the papers, and responded with insightful questions and comments resulting in a fruitful exchange among the public and the scholars. We hope that this volume will be of interest to general readers and serve as a useful textbook or supplemental source for the study of the context of, content of, and interpretive approaches to the New Testament in the light of the Old Testament and to its relevance to the contemporary church. We also trust that it makes a cogent contribution to the ongoing discussion of this important topic and fills a gap by adding voices to the relatively small but growing scholarship that addresses biblical social justice.

The Bingham Colloquium is named after Dr. Herbert Henry Bingham, who was a noted Baptist leader in Ontario, Canada. His leadership abilities were recognized by Baptists across Canada and around the world. His qualities included his genuine friendship, dedicated leadership, unswerving Christian faith, tireless devotion to duty, insightful service as a preacher and pastor, and visionary direction for congregation and denomination alike. These qualities endeared him both to his own church members and to believers in other denominations. The Colloquium has been endowed by his daughter as an act of appreciation for her father. We are pleased to be able to continue this tradition.

The volumes in this series are published by McMaster Divinity College Press, in conjunction with Wipf & Stock Publishers of Eugene, Oregon. We appreciate this active publishing relationship.

Finally, we wish to express our thanks to the many scholars, students, and church leaders who attended and contributed to the Bingham Colloquium on The Bible and Social Justice. Special appreciation goes to Stanley E. Porter, the convener of the Bingham Colloquium, who encouraged the proposal of this topic for the 2012 meeting and graciously allowed us to organize and oversee the event. It is our prayer that the papers from this conference, collected in this volume, will encourage further thinking and academic study of the theme of God's justice within the words of Scripture. We further hope that these papers will challenge us as individuals, and collectively as the church, to live out God's clear call to seek out justice in our time and context.

Contributors

Shannon E. Baines (PhD McMaster Divinity College) wrote her dissertation on social justice within the Minor Prophets and the Pentateuch in the Old Testament. Her Master of Religion thesis was titled "Provisions for the Poor in the Laws of Deuteronomy." Shannon has worked at Yonge Street Mission as a Resource Worker serving the poor in downtown Toronto and was involved in the Mission's church for a number of years.

Mark J. Boda (PhD University of Cambridge) is Professor of Old Testament at McMaster Divinity College. He has authored 9 books, edited 17 volumes of collected essays, and written over 90 articles on various topics related to the Old Testament and Christian Theology. Key areas of his interest include Old Testament Theology, prayer and penitence in Old Testament and Christian Theology, and Babylonian and Persian Period Hebrew Books and History.

M. Daniel Carroll R. (PhD University of Sheffield) is Blanchard Professor of Old Testament at Wheaton College. Prior to this, he taught at Denver Seminary for many years. Before going to Denver, he was professor of Old Testament and ethics at Seminario Teológico Centroamericano in Guatemala City, Guatemala, and continues as adjunct there. He has written extensively on Old Testament ethics, focusing especially on the prophetic literature. Related to his work on prophetic ethics, he is involved in efforts to reform immigration legislation in the USA.

Bryan R. Dyer (PhD McMaster Divinity College) wrote his dissertation on the topics of suffering and death in Hebrews. Prior to this he worked for four years in full-time ministry and earned his MA from Denver Seminary. He is the co-editor of *Paul and Ancient Rhetoric* and currently works for Baker Academic as an Acquisitions Editor.

Contributors

CRAIG A. EVANS (PhD Claremont University) is the John Bisagno Distinguished Professor of Christian Orgins at Houston Baptist University. He taught at Acadia Divinity College for many years and also McMaster University and Trinity Western University. He has published many books and scholarly articles on Jesus and the Gospels, including "Jesus' Ethic of Humility," *Trinity Journal* 13 (1992) 127–38, which in 1993 was awarded a Templeton Prize in Humility Theology.

PAUL S. EVANS (PhD University of St. Michael's College) is Assistant Professor of Old Testament at McMaster Divinity College. He also taught biblical Studies at Ambrose University College and Seminary in Calgary, Alberta. He has published several articles on the books of Kings and Chronicles as well as an award-winning book on 2 Kings. He emphasizes the theological significance of the Old Testament and the value of its application for the church today.

DAVID L. MATHEWSON (PhD University of Aberdeen) is Associate Professor of New Testament at Denver Seminary. He has taught at Gordon College, Wenham, MA and at Gordon Conwell Theological Seminary. Dave has authored books and articles on Revelation, the Old Testament in the New Testament in Revelation, Greek grammar and linguistics, and verbal aspect, as well as difficult New Testament issues that can be resolved by linguistic analysis.

STANLEY E. PORTER (PhD University of Sheffield) is President, Dean, and Professor of New Testament at McMaster Divinity College. He has taught for over thirty years in post-secondary institutions in Canada, the USA, and the UK. His publications include 18 authored books and over 250 journal articles and chapters, along with over a hundred other shorter pieces; he has also edited nearly 80 volumes. Stan has a wide range of academic specialties. One of his recent publications is *How We Got the New Testament: Text, Transmission, Translation.*

CYNTHIA LONG WESTFALL (PhD University of Surrey) is Assistant Professor of New Testament at McMaster Divinity College. She has taught at all levels in institutions in North America, including Denver Seminary and Colorado Christian University. She has written and edited several books and written numerous articles about topics including Hebrews, Jewish

Christianity, discourse analysis, linguistics, and gender. In Denver and Hamilton, Ontario she has focused on urban discipleship and has ministered to those who are at risk for homelessness in the urban community.

Abbreviations

AB	Anchor Bible
ABD	*Anchor Bible Dictionary*, edited by David Noel Freeman. 6 vols. New York: Doubleday, 1992.
ABRL	Anchor Bible Reference Library
ANET	*Ancient Near Eastern Texts Relating to the Old Testament*. Edited by James B. Pritchard. 3rd ed. Princeton: Princeton University Press, 1969.
ASV	American Standard Version Bible
BBB	Bonner biblische Beiträge
BBR	*Bulletin for Biblical Research*
BBRSup	Bulletin for Biblical Research Supplements
BCOTWP	Baker Commentary on the Old Testament Wisdom and Psalms
BDB	Francis Brown, S. R. Driver, and Charles A. Briggs. *Hebrew and English Lexicon of the Old Testament*. Oxford: Clarendon, 1907.
BECNT	Baker Exegetical Commentary on the New Testament
BETL	Bibliotheca Ephemeridum Theologicarum Lovaniensium
Bib	*Biblica*
BibInt	Biblical Interpretation Series
BT	*The Bible Translator*
BZAW	Beihefte zur Zeitschrift für die alttestamentliche Wissenschaft
BZNW	Beihefte zur Zeitschrift für die neutestamentliche Wissenschaft
CBQ	*Catholic Biblical Quarterly*
ch(s).	*chapter(s)*
CHANE	Culture and History of the Ancient Near East

Abbreviations

DOTP	*Dictionary of the Old Testament Prophets*, edited by Mark J. Boda and J. Gordon McConville. Downers Grove, IL: InterVarsity, 2012.
esp.	especially
EvT	*Evangelische Theologie*
HBT	*Horizons in Biblical Theology*
IBC	Interpretation: A Bible Commentary for Teaching and Preaching
ICC	International Critical Commentary
Int	*Interpretation*
JBL	*Journal of Biblical Literature*
JETS	*Journal of the Evangelical Theological Society*
JGRChJ	*Journal of Greco-Roman Christianity and Judaism*
JJS	*Journal of Jewish Studies*
JSNT	*Journal for the Study of the New Testament*
JSNTSup	Journal for the Study of the New Testament Supplement Series
JSOT	*Journal for the Study of the Old Testament*
JSOTSup	Journal for the Study of the Old Testament Supplement Series
LBS	Linguistic Biblical Studies
LHBOTS	The Library of Hebrew Bible / Old Testament Studies
LNTS	The Library of New Testament Studies
MNTS	McMaster New Testament Studies
MT	Masoretic Text
n	note
NAC	New American Commentary
NCBC	New Century Bible Commentary
NIBCOT	New International Biblical Commentary on the Old Testament
NICNT	New International Commentary on the New Testament
NICOT	New International Commentary on the Old Testament

NIDB   *New Interpreter's Dictionary of the Bible*, edited by Katharine Doob Sakenfeld. 5 vols. Nashville: Abingdon, 2006–9.

NIDOTTE *New International Dictionary of Old Testament Theology and Exegesis.* Edited by Willem A. VanGemeren. 5 vols. Grand Rapids: Zondervan, 1997.

NIGTC   New International Greek Testament Commentary

NIVAC   New International Version Application Commentary

NTL   New Testament Library

NTM   New Testament Message

NTS   *New Testament Studies*

OBT   Overtures to Biblical Theology

OTL   Old Testament Library

PNTC   Pelican New Testament Commentaries

RBL   *Review of Biblical Literature*

SBL   Society of Biblical Literature

SBLDS   Society of Biblical Literature Dissertation Series

SBG   Studies in Biblical Greek

SNTA   Studiorum Novi Testamenti Auxilia

SNTSMS   Society for New Testament Studies Monograph Series

SOTSMS   Society for Old Testament Studies Monograph Series

STDJ   Studies on the Texts of the Desert of Judah

TDNT   *Theological Dictionary of the New Testament*, edited by Gerhard Kittel and Gerhard Friedrich. Translated by Geoffrey W. Bromily. 10 vols. Grand Rapids: Eerdmans, 1964–76.

TDOT   *Theological Dictionary of the Old Testament*, edited by G. Johannes Botterweck and Helmer Ringgren. Translated by John T. Willis et al. 8 vols. Grand Rapids: Eerdmans, 1974–2006.

THKNT   Theologischer Handkommentar zum Neuen Testament

TLNT   *Theological Lexicon of the New Testament*, by C. Spicq. Translated and edited by J. D. Ernest. 3 vols. Peabody, MA: Hendrickson, 1994.

TNTC	Tyndale New Testament Commentaries
TTZ	*Trierer theologische Zeitschrift*
UNICEF	United Nations Children's Fund
v(v).	verse(s)
VT	*Vetus Testamentum*
WBC	Word Biblical Commentary
WUNT	Wissenschaftliche Untersuchungen zum Neuen Testament
YNER	Yale Near Eastern Researches
ZAW	*Zeitschrift für die alttestamentliche Wissenschaft*
ZNW	*Zeitschrift für die neutestamentliche Wissenschaft und die Kunde der älteren Kirche*

Introduction

CYNTHIA LONG WESTFALL AND BRYAN R. DYER

IT HAS BEEN ARGUED that a cry for justice is heard throughout the pages of Scripture. It is found in Israel's laws and commands, explored in its wisdom literature, and demanded by its prophets. It can be found in the teachings of Jesus, then repeated throughout the writings of the early church, and it serves as the background for Paul's teaching and exhortations. The call to implement God's justice here on earth, what we might deem "social justice," remains vital to the church in its present context, but it needs definition and further discussion. In recent years, the term *social justice* has become politicized, criticized, and often used with a variety of meanings and for a variety of causes.

Our understanding of biblical social justice is this repeated cry for God's justice throughout Scripture that targets conditions and behavior in the biblical writers' days that correspond to conditions and oppression in our current local and global context. Often, however, social justice is defined not by words but by action: helping the poor, caring for the outcast, and giving a voice to the oppressed. It incorporates exposing injustice and confronting the systems that bring about oppression. This is no small task, and the pages of Scripture testify to its significance. Surprisingly, however, an exploration of this theme in the Bible is lacking in most academic and church circles. Such an important biblical concept deserves faithful and earnest attention by scholars who take the Bible's cry for justice seriously with an eye to how it might be lived out in today's context.

To meet this need, the 2012 Bingham Colloquium focused on the topic "The Bible and Social Justice." The colloquium brought together scholars from across North America to present substantial papers exploring the biblical theme of social justice. Each paper was presented to a room of academic scholars, graduate students, and church practitioners. The conversations following each paper were lively and constructive and discussions continued well after the colloquium concluded. Our hope is that rigorous study of the biblical theme of social justice was met with practical concerns for how the church might respond to our world's cry for justice in the name of Christ. The eight papers are collected here in an effort to extend this conversation and to contribute to the much-needed resources concerning social justice for both academic and church study.

The first paper, by Paul S. Evans on the Covenant Code in Exodus 21–23, examines the role of Old Testament law in developing a biblical theology of social justice. By focusing on this particular law code, held by some to be the most ancient in biblical literature, Evans fleshes out the concern for justice in a text that often seems to have little contemporary relevance. To gain better understanding, Evans first places Exodus 21–23 within the context of other law codes in the ancient Near East. Such legal literature was common in the ANE and Israel's concern for the marginalized went beyond what was found in the surrounding cultures. Looking at the purpose of the law code, Evans argues that instead of functioning as true laws, the code was created—at least partially—to teach the principles behind legislative laws.

The bulk of Evans's paper consists of a comparative reading of the Covenant Code and other ANE law codes. Examining such issues as class distinctions, concern for the vulnerable, slavery, and punishments, he concludes that Israel's law code demonstrates a higher concern for justice than other ANE documents. This has implications for the church today, and Evans brings attention to how the principles of the Covenant Code translate to contemporary issues—including care for the poor, alien, widow, orphan, and slave. Movement to contemporary culture brings certain tensions, however, as Israel's law code often fails to meet the ethical standards of the twenty-first century. The morality of the Covenant Code therefore has certain limitations, as many of its laws fall short of full rights for the marginalized and implementation of ethical ideals. In response to this, Evans points to the hermeneutic of suspicion, demonstrated by Jesus in Matthew 19 regarding divorce. If the Mosaic law on divorce, while demonstrating a higher ethic than its ANE counterparts, can be understood as an accommodation to hard-heartedness and not an ethical ideal, might we not also see aspects of the Covenant Code in this light? If so, Evans argues, approaching these texts with a similar "suspicious reading" allows for identifying the redemptive direction of Israel's laws while noting their limitations. While not easy, this is the task set before modern Christians when examining these sometimes difficult passages of sacred Scripture.

In the second paper, Mark J. Boda and Shannon E. Baines examine the relationship between social justice and the Old Testament Wisdom Literature. Their exploration is positioned in relationship to recent scholarship—particularly that of Pleins, Malchow, and Houston—which disagree on the degree to which this literature addresses the issues of poverty/wealth and justice/injustice. Boda and Baines begin with the book of Proverbs—showing that through the genre of pithy sayings the book articulates a concern for justice in all facets of life. While recent studies have limited concepts of social justice to matters pertaining to aspects of poverty, Proverbs also speaks to justice in matters of honest living and fair treatment of others.

Moving to the more philosophical stream of wisdom literature, Boda and Baines show how Ecclesiastes presents the sobering realities of human existence—particularly in relation to justice and economics. The author's strategy is first to recognize the futility of life given these realities and then to present a mediating view between valuing wealth and praising poverty. In addition, the author encourages the readers to live in the assurance that God will judge oppression. The book of Job, according to Boda and Baines, affirms the significance of social justice within the wisdom tradition while at the same time challenging its notions of justice. Further, Job demonstrates a movement away from an anthropocentric fixation on humanity, with a reminder of humanity's place within the cosmos.

The third paper, by M. Daniel Carroll R., turns our attention to the prophetic literature with its cry for justice and emphatic defense of the vulnerable. Focusing on Amos 5:1–17, Carroll identifies the essential elements of the message of justice found throughout the prophetic literature. He identifies this section of Amos as a chiasm and uses each of its corresponding sections to draw out the concern for justice found within. The outside sections of this passage (5:1–3, 16–17) are concerned with the punishments and violence of God toward injustice and those who perpetuate it—a topic of much debate. As Carroll points out, it is often emphasized that God demands justice but rarely do such discussions delve into *how* God responds to injustice with punishment within history. As these verses make clear, a commitment to justice demands a developed theology of divine judgment.

The second set of verses in the chiasm (5:4–6, 14–15) makes clear that justice is a vital part of acceptable religion before Yahweh. Religion must include a desire for justice, a call for virtue, and a future hope for global justice. Amos 5:7 and 5:10–13 make up the next set of verses, which describe the abuse of justice in Israel. As such, these verses specify what justice entails in practice. As Carroll points out, justice must be tied to legal principle along with moral principle—while the legal aspect may change in different contexts, the moral principle remains the same. Finally, Amos 5:8–9, the center of the chiasm, grounds the concept of justice in the person of Yahweh. The demand for justice is established in the heart of God and his absolute sovereignty guarantees future global justice.

The fourth paper, by Craig A. Evans, looks at the language of "justice" or "righteousness" (δικαιοσύνη, δίκαιος) in the Gospels of Mark and Matthew. As Evans points out, this vocabulary, and the theological concepts to which it gives expression, is complex and the Greek words are often translated in a variety of ways. With this understanding, Evans explores each occurrence of justice and righteousness language in Mark and Matthew—along with references to these concepts without the presence of these particular words. This last point is especially significant for the Gospel of Mark, where the notions of justice and righteousness are presupposed in the narrative and presentation of Jesus' teaching. While words from the δίκαιος family appear just twice in Mark's Gospel, Evans demonstrates how the concepts find expression in other ways. Mark could have been more explicit in his inclusion of justice/righteousness concepts but was content to let the implications of Jesus' teaching speak for themselves.

The Gospel of Matthew contains substantially more references to δίκαιος and its cognates than Mark (28 appearances). Dividing these occurrences into the material Matthew inherited from Mark and Q along with the material unique to Matthew's Gospel, Evans first surveys the material and then explores the meaning in each use. Evans argues that most occurrences of δίκαιος and δικαιοσύνη refer to ethical requirements—things that God and/or Jesus expect of his people. This does not account for all of the uses, as Evans also shows where God's own righteousness is being referred to.

In the fifth paper, Bryan R. Dyer examines the theme of justice in the life and teaching of Jesus and his earliest followers in Luke–Acts. Looking first at how justice was understood in Old Testament prophetic literature, Dyer argues that this served as the background upon which Luke presented Jesus' ministry. In the Gospel of Luke, quotations, allusions, and appeals to this prophetic literature—especially Isaiah—become the lens through which the author portrays Jesus' emphasis on justice. Among many passages in Luke's Gospel, 4:18–19 is significant in that Jesus quotes from Isaiah to initiate and orient his public ministry as "good news for the poor." Jesus' concern for the poor—a term that includes various marginalized groups—certainly has a spiritual dimension, but Dyer argues that meeting people's physical needs is a genuine concern for Jesus in Luke's Gospel.

In the Acts of the Apostles, the emphasis on justice is continued by the early Christian community—although references to the prophetic tradition are noticeably fewer. Yet the author presents the community as one where "there was not a needy person among them." This description not only met an ideal of Greco-Roman society, but also fulfills Yahweh's standard of justice. Further, in Acts, Luke emphasizes the practice of almsgiving as a counter-cultural response to the poor and needy. More than simply a one-time monetary donation, almsgiving, according to Dyer, should be understood as genuine solidarity with those in need and an undermining of cultural norms that perpetuate injustice.

The sixth paper, by Stanley E. Porter, examines the notion of social justice in Paul's letters. He begins by noting the shortcomings of the term "social justice" and reframes his use within a larger conception of human behavior in relation to God. This certainly has a social dimension, and Porter continues by setting the stage of the social world into which Paul's letters speak. Three groups are highlighted as particularly disenfranchised by means of their socio-economic position within Roman society—women, slaves, and foreigners (including the Jews). Porter shows how Paul spoke directly to the heart of this socio-economic imbalance in the Roman world, focusing particularly on Gal 3:28.

Porter points out that Paul's response to the Roman socio-economic structure is the competing institution of the church. All of the major statements by Paul on socio-economic relations are grounded within the framework of what it means to be a follower of Christ. This causes believers to transform their own relationships into bonds within a new family—with God or Christ as the *paterfamilias*. Membership within this community carries its own obligations—one of which is the care of other members in appropriate ways. Porter argues that in Paul's writing, caring for those in need begins within the body of Christ and has the goal of each member getting to a place where they too can contribute. Traditional barriers and boundaries were transformed within the church as new standards were developed. Thus, according to Paul, true civility could only occur within the church, where members lived with respect and love for each other in the expectation of the return of their Lord and Master, Jesus Christ. As Porter points out, this is a compelling model for believers today and may be the catalyst for the contemporary church to become more vibrant and distinctive within their surrounding culture.

In the seventh paper, Cynthia Westfall describes how the letters and homilies of the General Epistles and Hebrews bring forward the prophetic voices of the Old Testament on social justice and address them directly to the church. She claims that these letters and homilies are issued from and directed toward a Jewish worldview in which the Old Testament concepts of social justice resonate and are relevant in the new contexts. Their attitude toward the Roman Empire reflects Old Testament attitudes towards the oppressive empires of earlier times. In addition, Jewish Christianity in the first century experienced a higher degree of marginalization than the non-Christian Jewish communities or the Gentile churches, so that they represented the needy, the oppressed and the marginalized. She proposes a working definition of social justice that reflects the elements found in the documents of the early Jewish Christian communities: It is "The provision by the individual believer and the church community of appropriate care for those suffering from need and oppression within the sphere of the community's responsibility and influence."

Westfall suggests that the Jewish Christian community represented by Hebrews and the General Epistles could be taken as synonymous with "the poor." They represent believers who suffer from need and oppression, because they experienced poverty, victimization, and suffering as well as identified with the difficult experiences of the refugee or resident alien. The Jewish Christian corpus offers suggestions for appropriate care within the community in terms of hospitality, the provision of life's necessities, equalization, prophetic and theological teaching on justice, practical and theological correction of injustice, and the maintenance of a biblical narrative that frames the life and actions of the Christian community. Westfall describes how the Jewish Christian corpus mandated taking responsibility for ensuring social justice where injustice was encountered. The pragmatic capability in terms of resources and scope of the Jewish Christian communities for social justice was limited, but they enacted social justice beyond what could be expected. In contrast, Westfall asserts that believers in North America have comparatively vast social, economic, and political resources to bring to global participation with commensurate responsibility.

In the eighth and final paper, David Mathewson explores the concern for social justice in Revelation. While the presence of this concern in Revelation is contested by some, Mathewson argues that Revelation addresses issues of social justice in a more implicit fashion that other biblical texts. John does not explicitly address care for the poor, widows, and others in need, but rather exposes the underlying system of injustice and violence within Rome. As such, Mathewson argues, Revelation addresses social justice by focusing on the broader issues of power and idolatry. As an apocalypse, or unveiling, Revelation exposes the true nature of things by critiquing imperial Roman rule. John's critique is an ideological one that identifies Rome's oppressive and exploitive practices.

One way that John accomplishes this is by contrasting the Roman imperial cult and worship with worship of the true God. Throughout Revelation it is God, or the Lamb, who is seated on the throne—not the emperor. It is God who is sovereign and the bringer of peace—not Rome. In essence, then, John is exposing the arrogance and idolatry of Rome in light of true worship of God. Mathewson identifies a second way that John critiques Rome's oppressive ideology: by addressing economic and social injustice. Focusing on three sections in Revelation (chs. 6, 17–18, 21–22), Mathewson shows how John portrays the Roman Empire as exploitative and unjust in its economic practices while offering a counter vision of a just and perfect society. As such, Revelation calls readers to actively confront the unjust and exploitative practices of empire while also identifying with the oppressed and victims of such injustice. In this way, according to Mathewson, Revelation—a book claiming to be an "unveiling"—may function to unveil our own commitments.

The contributions described above extend the conversation on biblical social justice to new ground. Academic discussions on biblical social justice have occurred primarily in the venue of Catholic scholarship due to both a historic focus and a more recent interaction with Liberation Theology. On the other hand, in Protestant circles, there has been less of a distinctive focus in academic work, though certain groups have rallied around issues of social justice. Methodism has had a strong continuing tradition of social action. In North America, there was significant involvement with the abolitionist movement that ended slavery in the nineteenth century and in the civil rights movement in the mid-twentieth century. In the last quarter of the twentieth century, a movement for biblical social justice within the evangelical community was initiated by the publication of Ronald Sider's

Rich Christians in an Age of Hunger in 1977. However, the stress has largely been on activism and the conversation has primarily taken place in the domains of theology and ethics, while there has been a lack of robust discussion, if not neglect, by Protestant scholars in biblical studies. It is our hope and prayer that this volume will lay a foundation for further discussion.

Imagining Justice for the Marginalized

A Suspicious Reading of the Covenant Code
(Exodus 21:1—23:33) in Its Ancient Near Eastern Context

PAUL S. EVANS

INTRODUCTION

IT IS FOR GOOD reason that social justice is a topic of great concern in both the church and broader society today. For the church, at least, the roots of this concern go back to the literature of both the Old and the New Testaments. In the Old Testament there is tremendous emphasis on social justice in each of its major sections, with the most obvious and sustained emphasis being found in the prophetic books. However, the prophetic concern with social justice goes back further to Old Testament legal collections. This should not be too surprising, given that ancient Jewish tradition held that the prophets in their missions to Israel and Judah were merely exponents of the concerns of the Torah. In order to bring out this concern with social justice in the Torah itself, this essay will examine the legal collection contained in Exod 21:1—23:33 with a view to finding its contribution to a biblical theology of social justice. This section of Exodus has been called the

Covenant Code (hereafter, CC) by scholars,[1] and is widely held to consist of some of the most ancient laws in biblical literature.[2]

The labeling of these chapters as a "code," that is, a law code, reflects best the dominant assumption among most modern readers that the CC is a collection of laws that served as part of the actual law code to which judges appealed in adjudicating legal decisions in ancient Israel. Unfortunately, the understanding of it as a document that was to function in this way for an ancient community often undermines attempts at underscoring its relevance for Christians today. After all, we are not ancient Israel and many of these laws clearly apply only to them. Furthermore, Christians often fall into one of two camps regarding the actual morality of Old Testament law. Some Christians, based on their strong faith in the character of the Scriptures as God's word, hold firmly to the belief that the laws uphold the highest ethical ideals, and some, given the chance, would even support putting many of these laws into practice today. Others have found the morality contained within these laws difficult to accept and falling below a modern ethical understanding of social justice.

However, scholarly research on biblical legal literature has undermined these understandings of biblical law in important ways. This paper will critically engage salient points of this scholarly research on the CC in order to offer further insights, and then suggest relevant implications regarding the role of the CC in developing a biblical theology of justice.

THE GENRE OF THE COVENANT CODE

The common view of these chapters, as suggested by the scholarly title, is that these laws were an actual legal code that was appealed to by the judiciary in making legal decisions in ancient Israel. However, scholarly research on biblical legal literature has undermined this understanding of the CC. Two related issues are relevant here: the relationship between biblical legislation and other law codes from the ancient Near East (hereafter,

---

1. Another popular label for these chapters is "The Book of the Covenant," which derives its name from the narrative describing Moses' descent from Mount Sinai with the tablets containing the Ten Words and additional laws. "Then he took the Book of the Covenant and read it to the people. They responded, 'We will do everything the LORD has said; we will obey'" (Exod 24:7).

2. Olson, "Jagged Cliffs," 251. Van Seters has argued for an exilic date (*Law Book*) but see the compelling critiques by Levinson ("Is the Covenant Code an Exilic Composition?"), and Otto (Review of *Law Book*).

ANE), and the question of whether these laws were really a law code or ever enforced at all.

The CC and ANE Laws

Until the early twentieth century, biblical laws were the only legal literature from the ANE known to interpreters. However, in the winter of 1901–2, French archaeologist Jacques de Morgan discovered a stele inscribed with the laws of the Babylonian king Hammurabi, which date to approximately 1700 BCE.[3] Subsequently, other legal material from the ANE (e.g., Sumerian, Assyrian, and Hittite) was discovered, the majority of which predates the biblical material.[4]

Shortly after their discovery many parallels between the ANE codes and the biblical legal literature were noticed. These similarities led most scholars to accept that there was a measure of dependence of biblical law on ANE legal literature. Some[5] saw ANE codes as actual sources of biblical legislation,[6] though most have stopped short of such conclusions as they have proved impossible to demonstrate with any certainty.[7] Similarly, others[8] suggested that the Israelite laws depended on their Mesopotamian predecessors as a result of cultural diffusion. However, this hypothesis is equally speculative and unable to be documented.[9] More plausible is the suggestion of a common Near Eastern or Semitic legal tradition inherited by the Israelites, which alleviates the need to posit actual literary dependence or cultural diffusion to explain similarities between ANE and biblical legislation.[10] As Marshall writes:

3. They were engraved near the beginning of his reign (ca. 1728–1686 BCE) (Blenkinsopp, *Wisdom and Law*, 95–96).

4. Only the laws from the Neo-Babylonian Empire are more recent (ibid., 96).

5. E.g., Alt suggested that the fundamental components of the CC were likely borrowed from the Canaanites ("Origins"). Similarly, Meek, "Origin of Hebrew Law."

6. E.g., Wright (*Inventing God's Law*) has recently argued that the CC relies explicitly on the Code of Hammurabi. Meyers notes parallel laws regarding stolen goods, bringing the case to god and paying back double. She concludes, "such correspondences suggest a direct textual dependence of the Exodus rulings on the Code of Hammurabi" (*Exodus*, 184).

7. Marshall, *Israel and the Book of the Covenant*, 19.

8. Bright, *History*, 89.

9. Marshall, *Israel and the Book of the Covenant*, 19.

10. Boecker suggests a common Semitic tradition (*Law and the Administration of Justice*, 77). Others suggest Israel shared in a continuing tradition of a Near Eastern

Given the geographical proximity of the ancient Near Eastern cultures producing these codes, the influence that the similar environmental context must have had on social development and thus indirectly, its laws, and the reciprocal influence among groups sharing the common Semitic tradition, such similarities may be expected.[11]

In sum, there is a general consensus in biblical scholarship that Israel's legal literature was not invented out of whole cloth but grew out of the already existing legal traditions of the ANE.[12] Moreover, Israel's concern for social justice was not unique but was something held in common with the surrounding cultures.[13] It is evident that protecting the poor, widows, and orphans was common legal policy in ANE legal texts.[14] This can be seen even in Sumerian times in Mesopotamia,[15] in Egypt,[16] and in Ugaritic texts.[17]

In giving these laws to Israel, it is abundantly clear that God communicated through legal and social norms common in the ANE.[18] While

common law. However, the details are difficult to discover. Cf. Finkelstein, *Ox*, 17–20.

11. Marshall, *Israel and the Book of the Covenant*, 20. In many ways, the following statement by Blenkinsopp is fairly representative: "While in no case is it possible to derive Israelite law directly from this mostly earlier material, it is now quite clear that early Israel inherited a legal tradition which can be traced back to Mesopotamia of the third and second millennium BCE" (*Wisdom and Law*, 96).

12. As Baker writes: "Although it is doubtful whether the compilers of the Old Testament laws were familiar with the Mesopotamian and Hittite law collections as such, it is likely that they were aware of legal principles common throughout the ancient Near East" (*Tight Fists*, 306).

13. Fensham, "Widow, Orphan," 129; Waldow, "Social Responsibility," 184–85; Havice, "Concern for the Widow."

14. Malchow, "Social Justice," 299. For example, the Teachings of Amenemope (Egyptian) forbid stealing from the poor, cheating cripples, or encroaching on the field of a widow. Cf. Lichtheim, "Instruction of Amenemope," 116. The "Speech of the Eloquent Peasant" (Egyptian) describes a magistrate as "a father to orphans and a husband to the widow." Cf. Shupak, "Eloquent Peasant," 100.

15. Kramer, *Sumerians*, 264; Fensham, "Widow, Orphan," 130–31.

16. *ANET* 407–410, 412–419, 421–424, 441–444.

17. *ANET* 149, 151.

18. Blenkinsopp also notes the narrative context of the CC, pointing out that just before these chapters the narrative describes "Moses' father-in-law, Jethro, a Midianite and hence a non-Israelite, offering guidance to Moses concerning matters of judicial administration (Exod 18:1–27)" already providing a precedent for "God's wisdom mediated through a non-Israelite culture." He rightly comments, "A robust understanding of God as Creator ought to be open to considering and testing the wisdom, guidance

this should not be too surprising, it is important to keep in mind moving forward. The wheel did not need to be reinvented. In dealing with similar legal concerns "Israel did not start from scratch in working out the answers to such questions."[19] Of course, belief in the inspiration of Scripture means we believe that God guided them in working out the answers to these questions. But the biblical writers clearly believed that God was at work in the other nations.[20] This truth is ever relevant in modern issues related to social justice, as it sets a precedent for seeing God at work in non-Christian efforts in the area of social justice. Furthermore, the way the CC draws on secular legislation of its day models the way forward for meaningful partnership with secular humanitarian work today.

THE ANCIENT FUNCTION OF THE COVENANT CODE

Another issue that scholarly study has brought to the fore concerns the genre of both ANE and biblical law codes. Recent research has questioned whether any of these law codes were actually used to settle legal disputes at all.[21] First, there are no extant texts that suggest verdicts were settled by reference to law codes.[22] Thousands of court cases and legal transactions are evidenced in extant Mesopotamian documents, yet it is clear that they were not based on the rulings of these ANE law codes.[23] Similarly, biblical evidence suggests that biblical legal literature was seldom (if ever) used for settling legal disputes or implemented in any way. This can be seen in biblical narratives, as they show very little correspondence with biblical legal material.[24] For example, when Ahab seeks Naboth's vineyard, there is no reference to biblical legislation (such as Num 36:7–8), though it was very applicable.[25] When David commits adultery (2 Sam 12:1–15) or other

---

and laws offered by other cultures, nations and communities that may not be our own" (*Wisdom and Law*, 98–99).

19. Goldingay, *Israel's Life*, 38.

20. That the CC is similar to other ANE legal material "bears testimony to Israel's conviction that the Creator God is at work in the surrounding cultures; those societies are understood to be ordered in some ways congruent with God's intentions for the world apart from specific divine revelation" (Fretheim, *Exodus*, 241).

21. Marshall, *Israel and the Book of the Covenant*, 21.

22. Greengus, "Law in the OT."

23. Meyers, *Exodus*, 183.

24. Patrick, *Old Testament Law*, 193–98.

25. Rofé, "Vineyard of Naboth," 90; Marshall, *Israel and the Book of the Covenant*, 21.

characters commit acts (e.g., worshipping false gods, murder) deemed worthy of capital punishment according to biblical law, these people are not sentenced in this way.[26] Furthermore, Jer 34:8–23 gives clear evidence that biblical laws were not actually enforced, as it notes that people were not obeying legislation regarding the emancipation of slaves after their set term of a maximum of six years.[27]

Second, neither biblical nor ANE law codes appear sufficient to service all the legal needs of their respective people. This can be clearly seen when one compares the Eshnunna Laws (hereafter, LE)[28] and the Code of Hammurabi (hereafter, CH).[29] Both are Babylonian and written within a century of each other but each fail to cover valid cases the other gives. For example, both codes mention cases regarding the hiring of boats (LE §§3–5; CH §§236–239, 275–277) but only the CH (§240) deals with a case concerning the collision of a boat resulting in it sinking. The LE (§6) instead has a different case, not covered in the CH, regarding someone damaging a boat while using it without the owner's permission. If either law code attempted to be complete, one would expect both cases to be represented in it.[30] Similarly, while the CC focuses on some important cases, it hardly covers the plethora of legal problems that would have arisen in ancient Israelite society.[31] Most scholars[32] therefore believe that the CC is an incomplete collection. Of course no law code is completely comprehensive, especially in ancient times where much law was transmitted orally.[33] But it is clear that

26. Goldingay, *Israel's Life*, 38. McKeating, "Sanctions."

27. Sprinkle, *Book of the Covenant*, 66–67.

28. See *ANET*, 161–163.

29. See *ANET*, 163–180.

30. Greengus, "Biblical and ANE Law," 245.

31. As Blenkinsopp writes: "They hardly qualify as law codes, since they are in no way comprehensive. They contain, for example, no legislation on marriage and divorce, with the exception of Deut. 24:1–4, which presupposes divorce but says nothing about who may initiate it, under what circumstances, and with what consequences" (*Sage*, 39).

32. E.g., Boecker, *Law and the Administration of Justice*, 137–38; Patrick, *Old Testament Law*, 198–200.

33. As Meyers asserts, this is probably due to the fact that "many standard, widely accepted, and uncomplicated legal materials were probably transmitted in oral form" (*Exodus*, 183). Furthermore, as Greengus writes: "It is apparent . . . that the validity of the Babylonian laws did not depend upon their being written down" ("Biblical and ANE Law," 246).

both ANE and biblical law collections "were not intended to be complete codes of law."[34]

If the CC was not meant to be a complete law code, what was its purpose? The intended role of the law can be seen in the abundance of so-called "motive clauses" found within biblical legal material.[35] A motive clause is a phrase added to a command in order to give a rationale.[36] For example, several laws concerning the oppression of non-Israelites provide a motive clause encouraging empathy by reminding the audience of their former status of being "aliens in the land of Egypt" (e.g., Exod 22:21; 23:9).[37] Other motive clauses encourage sympathy regarding the plight of others, such as the law requiring the return of the garment taken in pledge ("it may be your neighbor's only clothing" Exod 22:26–27). Several other motive clauses can be found, some of which simply provide an explanation (e.g., "so that your ox and donkey may have relief" Exod 23:12) or tie the law to salvation history in some way (e.g., Exod 23:15).

The abundance of motive clauses in the CC mark its legislation as distinct from otherwise similar ANE legislation. Only approximately 5 to 6 percent of stipulations in comparable ANE material provide such motive clauses, while in biblical legal literature nearly half of the stipulations contain such clauses.[38] The presence of these motive clauses probably points to the intended function of these laws to teach moral standards to a broader audience, rather than to be used by the judiciary.[39] The CC functioned to motivate ancient Israelites to implement the "justice" that these laws represent.[40] That is, biblical law functions to "develop the conscience of the community."[41] As Haas has put it, biblical law "does not so much tell us what to do as it teaches us how to think about what to do."[42] Therefore, this

---

34. Greengus, "Biblical and ANE Law," 246.

35. Meyers, *Exodus*, 185.

36. Cf. Sonsino, *Motive Clauses*.

37. Meyers, *Exodus*, 185.

38. Ibid.

39. Ibid., 185–86.

40. Patrick, *Old Testament Law*, 198–200.

41. Bauckham, *Bible in Politics*, 39. Blenkinsopp similarly writes: "their intent was primarily didactic; the collections were put together to serve the purpose of moral education" (*Sage*, 39).

42. Haas, "Quest," 153.

suggests that these laws were created at least partially in order to teach the principles behind the laws themselves.[43]

Understanding the purpose of these texts provides a key to their interpretation. If the CC was never meant to function as true law, two different approaches are undermined. First, and most obviously, any approach that attempts to implement them literally as law is obviously misguided (especially in light of the time-bound nature of the situations described therein). Second, an interpretive approach that would reject the relevance of the CC due to it being literally an ancient law code that was only applicable to its ancient Israelite audience should be re-examined.[44]

THE MORALITY OF THE COVENANT CODE

As noted above, some interpreters, influenced by theological presuppositions regarding their view of Scripture, hold that biblical legal literature represents a high morality that was uniformly superior to the morality of the day. Other interpreters find the morality of these laws suspect or even immoral at times. Previous to the early twentieth century, in the absence of comparative ANE material, both of these positions were equally plausible. At that time one could assert that Israelite laws were utterly unique in their morality, as it was impossible to assess whether the biblical legislation was humanitarian in nature when compared to other law codes of the time. However, modern comparative study of biblical and ANE legislation has brought new insights that impact both of these interpretive conclusions.[45]

43. Greengus, "Biblical and ANE Law," 246. Anderson notes that "the biblical laws . . . may not have been enforced within a judiciary system" but suggests that they were still quite influential and likely were employed at least for public shaming by the community (*Women, Ideology and Violence*, 82).

44. If calling for only literal implementation, one should recognize that biblical law "belongs in the life of Israel, which is distant from us" (Goldingay, *Israel's Life*, 41).

45. Of course there is no complete consensus concerning the results of comparative study of the legal literature of the Old Testament and the ANE. Some hold that Old Testament morality was more or less of the same nature as that found in other ANE law collections. Blenkinsopp's statement would be representative of this position. He writes, "A comparison of the laws in the Mesopotamian collections with those of the Covenant Code does not support the view that the latter are in all respects more advanced and humanitarian in character. Nor does it substantiate the liberal idea of a progressively enlightened approach to penal legislation . . . The Covenant Code stands apart not so much by virtue of its substance, but because of the historical-narrative context in which it is presented and its evolution, seen especially in the expansions" (*Wisdom and Law*, 98–99). Cf. Olson, "Jagged Cliffs," 256. First, it must be noted that part of the reason Blenkinsopp argues this way is due to his redactional analysis of the CC in which he

A comparative reading shows that much is held in common between the CC and ANE legislation. However, focusing on the ways in which the former departs from the latter aids interpreters in determining its distinct vision of social justice and in identifying underlying principles or, as Meyers puts it, "specifically Israelite values."[46] While the excavating of principles behind laws is an imprecise science,[47] it is more likely that principles actually did lie behind this legislation rather than that "they are random imperatives with no rationale beyond the desire to get Israel to live in obedience to God."[48] Therefore, this study will now undertake a brief comparative reading that will focus on the CC's distinctiveness in order to determine the principles and ideals it sets forth.[49]

---

separates "expansions" from the original versions of the laws, granting that the expansions show a movement towards higher morality. Blenkinsopp considers these "expansions" to be often of "a general ethical" nature and divides verses in two without a clear rationale or method for doing so. For example, he divides Exod 22:21 as follows: "You shall not wrong or oppress a resident alien, *for you were aliens in the land of Egypt* [italics indicating editorial 'expansions]" (*Wisdom and Law*, 98). Second, one of his main objections to biblical morality is the use of the death penalty. However, several recent studies undermine this position concerning the morality of biblical laws as compared to ANE law collections and in my opinion reveal the lack of sophisticated analysis (on the part of those who would hold to Blenkinsopp's position) of the biblical laws in their ancient context (cf. Marshall, *Israel and the Book of the Covenant*; Sprinkle, *Book of the Covenant*; Baker, *Tight Fists*).

46. Meyers, *Exodus*, 185.

47. Moshe Greenberg has undertaken a detailed study to discern principles underlying Israelite law and concluded that Israelite values conflicted with those of other ANE collections ("Some Postulates"). Hanson, on the other hand, has argued for two different value systems represented in the CC, one oppressive (the case laws) and one liberating (the apodictic laws), explaining the different values through a traditio-historical reconstruction running from the former to the latter ("Theological Significance"). Both studies have been criticized as "ignoring particularities and tensions" in the CC (Olson, "Jagged Cliffs," 256).

48. Goldingay, *Israel's Life*, 333.

49. Discerning the underlying values or principles can be accomplished, as Goldingay puts it: "By noting how its vision, its concrete examples and its teaching reaches beyond traditional societies and beyond the point where as "law" it ceases to hold" (*Israel's Life*, 41). My analysis of the laws in the CC will be not be exhaustive but will focus on laws that have direct bearing on social justice and the care for the deprived such as laws that concern the poor, marginalized, disenfranchised, and needy.

Differences Between Biblical and ANE Codes

Class Distinctions

The CC does not evince the same level of class-consciousness as ANE legal collections, where punishments routinely varied with class distinctions. For example, in the CH, laws concerning the "goring ox" stated that if the victim of the ox was a free person the owner was more liable than if the victim was a slave (CH §§250–253). Or in Hittite laws concerning attempted burglary, the guilty party was fined if he was a free man, but if he was a slave the culprit was fined *and* also mutilated (HL §§93–97).[50] Furthermore, punishments could vary from a fine to actual execution depending on whether the victim was a member of the nobility, a citizen, or simply a slave. For example, if a person was convicted of assaulting another person, the same injury the culprit inflicted on his victim was to be inflicted on the culprit. However, if the victim was a slave or of a lower class, instead of the retaliatory injury, a fine was imposed.[51] However, in the CC, punitive measures are meted out to all violators regardless of the social status of the one whose property is stolen or the status of the thief.[52] In sum, in the CC, all citizens are considered equal, resulting in punishments for a crime being "not hindered or magnified by class or wealth."[53]

Severity of Punishments

Generally speaking, the punishments in biblical legislation are more humane than those in ANE legal collections. For example, the punishments for violations of property rights in biblical legislation "never involve mutilation, beating or death."[54] Furthermore, the CC calls for capital punishment less often than other ANE legal literature.[55] For example, ANE law codes commonly mandate death for theft (e.g., CH §§6, 8, 21–22; LE §§12–13), which appears to "make property more valuable than human life."[56]

50. For the Hittite Laws see *ANET*, 188–197; Baker, *Tight Fists*, 19.

51. Meyers, *Exodus*, 186.

52. Baker, *Tight Fists*, 307.

53. Walton and Matthews, *Bible Background*, 97. As Meyers asserts, in Exodus, "comparable biblical materials have no class differentiations" (*Exodus*, 186).

54. Baker, *Tight Fists*, 307.

55. Meyers, *Exodus*, 186.

56. Ibid. The only theft worthy of capital punishment in the CC is the stealing of

The Sanctity of Human Life

A comparative reading of the CC with ANE law collections underscores the biblical view of the sanctity of human life. For example, in the case of the goring ox, only the CC demands that the ox who kills a human (slave or free) be stoned and its flesh not eaten. Comparable ANE legislation is concerned with economic loss, providing compensation to victims, or in the case of the death of a slave, compensation to the owner of the slave. However, the CC is less concerned with economic loss than with "blood-guilt, because human life is of inestimable value."[57]

Concern for the Vulnerable

Even a cursory reading of the CC reveals that it is deeply concerned with those who are most vulnerable in society (the poor, foreigners/aliens, widows and orphans, and slaves). As noted above, in ANE laws. the king was to be concerned with the protection of the vulnerable,[58] but the actual legislation gives limited rights to widows and orphans.[59] However, the CC has many distinctives in this regard that point to a deeper concern and higher morality than in contemporary ANE codes.

Concern for the Poor

Several laws within the CC clearly have the interests of the poor in view. There are laws concerned with lending money to the poor, and sharing produce with the poor. These laws not only aim to encourage provision for the poor but also to curb the growth of wealth, which would result in greater separation of the classes.

Lenders were not to charge interest to the poor.

---

persons (Exod 22:16), reflecting the value placed on human life. This is in regards to the suffering of both the one abducted and probably their parents. Abductions were most commonly of children and the parents would suffer greatly, not only emotionally but also materially, as they would have no one to take care of them in their old age. (This likely explains the literary location of this law after laws concerning striking of parents and before laws concerning cursing or repudiating parents.) (Sprinkle, *Book of the Covenant*, 76.)

57. Baker, *Tight Fists*, 307.

58. E.g., see the prologues of the Ur-Nammu code and CH, which clearly state that a "wise ruler" protects the rights of the poor, widows, and orphans.

59. Baker, *Tight Fists*, 308.

> If you lend money to my people, the poor among you, do not be
> like a moneylender—do not charge interest (Exod 22:25).[60]

In barring the charging of interest on a loan, this law not only favors aiding
the poor but also discourages the accumulation of wealth.[61] There is a clear
focus on the rights of the borrower rather than those of the lender. This is
contrary to ANE legislation, which simply assumes the right of the lender
to charge interest, and seeks to standardize interest rates. While interest
taking functioned to trap the poor into permanent poverty, this law seeks
to prevent such a state of affairs and prevent the rich from profiting from
the misfortune of others. But why would someone lend without any gain to
be had? The CC envisions an Israelite of means lending to the poor "as an
act of charity rather than for his own economic gain."[62]

Further concern for the poor is evidenced in the law concerning security for a loan.

> If you take your neighbor's cloak as security for a loan, you must
> return it to him before sunset (Exod 22:26).

Again, as in the law barring the charging of interest, the CC is more concerned with the needs of the borrower (the poor) than those of the lender
(the rich).[63] Here the law implies that taking something as a security deposit
is appropriate as long as it does not cause the borrower hardship. However,
since the poor would have little of value to give for security that they would
not desperately need, "this law virtually eliminates security in practice."[64]
That is, lenders are to loan to the poor without any guarantee that they will
be paid back.

Fallowing practices were aimed at sharing with the poor.

> You will sow your fields and harvest your crops for six years, but
> during the seventh year you will let the land lie unploughed and
> not use it, so that the poor among your people may eat from it,
> and what they leave, the wild animals can eat. You will do the same
> with your vineyard and your olive grove (Exod 23:10–11).

---

60. All biblical quotations in this essay are my own translations.

61. Meyers, *Exodus*, 186.

62. Sprinkle, *Book of the Covenant*, 171.

63. Baker, *Tight Fists*, 309.

64. Ibid.

The policy of allowing the land to lie fallow every seventh year similarly discourages wealth accumulation (by restricting the income derived from one's land) and also benefits the poor in making provision for those in need. While allowing the land to lie fallow is found in ANE legislations, it is always for agricultural purposes and has nothing to do with social welfare or concern for the poor.[65] Thus, the biblical laws in this regard are unparalleled in ANE legal collections.[66]

Of course, it is possible—if not likely—that it was known in Israel that the fallowing of the land was necessary for agricultural purposes (the reasons mentioned in ANE laws for allowing the land to lie fallow). If this is the case, the law here is giving a moral rationale for the practice and directs the community to the importance of social justice issues. This would concur with the next verse that provides a similar rationale for what originally was clearly a cultic law.

> Six days you will do your work, but on the seventh day do not work, in order that your ox and your donkey may rest and the slave born in your household may be refreshed and the resident alien also (Exod 23:12).

While the Decalogue (e.g., Exod 20:10–11; also 31:17) gives the rationale for the Sabbath as modelling God's example in resting after six days of creation, the CC Sabbath-keeping is done for the sake of giving rest to those who are disenfranchised (or beasts of burden).[67] By tying concern for the disenfranchised to one of the fundamental commandments of Israel's religion, the CC is clearly underscoring the importance of mercy and kindness to the powerless in society.

Concern for the Alien[68]

While concern for the poor, the widow, and the orphan is expressed in ANE legislation, concern for the foreigner or alien is unique to biblical

---

65. As Walton and Matthews explain: "In Mesopotamia fields were left fallow even more frequently to limit the impact of the salt in the water used for irrigation. The practice also helps to prevent exhaustion of the nutrients in the soil" (*Bible Background*, 118).

66. Baker, *Tight Fists*, 309.

67. Elsewhere, the rationale for the Sabbath being kept holy is that it is a sign between God and his covenant people (e.g., Exod 31:13–14; Ezek 20:12–24).

68. Structurally, Exod 22:20–27 and 23:1–9 are clear units within the CC that focus specifically on social justice. Significantly, laws concerning the alien form an inclusio around these units as the first unit begins with such laws and the second unit ends with

legislation.[69] The CC legislates care and concern for ethnic minorities in the Israelite community and reminds its readers that they too were once foreigners in a strange land.[70] In fact, the Torah warns about treatment of foreigners thirty-six times—that is more than commands regarding the Sabbath, circumcision, theft, falsehood, or loving God![71]

Exodus 22:21 states: "Do not mistreat or oppress an alien, for you were aliens in the land of Egypt." Here the law does not cite a hypothetical case to legislate but instead simply forbids mistreatment using an unconditional statement.[72] In some ways this is not really a law as much as it is an exhortation. It bars any oppression of ethnic minorities, even if such oppression would otherwise be legal. After all, foreigners could be oppressed by being paid extremely low wages or by being sold goods at prices far above standard rates (since aliens would not necessarily know the going rate).[73] Both of these practices could be legal (though immoral), but both are banned by this command.[74] Again, this is not really an enforceable law since illegal means of oppression would be hard to prove. This is a moral exhortation to the Israelite community to treat aliens well.

Concern for Slaves

The CC opens and closes with laws concerning slaves.[75] Before delving into the details of the legislation, it is important to first note that the type of slav-

---

the alien, clearly underscoring their importance (Sprinkle, *Book of the Covenant*, 182). Blenkinsopp argues that this structural arrangement is "indicative of the character and intent of the laws as a whole" (*Wisdom and Law*, 95).

69. As Sprinkle notes, this "enlightened attitude towards non-Israelites" has "no parallel in Mesopotamian law" (*Book of the Covenant*, 172).

70. Baker, *Tight Fists*, 308.

71. Leibowitz, *Studies in Shemot*, 380; Sprinkle, *Book of the Covenant*, 172.

72. This is, of course, what Alt referred to as apodictic law. Apodictic law, though not completely unique among ANE legislation as once thought, is still quite rare there compared to its frequency in Israel's legislation. As Meyers observes, "The appearance of so many non-juridical and unconditional exhortations in addition to the case rulings and rules is not typical of Near Eastern corpora" (*Exodus*, 185).

73. Sprinkle, *Book of the Covenant*, 171.

74. As Sprinkle writes, this verse then could "condemn an Israelite plaintiff even if he has every legal right to his judgment against a sojourner if, given the circumstances, he ought to have shown mercy" (*Book of the Covenant*, 185–86).

75. There has been some debate over what type of slavery is referred to here. While consensus is that the laws of Exod 21:1–11 concern debt slavery, some scholars (Greenberg, "Crimes and Punishments," 738; Sarna, *Exodus*; Chirichigno, *Debt-Slavery*, 148–85)

ery in view here is debt slavery (temporary enslavement). In the ANE, debt slavery occurred when those who found themselves in debt (commonly farmers, small landowners, etc.) for one reason or another (e.g., persistent drought or continued poor harvests) were forced into selling not only their land, but also a family member or themselves.[76] This type of slavery was meant to be only temporary, with the servitude lasting only until the debt was paid off. Thus it differed significantly from chattel slavery, where the servitude is permanent and the slave owner has "an absolute right of disposal over their slaves."[77]

Extant ANE documents legislate debt-slavery. The CH limited debt servitude to three years (CH §117). At Nuzi the term could last up to fifty years,[78] while Assyrian laws had no limitation on the length of the term. The fact that the CH limits the term as it does suggests that longer periods of service were probably common.[79] It is unknown whether this three-year rule was actually put into practice. The laws of Lipit-Ishtar (§14) inform us that a debt-slave had to serve an equivalent to twice the debt they owed.[80] In light of high interest rates, many debt-slaves were likely enslaved for longer or even permanent terms of servitude.[81]

ANE documents clearly show that debt-slaves were their master's property. In fact, extant legislation never prohibits masters from killing their slave.[82] Furthermore, if someone killed someone else's slave the ramification was merely a payment of the price of the slave to the owner (LH §116). This has led some to suppose an owner could kill his own slave with impunity.[83] At the least, it is clear that the master could maltreat a slave at will without fear of legal punishment.[84]

The CC permits a period of servitude up to a maximum of six years (Exod 21:2). The imperfect verb (יעבד) is probably "permissive," in that it

view the laws in Exod 21:20–21, 26–27 as concerning chattel slaves.

76. Walton and Matthews, *Bible Background*, 111.

77. Baker, *Tight Fists*, 136.

78. Eichler, *Indenture at Nuzi*, 20–21.

79. Sprinkle, *Book of the Covenant*, 68.

80. Baker, *Tight Fists*, 137.

81. Ibid.

82. Sprinkle, *Book of the Covenant*, 68.

83. Dandamaev et al., *Slavery in Babylonia*, 79, 460–64.

84. Sprinkle, *Book of the Covenant*, 68.

states how long a slave "may" serve rather than how long they "must" serve.[85] Presumably smaller debts could be paid off in shorter terms than six years.[86] In light of the lengthy terms permitted at Nuzi and in Assyria, the biblical legislation is far more favorable to the slave. However, as mentioned, in Babylon the CH limited the term to three years.

It is likely that the CC's term of six years with freedom granted in the seventh year patterned itself after the sabbatical principle. Furthermore, the term legislated may correspond to a standard wage of workers. Elsewhere the Old Testament notes that three years is the standard term, as Isa 16:14 equates three years to the "years of a hired laborer (שָׂכִיר)." Furthermore, Deut 15:18 states that when a slave is set free after six years the owner should be grateful, for the six year term provided "double wages" (מִשְׁנֶה שְׂכַר) to the owner. That is, a hired worker would have served only three years for that wage, but the debt-slave serves double that length of time. This is very similar to the legislation in Lipit-Ishtar, which says a slave has to pay back double before gaining freedom.[87]

Regarding a debt-slave's wife and children, Exod 21:3–6 has a charitable intent, though from a modern perspective it is more difficult to perceive. Two scenarios are introduced. First, if the slave was married before his indenture, his wife and children do not lose their freedom due to their association with him.[88] Second, if a slave is given a wife by his master, both she and any children born of their union remain slaves even when his term ends. Normally, a debt-slave would not be able to marry without the aid of his master since he could not afford the bride-price necessary to acquire a wife.[89] Therefore, this law allows a slave to have companionship and the joy of a family even in his state of servitude.[90]

However, that the slave must choose between freedom and his family is difficult to perceive as having a charitable intent. Again, the interpreter

85. Ibid., 69.

86. Thus the NLT translation of Exod 21:2: "If you buy a Hebrew slave, he may serve for no more than six years. Set him free in the seventh year, and he will owe you nothing for his freedom."

87. As Baker (*Tight Fists*, 148) writes: "six years' service to repay the debt means the creditor gets a worker at half the usual cost."

88. Sprinkle, *Book of the Covenant*, 70. He notes the same thing in Babylonia as a free woman married to a slave is not a slave (see 70 n. 1).

89. Ibid., 70.

90. It also benefits the slave owner as it may improve the attitude of his slave and also provide more slaves for the master through the children born of the union (ibid.).

must first attempt to see this law in all of its time-boundedness. Due to the harsh conditions in ancient times, a slave who had been freed after a six year period of servitude, who had no family when he entered his service and possibly little to no extended family (or else they might have prevented his indentured service), would likely have a daunting task ahead of him. As Sprinkle writes, the freedom to which he would leave "would be a precarious freedom, perhaps little more than freedom to be lonely or freedom to starve. Falling back into servitude again, possibly with a less congenial master, would not be unlikely."[91] Furthermore, from another perspective, this law may be implying that in Israel "slaves are to be looked after so well that they might prefer to continue in that status rather than claim their freedom."[92]

In light of this reality, the legislation offers a debt-slave an opportunity for securing his future by choosing to join the household on a permanent basis. Furthermore, it may be speaking into an environment where the master may simply want to exploit his servants for "breeding purposes" and then force them to leave.[93] By giving the slave the option of staying, it implies the master has no choice in forbidding him to stay. That is, the master cannot then give the slave's wife to another if the slave chooses to stay. Here it is significant that the slave is the one given the choice. Furthermore, the best chance for the children may be their staying with the master rather than departing with the emancipated slave, which could actually be why the text does not consider letting the slave's wife and children leave with him.[94] Of course, according to biblical legislation, when the Jubilee occurs all would be freed at that point anyway. Perhaps this law gives the slave the option of securing his family until the Jubilee comes (or his owner dies, at which point the slave and his family are thereby freed).[95] The CC legislates the option for temporary slaves once they have served their term.

Another hypothetical situation is of a father selling his daughter as a slave-wife, אמה (a difficult thing to imagine to someone living in the West today). This action was likely motivated by poverty and the resulting debt due to the fact that the father could not afford a dowry.[96] Of course this

---

91. Ibid.

92. Baker, *Tight Fists*, 308.

93. Sprinkle, *Book of the Covenant*, 71.

94. Ibid.

95. Ibid., citing Josephus, *Ant.* 4.28; *m. Qidd.* 1.2.

96. Sprinkle, *Book of the Covenant*, 71.

situation is very time-bound and assails our modern sensibilities in many ways. The daughter appears to have no choice in the matter, which is quite unacceptable from a modern Western point of view, though it does reflect the realities of life in ancient times.

This is not simply the same situation as the previous one, that is, she is not just a debt-slave with a different gender. The slave-wife (אמה) is likely best understood as a concubine (cf. Gen 20:17; 21:10, 13; 31:33; Exod 23:12).[97] As in the previous discussion regarding debt-slaves, some brief discussion regarding the status of a concubine in the ANE is necessary before assessing details in this law. Concubines normally had a higher status than slaves, as can be seen in the CH where it states that if a concubine attempts to be equal with her owner's wife, she is punished by being marked a slave (CH §146).[98] In fact, a concubine with children was really more like a second wife than like a normal slave.[99]

The duties of a concubine were generally to work in the home and produce children (thereby adding workers to the home).[100] Her status in comparison to the master's wife would always be secondary and inferior. Her children also would be of a secondary status, with no privileges of inheritance—though this could change in some instances.[101] A concubine who had borne her master children but was then sold as a debt-slave could be redeemed by her master (CH §119). A concubine and her children were freed upon their master's death (CH §171).

Contracts regarding the sale of a daughter as a slave-bride have been discovered at Nuzi.[102] While in Babylon and Assyria, children sold into slavery had no conditions attached to their situation, at Nuzi there was some protection for a daughter, as she was guaranteed to be married and not forced into prostitution.[103] She was promised to the master, a son, another man, or even a slave[104] and it appears that the daughter could be bought and kept for some time before it was decided whom she would marry.

---

97. Baker, *Tight Fists*, 152. Cf. Neufeld, *Ancient Hebrew Marriage Laws*, 121–24.

98. Baker, *Tight Fists*, 151.

99. Ibid.

100. Ibid., 150–51.

101. E.g., if the master married the concubine etc. (Lipit-Ishtar §26). Cf. Baker, *Tight Fists*, 151.

102. Mendelsohn, *Slavery*, 10–12 Neufeld, *Ancient Hebrew Marriage Laws*, 75–76.

103. Baker, *Tight Fists*, 152.

104. Baker notes that an Assyrian contract refers to a sale wherein the girl marries

In the scenario envisioned by the CC, it is clear that the girl was intended to be a concubine for either the master or his son, and not a debt-slave. A young woman/girl in such a situation was obviously very vulnerable and the CC seeks to ensure humane treatment for her in this situation. Specific standards of treatment are put in place. When the girl is given to the son, the purchaser is to treat her as a daughter (Exod 21:9)—that is, she must not be considered a slave but a genuine member of the family.[105] If the girl is to be the purchaser's concubine, she is to be given full rights as a wife. If the purchaser changes his mind regarding the woman, he is not permitted to sell her as a slave but must arrange for her redemption (Exod 21:8).[106] Lastly, if the purchaser takes another concubine, the CC legislates rights to food, clothing, and marital/conjugal rights for the first one (Exod 21:9). If the master fails to provide for her in this way she is to go free, and the debt that led to the arrangement is absolved (the text says this explicitly אין כסף).[107] Therefore, in the case of a concubine, her "slavery" is temporary, just as with male debt-slaves. If she is married, she is not a slave; if she is not to be kept as a concubine, she is either "redeemed" or set free and the debt forgiven.[108] As Baker observes, "This kindness towards concubines is in notable contrast to their utilitarian treatment in Mesopotamia."[109]

Regarding corporal punishment of slaves, two rules are found in the CC. The first concerns the beating of a slave (Exod 21:20–21) and the second concerns permanently injuring a slave (Exod 21:26–27). These laws are exceptional in their ANE context in that they are concerned about a master's abuse of a slave. While there are laws[110] regarding the treatment of slaves in ANE legal material, none are concerned with the master's treat-

---

"the purchaser's son" in order to "settle debts" (*Tight Fists*, 152).

105. Though this likely does not imply that she is the son's wife, as she remains the son's concubine (Baker, *Tight Fists*, 152).

106. This is the only use of פדה in the *hiphil* in the entire Old Testament. Normally פדה means "to redeem" or "be redeemed" but with the causative sense it is clear the owner is to "cause" this redemption. Exactly how this would happen is unspecified.

107. Westbrook, "Female Slave," 236.

108. As Sprinkle comments, this law, like the previous one, "works towards her freedom" and "reflects the text's humanitarian, moral concern" (*Book of the Covenant*, 72).

109. Baker, *Tight Fists*, 308.

110. For example, in CH §199, §220 there are laws concerning the blinding of someone else's slave or breaking one of their bones (the penalty for either is to pay the master half the price of a slave). If someone kills the slave of another, the culprit has to either replace the slave or pay the owner the price of a slave (§116, §214, §219).

ment of the slave, but only the abuse of someone else's slave. In ANE legislation, compensation is paid to the master, not the slave. In other words ANE laws "are not designed to protect slaves at all, but to protect masters from loss if their slaves are injured or killed by others."[111]

In the CC, there is regulation of how severely a master can beat a slave.

> If a man strikes his slave (male or female) with a rod, and he dies immediately, he must be avenged (Exod 21:20–21).

While beating with a stick was a common disciplinary action (e.g., Prov 10:13), even for children (Prov 13:24), this law is concerned with occasions where a master beats his slave to the point of death. If a master beats a slave so that the slave dies directly from the beating, the penalty is that "he shall be avenged" (Exod 21:20). While most translations read that the master "shall be punished" the Hebrew clearly states נקם ינקם "he shall certainly be avenged." This phrase normally implies death, and this was the understanding of both the Samaritan Pentateuch and ancient Jewish interpretation.[112] That the death of a slave should result in the death of the master is unparalleled in ancient legislation, for in the light of the principle of *talion*, such a verdict asserts that slaves are equal in value to their master. Furthermore, this applies to both male and female slaves.

> But if after a day or two, [the slave] gets up, he is not to be avenged, since [the slave] is his money (Exod 21:21).

In this scenario, the slave survives the beating, at least for a day or two. Two different translations are possible here: (1) after a beating the slave dies after a day or two; (2) the slave gets up and recovers after a day or two. If the former translation is preferred, the issue concerns whether the killing of the slave was intentional or unintentional. While the slave dying on the spot showed intentionality, the survival of the slave for a period of time showed that the master did not intend to kill the slave but merely punish the slave, as was his right (the slave is his money).[113] However, if the latter translation is preferred, the slave did not die at all, though he was severely injured.[114] In this case, the master would have to care for the slave until he was well again (for the slave is his money) just as in the previous law concerning the injury

---

111. Baker, *Tight Fists*, 122.

112. Ibid., 126.

113. E.g., this is the interpretation followed by Sprinkle, *Book of the Covenant*, 91.

114. Chirichigno, *Debt-Slavery*, 173–77. Baker, *Tight Fists*, 125, follows Chirichigno's interpretation.

of a free citizen (Exod 21:19).[115] Either way, the law makes the penalty the same whether the victim is a slave or a free person.

While the previous law covered scenarios where the slave either dies or recovers, another law covers instances where the slave is permanently injured.[116] Two examples of injuries are given: the loss of a slave's eye and the loss of a slave's tooth. While it may be questioned why a tooth should be worth as much as an eye, it is likely that these two examples serve as a word-pair giving upper and lower limits for applying the law.[117] While masters had the right to use corporal punishment, any permanent injury— from injuries as small as the loss of a tooth, to one resulting in permanent blindness—resulted in the slave being given their freedom. Though this does not apply the principle of *lex talionis*, the penalty greatly favors slaves as it gives them freedom even for something as small as the loss of a tooth. As Brueggemann writes, "The cost of an eye or a tooth to the master might deter brutality . . . the emancipation changes fundamental social relations."[118] Thus, this law concerning permanent injury would make masters quite cautious in doling out corporal punishment. This law combined with the laws concerned with the beating of slaves might function to discourage masters from using corporal punishment at all, given the possibilities of loss on their investment. More importantly for our purposes, once again the CC is seen as "treating marginal people as human beings."[119]

In summary, though slavery was not abolished in the CC, biblical legislation provided considerable protection for slaves and forbade their abuse.[120] While ANE laws treated slaves as property, in the CC slaves themselves had rights. The CC also encourages empathy for the slave, reminding the people that they were once slaves in Egypt (Exod 22:21; 23:9). Baker correctly writes:

> [A]lthough slavery was not abolished in ancient Israel, the laws move in the direction of ameliorating the condition of slaves . . . If put into practice, laws such as these would serve to limit the worst

---

115. Baker, *Tight Fists*, 125.

116. Ibid., 128.

117. Sprinkle, *Book of the Covenant*, 95–96; Baker, *Tight Fists*, 128.

118. Brueggemann, "Book of Exodus," 841.

119. Baker, *Tight Fists*, 129. This is also seen in the penalty for an ox goring a slave. The ox is still to be killed and its flesh to remain uneaten because a slave, like a free person, is human and human life is sacred.

120. Ibid., 308.

effects of slavery and ensure that even slaves have basic human rights.[121]

Concern for Widows and Orphans

In ANE legislation, widows and orphans are universally mentioned as classes of powerless people in society. Due to the harsh conditions in ancient times, with war, famine, and disease being commonplace, widows and orphans were ubiquitous. Widows could not inherit their deceased husband's property, and orphans could only inherit property (CH §191) or learn a trade if adopted.[122] Some Middle Assyrian laws legislate provision for a widow and give her the right to remarry if her husband is taken prisoner in war (and presumed dead).[123] Some Hittite laws legislated a levirate obligation by her dead husband's family, but most widows had to seek employment or attempt to find a new husband (e.g., Ruth).[124]

In the CC, as in the laws concerning aliens, an unconditional prohibition is given: "Do not abuse a widow or an orphan" (Exod 22:22). Again, because there were available legal means to abuse these disenfranchised people, the apodictic prohibition would be impossible to enforce. This is a clear moral exhortation. However, the case for protection is made even more strongly than in the case of an alien. The next verses read:

> If you do [oppress them] and they cry out to me, I will surely hear their cry. My anger will burn, and I will kill you with the sword; your wives shall become widows and your children orphans (Exod 22:23-24).

While lost in translation, the change from singular 'you' to plural 'you' in the Hebrew is very interesting in this verse. Basically it says "if you [singular] do this, you [plural] will pay the price—God will slay you [plural] with the sword." In other words, if an individual abuses the powerless, others will end up suffering on account of that act. The guilt would be not only on the individual but on the community.[125]

121. Ibid., 120.
122. Walton and Matthews, *Bible Background*, 116.
123. Ibid.
124. Ibid.
125. As Sprinkle writes, "If Israelites passively stand aloof and do not succor the afflicted when an Israelite oppresses his fellow, the nation as a whole by merit of its inaction can be held guilty of the offense" (*Book of the Covenant*, 169).

Assessment

In sum, a comparative reading of the CC in its ANE context shows that the CC consistently emphasizes compassion and justice for the marginalized and vulnerable. While some of the values in the CC can only be appreciated if their ANE context is taken into account, others transcend time as the CC "emphasizes compassion, encouraging positive action to supply the needs of the poor rather than simply fulfilling minimal legal requirements."[126] The CC evinces a deep concern to protect the vulnerable from abuse in a way that is "not characteristic of other ancient Near Eastern cultures or even of classical Greece and Rome."[127]

Coming back to the question of the morality of the CC, a negative judgment in this regard is not merited if its ancient cultural context is taken into account.[128] As our brief analysis has shown, in comparison to its ANE context, the CC shows a higher morality in its ancient cultural context and moves in a "redemptive direction."[129]

APPLYING THE COVENANT CODE
FOR A BIBLICAL THEOLOGY OF SOCIAL JUSTICE

In light of the above, the CC has much to contribute to a biblical theology of social justice. First, the motivations employed in the CC are still relevant today. The CC used "motive clauses" that appealed to God's authority, called for compassion, reminded Israelites how God saved them in the past, and exhorted Israel to emulate God's concern for the vulnerable in society. Such "motive clauses" are completely appropriate to similarly motivate Christians today.[130]

Second, as we have seen, these laws represent ways in which Israel sought to aid the vulnerable and marginalized in society. They attempted "to prevent unjust acts, to stimulate giving, and at least partially to equalize the

---

126. Baker, *Tight Fists*, 311.

127. Meyers, *Exodus*, 187.

128. This conclusion is contra those who would see CC law as merely conforming to or falling below the morality of its day. E.g., Hanson writes, "The case laws are typical of the ordinances found in the great cultures of Mesopotamia" (*The People Called*, 44). Cf. Blenkinsopp, *Wisdom and Law*, 98–99.

129. Lamb, *God Behaving Badly*, 63.

130. As Malchow writes, "Thus, the ancient legal codes of the Pentateuch can assist the modern church in its attempt to bring justice to the poor" ("Social Justice," 306).

position of the rich and poor."[131] Following the lead of the CC in these areas, believers are called upon to take comparable measures in today's society. How might we apply "those principles in equivalent regulations for our context"?[132]

Concern for the Poor

The concerns of the CC with aiding the poor have direct impact on the mission of believers today. Though the cultural context has changed, the task of Christians remains to find ways to aid the poor. As we have seen, the CC actually sets a precedent for charitable giving as it removes any monetary motivations for lending to the poor (no interest, no deposit, or expectation of payment back). Furthermore, through fallowing practices the economic prosperity of people of means is actually restricted in order to provide resources for the poor. The modern practice of higher income earners paying a higher percentage of tax may be seen as following this principle, provided that governments use these funds to provide for the poor. Finally, religious observances (the Sabbath) and business practices (fallowing the land) are reinterpreted to emphasize how they serve the poor, providing a strong rationale for viewing modern religious observances as serving the poor in direct ways (e.g., sharing church monies with the poor, acts of service to the poor as serving God).

Concern for the Alien

One does not have to look far to see modern analogues to the sojourner or the alien. In Canada today there are many new immigrants who are in need. There are many areas in which the church can serve such people, not only through providing programs (such as, for example, teaching English), but by embracing them as true fellow-citizens and welcoming them into our communities. From a global perspective, concern for the alien finds an analogue in the refugee. There are estimated to be 15.2 million refugees in the world today who are displaced due to political persecution, economic hardship, or on-going war.[133] In addition to refugees, it is estimated that there are over 26 million "internally displaced persons" who remain in their country but have been displaced due to armed conflict within their

---

131. Ibid.

132. Goldingay, *Israel's Faith*, 333.

133. Birkeland et al. *Global Overview*, 13. UNHCR, A Year of Crises, 3.

own land.[134] The church's efforts in overseas mission and charitable giving are vital in living out the implications of the CC today to take care of the sojourner and the alien. Solutions to these problems are not easy, but biblical ethics underscores the importance of working toward a solution and aiding these vulnerable people.

Concern for Widows and Orphans

The problems of widows and orphans remain in modern society. The United Nations Children's fund (UNICEF) and global partners generally define an "orphan" as a child who has lost one or both parents.[135] Using this definition, UNICEF estimates there are 153 million orphans on the planet today.[136] The biblical concern with widows and orphans translates directly into the call for action in aiding these vulnerable people. In some cases (where both parents have been lost) this may mean adopting children and supporting orphanages, but in most cases it means providing support for one-parent families and children in need.[137]

Furthermore, this concern with orphans and widows can be applied to victims of divorce and household abuse that results in women and children being in situations very similar to those of widows and orphans. Of course, in our society many women have been abandoned not by their legal husband but by their partner who is also the father of their child(ren). The local church must seek to live out the exhortation of the CC by coming to the aid of these often marginalized people, lest the church as a whole incur guilt.

Concern for Slaves

The concern for slaves in the CC has immediate relevance for our modern context. Despite the fact that the West has officially abolished slavery, it is estimated that there are approximately 20 million slaves in the world today. This is actually more slaves than there have been at any time in world history.[138]

---

134. UNHCR, A Year of Crises, 3.

135. UNICEF, "Orphans."

136. UNICEF, *State of the World's Children*, 103.

137. UNICEF points out that it is important to realize that most of the orphans are those who have lost one parent. "UNICEF's 'orphan' statistic might . . . lead to responses that focus on providing care for individual children rather than supporting the families and communities that care for orphans and are in need of support." (UNICEF, "Orphans").

138. Baker, *Tight Fists*, 120–21.

Furthermore, if we include the millions of child laborers, sweatshop workers, or those forced into the sex trade, the number is far larger.[139] Given the complex nature of the problem, no easy solution is envisioned, but the biblical call to justice for slaves rings out in the CC. As Webb writes, "Scripture sides heavily with the plight of the slave, the poor and the oppressed. This life-breathing spirit, which bettered the conditions for slaves in the ancient world, should also influence the application process today."[140] Similarly, even though in many instances it is not possible to abolish some types of slavery, at the minimum the church must be concerned with how best to ameliorate conditions for the marginalized and the oppressed as did the CC.

LIMITATIONS OF THE COVENANT CODE

Despite the high morality evinced by the CC in light of its ANE cultural context, the CC cannot be said to represent ethical ideals so that it would be appropriate for its laws to be applied literally in our modern context. Its laws "were *not* written to establish a utopian society with complete justice and equity. They were written within a cultural framework with limited moves toward an ultimate ethic."[141]

Limitations regarding the law's morality can be easily illustrated. For example, the CC appears to legitimate the practice of temporary or debt-slavery. While at first blush debt-slavery could appear to be a necessary evil that allowed those in debt to become solvent, the situation is not as neat as this might suggest. The fact is that most who ended up being slaves were made so simply due to extreme poverty.[142] Orphaned, abandoned, or kidnapped children were some of the most common sources of slaves in the ANE.[143] (Children born to slaves were actually the main source of slaves in the first millennium BCE.)[144] Not only this, but several studies have suggested that in most cases in the ANE, loans were made to poor peasants primarily in order to acquire the latter's land and/or enslave them.[145] Lenders were aware that the poor would likely be unable to pay

139. Ibid., 121.

140. Webb, *Slaves, Women*, 38.

141. Ibid., 31.

142. Mendelsohn, *Slavery*, 14–16.

143. As were criminals (slavery as their punishment) and prisoners of war (Sprinkle, *Book of the Covenant*, 68).

144. Mendelsohn, *Slavery*, 14–16; Dandamaev et al., *Slavery in Babylonia*, 111; Sprinkle, *Book of the Covenant*, 68.

145. Baker, *Tight Fists*, 138.

back what they owed and were motivated to lend in order to gain long-term laborers. In fact, the charging of interest may have been not just to make a profit on a loan but primarily in order to make the amount of the debt impossible to pay back.[146] Thus, although in theory the practice of debt-slavery was to be temporary, it often became permanent.

Furthermore, though the moral intent of the laws is evident when compared with ANE legal collections, in their specifics these laws do not go far enough.

1. The law concerning the right of the freed slave to stay with his master in order to retain his wife and children could very well be used simply to turn a temporary slave into a permanent one.

2. Of course the CC envisions a master-slave relationship wherein the treatment of the slave was so good that a freed slave might choose to stay on permanently, but this was clearly not the norm. The CC itself legislates situations where the master beats his slave and this is deemed to be fully allowable (Exod 21:21). Although the CC has more concern for the wellbeing of a slave than other ANE legislation (mandating freedom for a lost tooth), it does not bar physical beatings or the institution of slavery. In fact, that a fine is given for the death of a slave reinforces the institution of slavery (the slave is "his money"; Exod 21:21).

3. The practice of selling one's daughter as a bride due to poverty falls short of an ethical ideal to say the least. This makes a woman mere chattel, even if the laws legislating the practice aim to make such a woman gain her freedom, either by being treated as a daughter or a true wife, or by being granted her freedom. The CC still does not bar or discourage the practice. However, clearly the whole institution of slavery needed abolishing—both permanent slavery (chattel) and temporary slavery (debt-slaves or concubines).

JESUS' HERMENEUTICS OF SUSPICION

In light of the limitations of the CC's morality, with many of its laws falling short of full rights for the marginalized, drawing on the CC in constructing

---

146. Ibid.; Cornell, *Beginnings*, 281–83. Baker points out that the fact that a multitude of loan documents have been found from the ANE may suggest that debt-slaves served perpetually since such documents were to be destroyed when the debt was paid off. He writes, "The documents which have survived would therefore appear to represent loans that were never repaid, in which case it is likely that these debtors became permanent slaves of the creditors" (*Tight Fists*, 138).

a biblical theology of social justice is challenging. How might a modern interpreter understand its relevance for today? Furthermore, how are Christians best to understand how the CC functions as Christian Scripture?

Jesus' statements in Matthew 19 regarding the interpretation of Mosaic divorce law may provide a hermeneutical key to aid an interpreter in understanding the CC as Christian Scripture. Jesus himself noted the frequent tension between what was legislated by Moses and what was the ethical ideal. Jesus clearly stated that some parts of the law express ideals while others make allowance for human hard-heartedness. When asked about the morality of a man divorcing his wife, Jesus stated that the ideal was expressed in the beginning.

> [Jesus] answered, "Have you not read that the Creator from the beginning 'made them male and female,' and said, 'For this reason a man will leave his father and mother and be joined to his wife, and the two will become one flesh'? So they are no longer two, but one flesh. Therefore let no one separate what God has joined together" (Matt 19:4–6).

His interlocutors responded by pointing to Mosaic legislation regulating divorce, to which Jesus replied:

> Moses allowed you to divorce your wives because you were so hard-hearted, but from the beginning it was not this way (Matt 19:8).

Jesus' hermeneutical move here is significant, as it sets a precedent for a suspicious reading of Scripture itself.[147] Jesus states that this law concerning divorce was an accommodation to human hard-heartedness.[148] If this particular law was accommodating, it is likely that other laws were also. In Matthew 19 the Pharisees misunderstand Scripture "due to their expectation of a uniform ethic" wherein "They understood the words of Moses to reflect God's idealized will in every respect."[149] In other words, Jesus explicitly rejects interpretations of such laws as representing ethical ideals.

It is important to note that the Mosaic divorce law, like the CC, represented a higher ethic in its ANE context, as it was a move toward protecting

---

147. Goldingay, *Israel's Life*, 339.

148. As Goldingay writes: "There are tensions within the Torah, and one explanation is that parts of the Torah express how things were at the Beginning (how God designed humanity to be) while parts make allowance for human sinfulness or 'hardness of heart'" (*Israel's Faith*, 338).

149. Webb, *Slaves, Women*, 43.

the rights of the wife, who in that ancient patriarchal context needed to marry again in order to survive. Thus the law was "an attempt to minimize the damage of living in a fallen world."[150] While it showed a move towards compassion and support for the vulnerable (the woman who was being divorced) it also accommodated itself to human sinfulness, at least part of which we now recognize as patriarchy. While the law benefits the vulnerable (the woman) it also supports the powerful (the man) in allowing the divorce and according the man the power to divorce his wife (a power which the wife did not possess).

In other words, in seeking the role of the CC in a biblical theology of social justice, our study cannot end with an examination of this legislation in light of its historical context, but must re-read the CC suspiciously and ask whose interest this law serves, and look for ways in which the CC allows for human sinfulness.[151] This hermeneutic of suspicion is so essential that, without it, interpretations run the risk of allowing the CC to justify slavery and help maintain a patriarchal, hierarchical ideology.[152] A suspicious reading is called for lest the CC be used to construct gender roles, and/or class identities based on an ancient cultural context that the CC was *merely accommodating* and not attempting to promote. When one approaches with suspicion and questions whom the law benefits, and how it allows for human sinfulness, the redemptive direction of the laws can be seen to be instructive, while the limitations of the laws can be criticized and understood to be due to human stubbornness.

This approach is not to undermine this text as Christian Scripture, but simply to follow Jesus' lead in evaluating the continued relevance of biblical law for today. Furthermore, examining the way in which the CC approached and legislated ethical issues can serve as a model for implementing God's vision of social justice.

THE COVENANT CODE AS A MODEL FOR APPROACHING THE TASK OF SOCIAL JUSTICE TODAY

As we have seen the CC does not go so far as to represent an ethical ideal, but instead charts both a course (limited moves, some compromise, and

---

150. Ibid., 41.

151. Goldingay, *Israel's Life*, 339.

152. As Anderson laments, biblical law "has been used historically and is used today to maintain patriarchy's hierarchical ideologies and structures" (*Women, Ideology, and Violence*, 113).

awareness of the practicalities of life), and a destination (ethical ideals). However, this approach of accommodation and compromise is instructive. As Goldingay writes,

> [I]n seeking to be lenient without losing touch with God's ideals, and to keep hold of God's ideals without losing touch with the practicalities of where people are, [Old Testament law] is modeling a path of discipleship for us to follow.[153]

In our efforts towards social justice, the role of compromise must not be overlooked. Though we strive for ideals, in reality and in view of the fallen state of humanity, limited moves are often all that is possible.[154] In his book *From the Tower of Babel to Parliament Hill*, Brian Stiller discusses the "appropriate role of compromise" in engaging our culture, and gives the example of debate on the abortion bill "Bill C-43" (which was tabled November 3, 1989). Some pro-life groups opposed the bill because it did not "go far enough in protecting the unborn."[155] Bill C-43 viewed life as existing upon conception but still allowed abortion in a limited number of exceptions. While Stiller viewed it as allowing too many exceptions, he was in favor of the bill as it "was public policy pointed in the right direction" and he believed that "over time, the number of exceptions could be reduced. The right principle was in place, even if some of the specifics were flawed."[156] However, the bill was defeated by one vote in the Senate, leaving Canada with no law providing restrictions on abortion. Stiller attributes this to "those who wanted to do right [but] failed to understand the legitimate place of compromise in the writing of public policy."[157] The CC and other Old Testament laws represent a precedent for compromise, even within Christian Scripture. Just in case one thinks this is an "Old Testament" approach and therefore irrelevant, the New Testament also follows the lead of Old Testament law in this regard (e.g., in accommodating slavery).[158] Of course, our goal is to move towards the ideal, but starting where people are is the pastoral strategy modelled by Scripture itself.[159]

153. Goldingay, *Israel's Life*, 42.

154. As Goldingay writes: "We do not lay out utopia but suggest steps in a direction" (ibid., 340).

155. Stiller, *Tower of Babel*, 201.

156. Ibid., 202.

157. Ibid.

158. Goldingay, *Israel's Life*, 42.

159. Goldingay observes that "part of the Torah's pastoral strategy [is] to start where

This has implications for which laws should be supported, which policies created, or which direction taken in efforts toward social justice by Christians today. As we have seen, the CC did not forbid slavery, but it did seek to provide for the rights of slaves. Similarly, laws allowing abortion only in limited cases (in efforts to protect the lives of many or most of the unborn), or laws decriminalizing prostitution[160] (in efforts to protect sex-trade workers) *may* be viewed as following the spirit of the CC if these laws truly function to protect the vulnerable. Neither uphold an ethical ideal, and the laws themselves may need rewriting or eventually abolishing, but such approaches cannot be rejected *a priori* just because they do not uphold the ethical ideal.

CONCLUSION

In light of our discussion concerning the genre of the CC, its evident concern for the marginalized, and its approach in working toward—though not legislating—ethical ideals, interpreters who understand it to be Christian Scripture have greater demands placed on them than if this text simply asked us to literally implement certain laws. As Goldingay writes:

> If the teaching expresses a vision or provides illustrations of how principles may be embodied in life or teaches us about the way God wants us to look at different areas of life . . . We have to ask how we could redream and implement this vision, how we could embody it, how we need to change our thinking in the light of it.[161]

While literally implementing the laws would be difficult, in many ways it would be easier than having to think hard about the relevance of the principles contained therein and reimagining how such principles could be worked out in a modern context. The modern task is to imagine how we can work toward social justice today. Thus, the hermeneutical approach requires not only awareness of the ancient cultural context of the CC but also astute awareness of the interpreter's own context. An "'act of imagination' is

---

people are" (ibid., 339).

160. Some opponents of prostitution advocate decriminalization for prostitutes, but continued laws against pimps and johns (Lucas, "Race, Class"). Also, radical feminists argue that prostitution is an example of the subordination of women and not representative of women making a choice of what to do with their bodies, since they are coerced into it by men or economic factors. However, they push for its decriminalization (Sullivan, "Women's Movement").

161. Goldingay, *Israel's Life*, 41.

required to bridge these two contexts."[162] Nobody said it was an easy task, but it is the task that the CC exhorts modern Christians to embrace. We must imagine justice for the marginalized and work in faith toward making the dream one day a reality.

BIBLIOGRAPHY

Alt, Albrecht. "The Origins of Israelite Law." In *Essays on Old Testament History and Religion*, translated by R. A. Wilson, 101–71. Garden City, NY: Doubleday, 1967.

Anderson, Cheryl B. *Women, Ideology, and Violence: Critical Theory and the Construction of Gender in the Book of the Covenant and the Deuteronomic Law*. JSOTSup 394. London: T. & T. Clark, 2004.

Baker, D. L. *Tight Fists or Open Hands? Wealth and Poverty in Old Testament Law*. Grand Rapids: Eerdmans, 2009.

Bauckham, Richard. *The Bible in Politics: How to Read the Bible Politically*. Third Way Books. London: SPCK, 1989.

Birkeland, Nina M., et al. *Global Overview 2011: People Internally Displaced by Conflict and Violence*. Geneva: Internally Displaced Monitoring Centre, Norwegian Refugee Council, 2012. Online: http://www.internal-displacement.org/publications/global-overview-2011.pdf.

Blenkinsopp, Joseph. *Sage, Priest, Prophet: Religious and Intellectual Leadership in Ancient Israel*. Louisville: Westminster John Knox, 1995.

———. *Wisdom and Law in the Old Testament: The Ordering of Life in Israel and Early Judaism*. Rev. ed. Oxford Bible Series. Oxford: Oxford University Press, 1995.

Boecker, Hans Jochen. *Law and the Administration of Justice in the Old Testament and Ancient East*. Minneapolis: Augsburg, 1980.

Bright, John. *A History of Israel*. 3rd ed. Philadelphia: Westminster John Knox, 1981.

Brueggemann, Walter. "The Book of Exodus: Introduction, Commentary, and Reflections." In *New Interpreter's Bible: A Commentary in Twelve Volumes*. Edited by Leander E. Keck et al., 1:675–982. Nashville: Abingdon, 1994.

Chirichigno, Gregory C. *Debt-Slavery in Israel and the Ancient Near East*. JSOTSup 141. Sheffield: JSOT, 1993.

Cornell, Tim J. *The Beginnings of Rome: Italy and Rome from the Bronze Age to the Punic Wars (c. 1000–264 BC)*. Routledge History of the Ancient World. London: Routledge, 1995.

Dandamaev, M. A., et al., *Slavery in Babylonia: From Nabopolassar to Alexander the Great (626–331 BC)*. Translated by V. A. Powell. Edited by Marvin A. Powell and David B. Weisberg. Rev. ed. DeKalb, IL: Northern Illinois University Press, 1984.

Eichler, Barry Lee. *Indenture at Nuzi: The Personal Tidennutu Contract and Its Mesopotamian Analogues*. YNER 5. New Haven: Yale University Press, 1973.

Fensham, F. Charles. "Widow, Orphan, and the Poor in Ancient Near Eastern Legal and Wisdom Literature." *Journal of Near Eastern Studies* 21 (1962) 129–39.

Finkelstein, J. J. *The Ox That Gored*. Philadelphia: American Philosophical Society, 1981.

Fretheim, Terence E. *Exodus*. IBC. Louisville: Westminster John Knox, 1991.

Goldingay, John. *Israel's Faith*. Downers Grove, IL: InterVarsity, 2006.

---

162. Ibid., 333.

———. *Israel's Life*. Old Testament Theology. Downers Grove, IL: InterVarsity, 2009.

Greenberg, Moshe. "Crimes and Punishments." In *Interpreter's Dictionary of the Bible*, edited by G. A. Buttrick, 1:733–44. New York: Abingdon, 1962.

———. "Some Postulates of Biblical Criminal Law." In *Yehezkel Kaufmann Jubilee Volume: Studies in Bible and Jewish Religion*, edited by M. Harán, 5–28. Jerusalem: Magnes, 1960.

Greengus, Samuel. "Biblical and ANE Law." In *ABD*, 4:242–52.

———. "Law in the OT." In *Interpreter's Dictionary of the Bible: Supplementary Volume*, edited by K. Crim, 532–36. Nashville: Abingdon, 1976.

Haas, Peter J. "The Quest for Hebrew Bible Ethics: A Jewish Response." *Semeia* 66 (1994) 151–59.

Hanson, Paul D. *The People Called: The Growth of Community in the Bible*. San Francisco: Harper & Row, 1986.

———. "Theological Significance of Contradiction within the Book of the Covenant." In *Canon and Authority*, edited by George W. Coats and Burke O. Long, 110–31. Philadelphia: Fortress, 1977.

Havice, Harriet Katherine. "The Concern for the Widow and the Fatherless in the Ancient Near East: A Case Study in Old Testament Ethics." Unpublished PhD diss. Yale University, 1978.

Kramer, Samuel Noah. *The Sumerians: Their History, Culture, and Character*. Chicago: University of Chicago Press, 1963.

Lamb, David T. *God Behaving Badly: Is the God of the Old Testament Angry, Sexist, and Racist?* Downers Grove, IL: InterVarsity, 2011.

Leibowitz, Nehama. *Studies in Shemot*. Translated by Aryeh Newman. Jerusalem: World Zionist Organization, 1976.

Levinson, Bernard. "Is the Covenant Code an Exilic Composition? A Response to John Van Seters." In *In Search of Pre-Exilic Israel*, edited by John Day, 272–325. London: T. & T. Clark, 2004.

Lichtheim, Miriam. "Instruction of Amenemope." In *The Context of Scripture*, edited by W. W. Hallo and K. Lawson Younger, 1.47:115–22. Leiden: Brill, 1997.

Lucas, Ann M. "Race, Class, Gender, and Deviancy: The Criminalization of Prostitution." *Berkeley Women's Law Journal* 47 (1995) 47–60.

Malchow, Bruce V. "Social Justice in the Israelite Law Codes." *Word & World* 4 (1984) 299–306.

Marshall, Jay W. *Israel and the Book of the Covenant: An Anthropological Approach to Biblical Law*. SBLDS 140. Atlanta: Scholars, 1993.

McKeating, Henry. "Sanctions against Adultery in Ancient Israelite Society, with Some Reflections on Methodology in the Study of Old Testament Ethics." *JSOT* 11 (1979) 57–72.

Meek, Theophile James. "The Origin of Hebrew Law." In his *Hebrew Origins*, 49–81. New York: Harper & Row, 1960.

Mendelsohn, Isaac. *Slavery in the Ancient Near East: A Comparative Study of Slavery in Babylonia, Assyria, Syria, and Palestine from the Middle of the Third Millennium to the End of the First Millennium*. London: Oxford University Press, 1949.

Meyers, Carol L. *Exodus*. New Cambridge Bible Commentary. Cambridge; New York: Cambridge University Press, 2005.

Neufeld, E. *Ancient Hebrew Marriage Laws: With Special References to General Semitic Laws and Customs*. London: Longmans, Green, 1944.

Olson, Dennis T. "The Jagged Cliffs of Mount Sinai: A Theological Reading of the Book of the Covenant (Exod 20:22—23:19)." *Int* 50 (1996) 251–63.

Otto, Eckart. Review of *A Law Book for the Diaspora: Revision in the Study of the Covenant Code*, by John Van Seters. *RBL* (2004). Online: http://www. bookreviews.org/ pdf/3929_3801.pdf.

Patrick, Dale. *Old Testament Law*. Atlanta: John Knox, 1985.

Rofé, Alexander. "The Vineyard of Naboth: The Origin and Message of the Story." *VT* 38 (1988) 89–104.

Sarna, Nahum M. *Exodus: The Traditional Hebrew Text with the New JPS Translation*. 1st ed. The JPS Torah Commentary. Philadelphia: Jewish Publication Society, 1991.

Shupak, Nili. "The Eloquent Peasant." In *The Context of Scripture*, edited by W. W. Hallo and K. Lawson Younger, 1.43:98–104. Leiden: Brill, 1997.

Sonsino, Rifat. *Motive Clauses in Hebrew Law: Biblical Forms and Near Eastern Parallels*. SBLDS 45. Chico, CA: Scholars, 1980.

Sprinkle, Joe M. *The Book of the Covenant: A Literary Approach*. JSOTSup 174. Sheffield: JSOT, 1994.

Stiller, Brian C. *From the Tower of Babel to Parliament Hill: How to Be a Christian in Canada Today*. Toronto: HarperCollins, 1997.

Sullivan, Barbara. "The Women's Movement and Prostitution Politics in Australia." In *The Politics of Prostitution: Women's Movements, Democratic States and the Globalisation of Sex Commerce*, edited by Joyce Outshoorn, 21–40. New York: Cambridge University Press, 2004.

UN High Commissioner for Refugees (UNHCR). A Year of Crises: Global Trends 2011. June 18, 2012. Online: http://www.unhcr.org/4fd6f87f9.html

UNICEF (United Nations Children's Fund). "Orphans." No pages. Online: http://www. unicef. org/emailarticle/media/media_45279.rhtml.

———. *State of the World's Children 2012: Children in an Urban World*. UNICEF: February, 2012. Online: http://www.unicef.org/sowc2012/pdfs/SOWC%202012-Main%20Report_EN_13Mar2012.pdf.

Van Seters, John. *A Law Book for the Diaspora: Revision in the Study of the Covenant Code*. Oxford: Oxford University Press, 2003.

Waldow, Hans Eberhard von. "Social Responsibility and Social Structure in Early Israel." *CBQ* 32 (1970) 182–204.

Walton, John H., and Victor Harold Matthews. *The IVP Bible Background Commentary: Genesis—Deuteronomy*. Downers Grove, IL: InterVarsity, 1997.

Webb, William J. *Slaves, Women and Homosexuals: Exploring the Hermeneutics of Cultural Analysis*. Downers Grove, IL: InterVarsity, 2001.

Westbrook, Raymond. "The Female Slave." In *Gender and Law in the Hebrew Bible and the Ancient Near East*, edited by Victor H. Matthews, et al., 214–38. Sheffield: Sheffield Academic, 1998.

Wright, David P. *Inventing God's Law: How the Covenant Code of the Bible Used and Revised the Laws of Hammurabi*. Oxford: Oxford University Press, 2009.

2

Wisdom's Cry

Embracing the Vision of Justice
in Old Testament Wisdom Literature

MARK J. BODA AND SHANNON E. BAINES

INTRODUCTION

ONE CAN DISCERN AN increasing interest in research on the relationship between Old Testament Wisdom Literature and social justice over the past two decades. Three works in particular help to orient us to some of the basic issues and especially the variety of views on social justice in the three main wisdom books: Proverbs, Ecclesiastes, and Job.

In his broader work on the social visions of the Hebrew Bible, David Pleins evaluates the wisdom tradition the most negatively among the main Jewish traditions, especially in contrast to the prophetic and priestly traditions. Within the wisdom tradition, the book of Proverbs receives the greatest critique as Pleins caricatures it as possessing a message against the poor, especially because its "rhetoric lacks the sociologically overt boundary-line drawing that we find in the prophets."[1] Any evidences of a similar prophetic approach in Proverbs, what he considers "prophetic chinks in the proverbial armor," are explained away as from a later period and unreflective of the foundational and traditional wisdom tradition.[2] For Pleins, Job is the wisdom text of choice, for there he finds a sensitivity in line with the prophetic social critique, since it focuses on the exploitation of the poor

1. Pleins, *Social Visions*, 465.
2. Ibid., 474.

35

and the need for solidarity with the poor.[3] While Pleins appreciates Qoheleth's sensitivity to the futility of poverty, he finds Qoheleth falling short of "the radical solidarity with the poor" evidenced in Job.[4]

Pleins has been criticized by both Bruce Malchow and Walter Houston.[5] Of the two, Malchow displays the greater difference from Pleins as he traces the attitudes toward wealth, approaches to the poor, and motivations for social justice and charity across Proverbs, Ecclesiastes, and Job, without distinguishing the particular nuances of each book.[6] According to Malchow, while the wisdom tradition does teach respect for the power of money, encourages people to enjoy abundance, and adheres to retribution theory, it places greater emphasis on the limits of wealth's power and the problems of riches, and warns that trusting in wealth is wrong.[7] The wisdom tradition recommends charity, but also exhorts the reader to seek justice for the poor by avoiding maltreatment of them and then actively doing what is right.[8] Malchow attacks Pleins especially in his claim "that Proverbs never goes beyond charity and reaches the level of social justice," noting the evidence of Prov 13:23; 22:22; 29:7, 14; 30:13–14; and 31:9.[9] For Malchow "there is concern for social justice in Proverbs and in the rest of the Wisdom literature."[10] Although Houston is disturbed by the lack of references to the poor in Proverbs 1–9,[11] he catalogues the many proverbs related to poverty in chs. 10–31 that "give the lie to Pleins' assertion that Proverbs launches 'a veritable attack on the poor,' and that the main role they play in the book is to function as a dreadful warning of the dangers of laziness."[12] Houston admits that "the wise are not interested in the origins of the social system, nor are they interested in changing it," that is, "the Proverbs writers were no 'advocates' for the poor." But Houston does track the disapproval of the writers concerning oppression through economic exploitation, insult of the poor, and ignoring the needs of the needy, while

---

3. Ibid., 501–3.

4. Ibid., 510.

5. For Malchow's critique, see further Malchow, "Role of the Poor."

6. See Pleins's critique of this in Pleins, *Social Visions*, 471–72.

7. Malchow, *Social Justice*, 65–66.

8. Ibid., 67–71.

9. Ibid., 72.

10. Ibid.

11. Houston, *Contending for Justice*, 118.

12. Ibid., 121.

noting the encouragement of charity.[13] Although he notes the importance of the doctrine of retribution in Proverbs, he also draws attention to what he calls "a serious tension within the book of Proverbs": "On the one hand, we are assured that the just will receive material rewards and the unjust will be deprived of them. On the other, we learn that those that rule over the poor, give them harsh answers and exploit them . . . are the rich!"[14] Houston finds this same tension made explicit in the dialogue of Job, coming to a head in the exchanges in Job 20–24, especially in Job's disillusionment with God's actions: "By questioning the will of God to judge justly, the Job dialogue [24:1–17] pulls the rug out also from under the ideological justification of a hierarchical society." For Houston, however, "it would not be argued, I think, that the parts of the book that follow offer any way of restoring it." Yahweh's speeches, in particular, articulate an understanding of divine justice that is "very different from that which the friends had assumed and Job had demanded."[15] The view of justice that emerges is one "not determined by human demands, and therefore no foundation for human social order in the way in which the human characters of the book conceive it."[16]

These key studies have prompted us to make a fresh analysis of the data of the biblical Wisdom books so that we can assess the accuracy of the previous overviews. Our analysis will begin with the practical wisdom tradition embedded within the book of Proverbs before moving on to the philosophical stream of the Hebrew wisdom tradition represented by the books of Ecclesiastes and Job.

PRACTICAL WISDOM: PROVERBS

The book of Proverbs provides practical instructions for its audience on how to live in the world—to prosper and attain success in honest ways, and to avoid poverty. The teachings do not advocate a change in the social structures but say that people should be generous to the poor. Proverbs is primarily directed towards life in the public sphere, where men gather together, acquire counsel, and direct the course of their lives.[17] Though

---

13. Ibid., 123.

14. Ibid., 125.

15. Ibid., 131.

16. Ibid.

17. Due to the prominence of instructions given to the "son" in Proverbs, and in general, its overtly male audience, gender inclusive language has not been used in this paper.

this audience was predominantly the upper class, it was not necessarily comprised of government officials only. However, some of the teachings directly address how kings and rulers should act.[18] The primary target audience consists of the young man, the naïve person (1:4), and those who are already wise can become increasingly wise by adhering to the wisdom instructions.[19]

The fear of the Lord is recognized as the beginning of wisdom; wisdom being the ultimate teacher "who forms the conscience of the people in the fear of the Lord as the only path to true success."[20] The "fear of the Lord" is so central to the understanding of wisdom that it occurs fourteen times in the book of Proverbs.[21] Additionally, the fear of the Lord forms an inclusio around the foundational chapters 1–9 (1:7; 9:10) as well as the entire book (1:7; 31:30), so that the heart of the cry of Lady Wisdom in ch. 9 is the fear of the Lord and "the woman presented in 31:10–31 is the embodiment of 'the fear of the Lord' in 1:7 from a human perspective."[22]

Chapters 1–9 prepare the audience for what can be expected in chs. 10–31, establishing the framework within which to read the wisdom presented predominantly through pithy statements in chs. 10–31.[23] Roland Murphy argues that wisdom has two aspects in Proverbs: wisdom calls in chs. 1–9, but people need to respond to wisdom in chs. 10–31.[24] In particular, Prov 1:1–7 provides an introduction and overview to the entire book by including its title (v. 1), purpose (vv. 2–6), and foundation (v. 7).[25] Verses 2–6 each begin with an infinitive construct and each refers back to v. 1, representing a different purpose of the proverbs.[26] The purposes of wisdom are as follows: (1) to know (wisdom, instruction, v. 2a), (2) to discern (sayings of understanding, v. 2b), (3) to receive (instruction in wise behavior: righteousness, justice, and equity, v. 3), (4) to give (prudence,

18. Houston, *Contending for Justice*, 119.

19. Berry, *Introduction to Wisdom*, 129.

20. Nardoni, *Rise Up, O Judge*, 135.

21. Bartholomew and O'Dowd, *Old Testament Wisdom Literature*, 80.

22. Ibid., 81.

23. Berry, *Introduction to Wisdom*, 127; Waltke, *Book of Proverbs: Chapters 1–15*, 10. This viewpoint is reiterated and further expanded by Murphy: chs. 1–9 provide the "hermeneutical key" for the remainder of the book (Murphy and Huwiler, *Proverbs, Ecclesiastes, Song of Songs*, 5).

24. Murphy, *Tree of Life*, 29.

25. Waltke, *Book of Proverbs: Chapters 1–15*, 10.

26. McKane, *Proverbs*, 263.

knowledge, and discretion to the naïve and to youth, v. 4; [a wise man will hear and increase in learning, and a man of understanding will acquire wise counsel, v. 5]), and (5) to understand (a proverb, a figure, words of the wise, and their riddles, v. 6). Verse 3 stands out in its immediate context because it addresses behavior or actions, not internal personal qualities.[27] What is striking is that this one reference to wise behavior emphasizes behavior that consists of righteousness, justice, and equity, thus establishing a strong relationship between wisdom and justice.[28] As in v. 3, the words "righteousness," "justice," and "equity" occur again in 2:9 and are presented to the son as some of the results of wisdom; the one who finds wisdom will be able to discern "righteousness and justice and equity and every good course."[29]

This relationship between wisdom and justice is not only firmly established at the beginning of Proverbs but is also repeated in 8:15, 16, and 20. Wisdom is personified as a woman. She describes her relationship with justice in the following way: by wisdom, kings reign (v. 15a), rulers administer justice (v. 15b), and princes and nobles rule--"all who judge rightly" (v. 16). Wisdom also describes herself as walking "in the midst of the paths of justice" (v. 20b). This data from key sections within the foundational chapters (1–9) of Proverbs reveals from the outset the key role that justice plays within the wisdom worldview. As we investigate the practical wisdom on justice articulated throughout the book of Proverbs we will first look at the broader issue of wealth and poverty, since economics was the dominant arena where acts of justice and injustice were carried out in ancient Israel. This will provide a foundation for a consideration of explicit references to justice and injustice.

Wealth and Poverty

CAUSES OF WEALTH

Proverbs identifies both admirable and unjust means that lead to wealth. Admirable ways include adhering to the teachings of wisdom and instruction, giving back to God, being diligent and hard-working, using oxen in the fields, receiving a blessing from God, being generous, being righteous, trusting in God, being humble and fearing God, planning, and inheriting.

27. Berry notes that v. 3 "identifies the practical aims of the collection [Prov 1–9]" (*Introduction to Wisdom*, 129).

28. This paper will primarily focus on only one of these components: justice.

29. Unless otherwise stated, all Scripture will be quoted from the NASB.

In contrast, Proverbs also identifies injustice (Prov 15:27; 16:8b; cf. 11:16b) and the oppression of the poor (22:16a)[30] as dishonest means, specifically, robbery, fraud, and charging interest. For the purposes of this paper, injustice and oppression will be explored only as a cause of wealth and in the following section, a cause of poverty.

In Prov 1:10–15, the son is warned against being enticed to join in with sinners who desire to harm people and steal their possessions. The would-be offenders tempt the son with the prospect that many valuable items can be obtained to fill their houses, and that they can pool their resources together so they will have "one purse" (v. 14).

Fraud is a means of acquiring wealth (Prov 13:11a).[31] Though the word מֵהֶבֶל is translated "fraud" in the NASB, scholars are uncertain about how to translate it. מֵהֶבֶל may be translated as "meaninglessness" or "hastiness," implying that the wealth was attained through nothingness (without labor), but likely, through dishonest means.[32] Wealth gained dishonestly at other people's expense will come and go quickly.[33] Moreover, Prov 21:6 likens telling lies to attain wealth to "a fleeting vapor, the pursuit of death" ; the punishment for this behavior will be the disappearance of wealth and, ultimately, death.[34]

Proverbs 28:8 indicates that those who acquire wealth through interest and usury store it up for someone who will be gracious to the poor. Interest was prohibited on loans made to fellow Israelites (cf. Exod 22:25; Lev 25:36–37; Deut 23:19–20) because loans were given to people in need; they had to borrow to feed themselves and their families. The person providing a loan was not to profit from another's misfortune. The image of wealth being

30. Though there is an unequal relationship between the oppressed and the oppressor, Prov 29:13 identifies a commonality between the two: "The Lord gives light to the eyes of both." Light is a metaphor for God's gift of life to people, including the oppressed and the oppressor (Perdue, *Wisdom Literature*, 67).

31. In the NIV, מֵהֶבֶל is translated as "dishonest"; ESV, "hastily"; ASV, "vanity"; NLT, "get-rich-quick schemes."

32. Koptak, *Proverbs*, 358. Cf. also Murphy, *Proverbs*, 97; Murphy and Huwiler, *Proverbs, Ecclesiastes, Song of Songs*, 65; Whybray, *Proverbs*, 204. Waltke suggests that מֵהֶבֶל is used metaphorically in this verse to denote a lack of permanence (*Book of Proverbs: Chapters 1–15*, 561).

33. Waltke, *Book of Proverbs: Chapters 1–15*, 561.

34. Longman, *Proverbs*, 391.

gathered up may imply that God will ensure, either directly, or indirectly, through another person, that the poor are repaid.[35]

Causes of Poverty

Several causes of poverty are identified in the book of Proverbs: laziness, sinfulness, selfishness, failure to heed discipline, failure to plan, injustice and oppression, the pursuit of pleasure over work, and contractual obligations.[36]

Proverbs 13:23 indicates that abundant food exists in the poor man's ground (field) but it is taken away through injustice. In this example, injustice keeps the poor man in his present condition of poverty, depriving him of the resources that could fulfill his needs. Poverty can also be the consequence for individuals who acted unjustly as indicated in 22:16: the one who oppresses the poor or gives to the rich (instead of to those who need resources) will succumb to poverty.

Contrasts between Wealth and Poverty

Some passages in Proverbs present wealth as a more favorable option than poverty. Proverbs 10:15 states that "the rich man's wealth is his fortress, the ruin of the poor is their poverty." In the first part of the verse, wealth can serve as protection for the rich just as a fortified city provides protection for those who reside within its wall (cf. 18:11). However, for those who are poor, poverty is their destruction. This passage does not provide any cause-effect relationship between good behavior and wealth, or bad behavior and poverty, but simply states the reality that wealth provides protection and poverty is destructive.[37]

Proverbs 14:20 indicates that the poor are shunned by their own neighbors but the rich have many friends (cf. 18:24). A similar saying is presented in 19:4, "wealth brings many friends but a poor man's friend deserts him," repeating the notion that poverty leads to social isolation. Social isolation means that the poor man does not have access to people who could help him; they want nothing to do with him because he may ask

35. Longman notes that the process of gathering up of wealth is not specified but that there may be an assumption that God will ensure that it occurs (ibid., 490). Proverbs 13:22b states that the "wealth of a sinner is stored up for the righteous."

36. Proverbs, unlike the prophetic literature, does not view injustice as the only cause of poverty but also "laziness and negligence . . . disordered behavior and bad habits" (Nardoni, *Rise Up, O Judge*, 134).

37. Hatton, *Contradiction*, 92–93.

for something.[38] Proverbs 19:7 states that both a poor man's relatives and his friends shun and avoid him, and that "though he pursues them with pleading, they are nowhere to be found."[39]

In addition, a person's manner of speech is influenced by his wealth or poverty. In Prov 18:23, a poor man needs to plead for mercy while a rich man can answer harshly. The poor person has to be careful how they speak because their livelihood (acquiring resources such as food for survival) depends on it, while the wealthy person has no such concern.

Another disadvantage of poverty is that the rich rule over the poor and the borrower (poor) is a servant to the lender (22:7). In ancient times, borrowing, unlike often in the West today, was for survival. People went into debt to buy food to support themselves and their family. If borrowers could not repay the loan, then they or their family members could become servants of the creditor, working to pay off the loan. Creditors could also sell defaulters to others who would then become the owners of the debtors.[40]

In contrast to wealth being a more favorable option than poverty, wealth can be detrimental to one's well-being. It can expose a person to being kidnapped for ransom, whereas the poor are not threatened in this manner due to a lack of wealth (13:8).[41]

WEALTH VERSUS CHARACTER TRAITS, REST, AND THE DAY OF WRATH

Wisdom, a dominant trait that permeates the book of Proverbs, is viewed as superior to wealth. It is described as more valuable than silver, gold, or jewels (cf. 3:14–15; 8:10–11; 16:16). Moreover, Proverbs views money as useless in the hands of a fool because a fool has no desire to acquire wisdom (17:16), and the fool should not even have wealth—i.e., to live in luxury (19:10).

Proverbs presents other traits that one should strive for and attain that are superior to wealth. For instance, Prov 15:16 observes that having a small amount of the fear of God is better than possessing great wealth with

38. Waltke, *Book of Proverbs: Chapters 1–15*, 599.

39. Murphy questions the type of friends mentioned in these pages, who gravitate toward the rich and avoid the poor. Are they the type of friends worth associating with? (Murphy and Huwiler, *Proverbs, Ecclesiastes, Song of Songs*, 13–14).

40. Waltke, *Book of Proverbs: Chapters 15–31*, 207.

41. However, regardless of the differences between the wealthy and the poor, both have in common the same maker, God (22:2). Hatton argues that 22:2 in effect devalues wealth (relatively) by stating that both the rich and poor are equal before God (*Contradiction*, 111).

turmoil, while 22:1 teaches that a good name or reputation (honor) is preferable to great wealth. Moreover, 20:15 states that lips that speak knowledge are more valuable than gold and many jewels.

Proverbs does not promote an ever-increasing desire for and pursuit of wealth, but actually provides good practical advice: "do not weary yourself to gain wealth, cease from your consideration of it" (23:4). In v. 5, wealth is portrayed as temporary, as it can vanish quickly and is likened to a bird making itself wings and flying heavenward like an eagle.[42] Wealth is portrayed as having no value or benefit on the day of wrath. It cannot save a person from death, but only righteousness can do this (Prov 11:4). The day of wrath may refer to a life-threatening situation, the wrath of God, or the wrath of an individual; this passage "fits in well with the pervasive teaching in the book that the righteous tend to escape difficulties, while the wicked seem to invite them."[43]

POVERTY IS A PREFERABLE STATE

Proverbs 16:8 teaches that it is better to be righteous and possess only a small amount (of income or wealth), than to have great wealth with injustice. This passage does not specifically mention poverty but is explicit that possessing less is preferable.

Proverbs 16:19 states that it is better to be lowly in spirit and to be among the oppressed (those who do not have the power or influence in society to defend themselves, i.e., the poor) than to share plunder with those who are proud.[44] In two other instances, things are better for a poor man who has integrity than for a person who speaks perversely and is a fool (19:1); and it is better for a man to be poor than a liar (19:22b). Likewise, Prov 28:6 establishes a contrast in that it is better for a poor man to have integrity than be someone who is crooked; the difference between this verse and the previous one is that it ends with the qualifier, "though he may be rich."

---

42. Longman and Garland, *Proverbs–Isaiah*, 197. In the ancient Near East, the image of a bird flying away was a symbol of "fleeting wealth" (ibid., 197).

43. Longman, *Proverbs*, 251.

44. Davis notes that passages such as 15:16, 16:8, and 16:19 are examples of the sages' teachings on temperance as a virtue, and that the "cumulative of these 'better . . . than' statements . . . means that one must want fewer material goods than we are generally disposed to want" ("Preserving Virtues," 194).

INDIFFERENCE TOWARDS WEALTH AND POVERTY

Proverbs 30:7–9 is a strong acknowledgement of the value of temperance in the pursuit of wealth in the form of a prayer to God, the only one that occurs in the entire book.[45] In 30:8b and c, the speaker does not desire poverty or riches, but only his daily bread, what is necessary to survive from day to day. His rationale is that if he has too much, he may deny or disown God, and if he becomes poor, he may steal and dishonor God's name.

SUMMARY OF WEALTH AND POVERTY

The theme of wealth and poverty is prevalent throughout the book of Proverbs. Though there are varying causes of wealth and poverty mentioned in Proverbs, the previous section has focused solely on one of these causes, namely, injustice. Injustice leads predominantly to wealth (or increased wealth) for the perpetrators and poverty (or the continuation of poverty) for the victims. However, in 22:16, this pattern is reversed in that the perpetrators of injustice experience poverty, not wealth.

Proverbial sayings are also provided that contrast wealth and poverty with each other, both being portrayed as positive, negative, or neutral. When wealth is compared to some aspects of life, it is evaluated negatively. However, when poverty is compared with other aspects of life, it is evaluated positively. These contrasts illustrate that varying viewpoints on wealth and poverty exist within the book of Proverbs.

Justice and Injustice

In the previous section, injustice was identified as one of the causes of wealth and poverty; forms of injustice included robbery, fraud, charging interest, and oppression. This section will examine the nature of justice and injustice as portrayed in Proverbs. It will include teachings pertaining to both the poor and those who are not identified specifically as poor.

Justice is associated with providing help for the poor and needy. Whoever is gracious and kind to the poor will be blessed but the nature of the blessing is not specified (Prov 14:21 and 22:9). Moreover, Prov 21:13 indicates that the cries of the poor need to be heeded. In this passage, consequences are also provided for inaction. If a man does not listen to the cries of the poor, then he will suffer the same fate: when he cries out, he will not be answered. Similarly, the person who gives to the poor will

45. Ibid.

never experience want, but the one who ignores the poor will receive many curses (28:27). Furthermore, one of the attributes of the noble wife is that she "extends her hand to the poor and stretches out her hands to the needy" (31:20). She is generous and gives to those in need.

Proverbs also addresses unjust actions towards the poor. Proverbs 22:22–23 instructs the audience not to rob (exploit) the poor because of their situation nor "crush the afflicted at the gate." The gate was the place where court cases were judged and justice was to be administered. This passage warns that if justice is denied to the poor or the afflicted, then God will rescue them and destroy their oppressors. Furthermore, 28:15–16a likens a wicked leader ruling over the poor to a "roaring lion and a rushing bear"; this oppressive leader lacks understanding. In another instance of oppression, a wicked man devours the afflicted and needy (30:14).

Proverbs identifies righteous people as those concerned about justice[46] and the rights of the poor. Conversely, the unrighteous do not have the same concern (29:7).[47] The righteous are described as rejoicing when justice has been implemented but the unrighteous are terrified of it (21:15). In fact, the righteous and unrighteous are so incompatible that they are an abomination to each other (29:27).

Proverbs teaches that treatment of the poor, whether just or unjust, is reflective of one's attitude toward God. Someone who oppresses the poor shows contempt for their maker but the one who is kind to the needy honors God (14:31). Proverbs 17:5 teaches that a person who mocks the poor taunts their maker. Proverbs 19:17 pushes the relationship between one's actions and God even closer together. A person who is kind to the poor, presumably by providing them with resources, is actually lending to God. As a result, the generous person will receive a reward (unspecified) from God.[48]

Proverbs also teaches that justice and injustice extend beyond treatment of the poor. Proverbs 3:27–28 instructs the son not to withhold good

46. Proverbs 12:6 states that "the thoughts of the righteous are just."

47. Cf. Prov 29:10: "Men of bloodshed hate the blameless, but the upright are concerned for his life."

48. Since it was unlikely that the poor would be able to repay these loans, God was solely responsible for repayment (Curtis and Brugaletta, *Discovering the Way of Wisdom*, 75). Moreover, Prov 19:17 is an indication of God's commitment to the poor, in that lending to them is the "most solid investment" because God will repay the loan in full. This assurance of full repayment provides an incentive for people with means to help the poor (Nardoni, *Rise Up, O Judge*, 133).

from people who deserve it when he has the resources to act. The son is to give at the time of the request instead of asking the person in need to return the next day. This verse does not specifically mention the poor (or needy). Someone can have an immediate need but it may not be reflective of their financial situation.[49]

The unjust act of robbery is not condoned in Proverbs. Robbery was identified as a cause of wealth (3:10–15) in the previous section but is mentioned again in 28:24. In this passage, the son who robs his mother or father and does not believe it is a sin is described as the "companion of a man who destroys."

Justice was also to be practiced in business transactions. Proverbs 16:11 teaches that honest scales, balances, and weights originate with God. These measuring devices were used in the marketplace where goods were traded but could easily be manipulated by the merchant in his favor to increase profits.[50] Deliberately inaccurate weights and measures are an abomination to God (cf. 11:1; 20:10, 23) and a means of injustice.[51] In the marketplace, merchants were the perpetrators of injustice and unsuspecting consumers were the recipients of injustice.[52]

Another context where justice was to be administered was the court system, even though injustices infiltrated it. Proverbs 17:15 states that God hates the (unjust) acts stemming from the court system where the guilty are acquitted of their wrongdoing and the innocent are condemned (found guilty): a complete reversal of justice. This situation could have resulted from a bribe used to manipulate the outcome of a case, which is a perversion

49. Duane Garrett notes that the recipients of the good that is due to them could be "laborers who have earned their pay, the poor who rightly plead for help, or suppliants at the city gates who call for justice. On the other hand, they could be those who have lent money and deserve to be repaid" (*Proverbs, Ecclesiastes, Song of Songs*, 84).

50. Deut 25:13 warns against possessing two different sets of weights and measures: one heavy and the other light.

51. Brown ("Pedagogy of Proverbs 10:1—31:9," 156–57) notes that the synonymous parallelism present in Prov 16:11; 20:10, 23, in the second half of the sayings attributed to Solomon (chs. 16–22), "expand upon what is encapsulated antithetically in the first proverb," namely 11:1, "a false balance is an abomination to the Lord, but a just weight is his delight." Proverbs 11:1 is situated within the first half of the sayings (chs. 10–15). Brown also notes that the theme of being a truthful witness, introduced antithetically in 12:17, is expanded upon in the latter half of the sayings in 19:5, 9, 28; 21:28 ("Pedagogy of Proverbs 10:1—31:9," 157–58).

52. The passages do not indicate whether the victims of this injustice were poor or not.

of justice (17:23).[53] Partiality to the wicked (guilty) and deprivation of justice for the innocent in the court system is condemned (cf. 18:5; 24:23–24; 28:21). Further, Prov 24:24b includes consequences that will befall those responsible for injustice. The one who declares the guilty innocent will be cursed by others and denounced by nations. In v. 25, those responsible for justice, who convict the guilty, will experience blessing.

Injustice within the court system can also result from a corrupt or lying witness who interferes with the implementation of justice (19:28; cf. 6:19; 12:17; 14:5; 25:18).[54] Proverbs 24:28–29 prohibits a person from being a witness against a neighbor without cause, and from deceiving through speech in order to seek revenge. However, justice will prevail in the end. Proverbs 21:28 states that a false witness and those who listen to him will not escape punishment; both will be destroyed forever (cf. 19:5, 9). Proverbs 3:30 further prohibits the misuse of the court system, with either a frivolous case or a case that falsely accuses a person of wrongdoing.[55]

Another context where justice was to be administered was in the maintenance of property lines. Stones were used to demarcate boundaries for people's land, which were applicable to future generations. Proverbs 22:28 prohibits the movement of boundary stones initially set up by ancestors. These stones could be moved unjustly to steal portions of the land. Widows and the fatherless were particularly vulnerable because they did not have an adult male in the household to protect and defend them. God would become their protector and advocate to "establish the boundary of the widow" (15:25a). Furthermore, Prov 23:10 prohibits both the movement of the stones and people trespassing on the fields that belong to the fatherless. Verse 11 provides the rationale for obeying these commands: God is their defender and he will take the case up against the offender. In other words, God will ensure that justice is administered.

---

53. Ambiguity exists surrounding the phrase "a wicked man receives a bribe from the bosom." The wicked man could be the person who received the bribe in secret, such as an unjust judge or other court official (Longman and Garland, *Proverbs–Isaiah*, 158; Murphy, *Proverbs*, 131); the wicked man could be the person who gave the bribe, who "takes the bribe from his own bosom to give it to an unjust official" (Murphy and Huwiler, *Proverbs, Ecclesiastes, Song of Songs*, 88); or the wicked man could be the giver or recipient of the bribe. Proverbs 17:23 is ambiguous. Either way, the practice is deemed wrong because the bribe is used to pervert justice (Longman, *Proverbs*, 350). Cf. 15:27b.

54. Several general references to the act of lying occur in Proverbs: 6:17; 10:18; 12:19b, 22; 14:25; 15:4; 17:4, 7; 26:28.

55. McKane, *Proverbs*, 300.

A further context for justice was in the leadership of Israel, especially the highest position, the king. The book of Proverbs addresses the responsibility that a king has to rule with integrity and uphold justice (cf. 20:8). A king should not betray justice or decree erroneous judgments (16:10b; cf. 29:12). It is by justice that a king provides stability for a country but the one who accepts bribes (perversion of justice) overthrows or destroys it (29:4). If a king judges the poor justly, then "his throne will be established forever" (29:14). The security of the king's reign is dependent upon his actions towards the poor.

Kingship and justice also appear near the end of Proverbs in the sayings of King Lemuel. Proverbs 31:4–5 instructs that kings and rulers should not drink wine or beer because it would cause them to forget the laws, which would then, in turn, deprive the oppressed of their rights. Verses 6–7 instruct Lemuel to give wine and beer to those who are perishing and experiencing anguish so that they will forget their current condition. Verse 8 instructs the king to speak up for those who cannot speak on their own behalf and speak for the rights of all people who are destitute. Verse 9 not only repeats the beginning of verse 8, "speak up," but instructs the king to judge fairly and defend the rights of the poor and needy.

Those who refuse to act justly will be taken away by the violence they inflicted upon others (21:7). This final passage does not specifically mention the poor but rather is a general comment about the consequences that will befall the wicked.

Observations on Wealth and Poverty and Justice

In Proverbs 1–9, justice is either associated with wisdom (1:3; 8:15, 20), or God, who guards "the paths of justice" and "preserves the way of his godly ones" (2:8). Proverbs 2:9 declares that if the son takes these words to heart, he too will be able to discern justice. What exactly constitutes justice or injustice is not revealed. In the same way, the poor and needy are not explicitly mentioned in Proverbs 1–9. There is no counsel on justice towards the poor.[56] However, it has been demonstrated above that references to (in)justice are present in chs. 1–9, specifically warnings against robbery, and exhortations to help one's neighbor.

Proverbs 10–31 provides further details on justice, especially in the areas of the marketplace, the courts, land boundaries, and the proper treatment of the poor. Throughout these chapters, the poor are mentioned

56. Houston, *Contending for Justice*, 118.

frequently in various types of wisdom sayings and instructions. Though mention of the poor is scattered, they are most often referred to in chs. 19, 22, and 28.[57] In some instances where treatment of the poor is addressed, the consequences are provided. Righteous behavior toward the poor results in a happy giver (14:21), blessing (22:9), and satisfaction (28:27). Unrighteous behavior towards the poor and needy results in poverty (22:16), death (22:22), and many curses (28:27). Furthermore, a few passages include an effect on God: he is taunted when the poor are oppressed (14:31a) and when the poor are mocked (17:5), but honored by those who are gracious to the needy (14:31b). Proverbs 19:17 includes both an effect on God and a consequence: those who are gracious to the poor lend to God and will be repaid in full. Proverbs 28:2 is the only reference in the entire book to a poor man oppressing the lowly--he is likened to a "driving rain which leaves no food." In addition, the widow and fatherless among the poor in ancient Israel appear separately in 15:25 and 23:10, both in reference to land boundaries.

Proverbs does not have one consistent or all-encompassing perspective on wealth and poverty. This is seen not only in the comparisons between wealth and poverty but also the comparisons evaluating other aspects of life in light of poverty and wealth.[58] Neither status is recommended as *the* absolute condition to attain in life, nor is wealth to be pursued recklessly and without restraint. The various positions, seemingly contradictory and clashing with one another, stand side by side in the book.[59]

Injustice has been identified as one of the causes of both wealth and poverty, but the wisdom instructions suggest, either explicitly or implicitly,

---

57. Houston notes that instructions for providing charity to those in need frequently occur in Prov 10:1—22:16 and chs. 25–29 (ibid., 118).

58. Longman identifies seven "snapshots" of wealth and poverty in Proverbs: (1) "God blesses the righteous with wealth," (2) "foolish behavior leads to poverty," (3) "the wealth of fools will not last," (4) "poverty is a result of injustice and oppression," (5) "those with money must be generous," (6) "wisdom is better than wealth," and (7) "wealth has limited value" (*Proverbs*, 573–75). Longman further states that "no single proverb can be taken as representing the teaching of Proverbs on wealth and poverty" (ibid., 576).

59. Murphy argues that the variation in views on wealth and poverty in Proverbs was likely a result of the "realities of life" that the sages reflected upon (Murphy and Huwiler, *Proverbs, Ecclesiastes, Song of Songs*, 13). Washington notes, "Expressions on wealth and poverty in Proverbs can be grouped into variations on a number of themes, such as 'wealth is an unqualified good,' as opposed to 'wealth is a liability'; 'poverty is a disgrace,' as opposed to 'the disgrace of X (dishonesty, cruelty, etc.) is worse than poverty'" (*Wealth and Poverty*, 179).

that God will bring justice into situations where injustice exists. However, humanity has a role to play in the area of justice. "[It] is through the divine gift of wisdom, enhanced by study, reflection, and action, that humans learn to actualize justice in social life."[60]

The book of Proverbs does not advocate for societal reform to eliminate poverty. It accepts that poverty is a reality in life but that people with resources are to be generous to the poor, performing acts of charity to sustain the lives of the poor. With the exception of Prov 30:7–9, those speaking in the book share a view common in the ancient Near East that wealth, in general, is a blessing, even though this belief is qualified in some of the instructions.[61]

PHILOSOPHICAL WISDOM: ECCLESIASTES AND JOB

The book of Proverbs provides a window into the core wisdom tradition of the Old Testament and reveals the diversity of thought on economic and justice themes. This is expressed mainly through the genre of the pithy saying, providing practical wise advice, exhortations, and observations on wealth/poverty and justice/injustice. But there is another key stream within the wisdom literature of the Old Testament, a more philosophical stream that considers the same issues from a different perspective and provides additional insights into these key themes.

Ecclesiastes

The voice of Qoheleth is linked to the wealthy and powerful elite, identified with the royal house from the outset. The autobiographical sections make clear that this Qoheleth has significant financial means and social power and throughout the book one finds deep reflection on both wealth/poverty and justice/injustice.

Wealth and Poverty

One of the first pursuits Qoheleth describes is that of pleasure—identifying himself as one able to build houses and plant vineyards, gardens, and parks, and to create ponds (2:4–6). He has the means to possess slaves, singers, and a harem, as well as herds and flocks, and precious metals (2:7–8). And yet his evaluation of such wealth is that it is *hebel*, futility, a "striving after

60. Perdue, *Wisdom Literature*, 74.
61. Whybray, *Wealth and Poverty*, 113.

wind" under the sun (2:11). While Qoheleth agrees with the aphorism that the fool abandons work to his own detriment (4:5), such rest is better than endless labor, which is but a striving after the wind (4:6). This vanity is illustrated by the example of the man continually working, finding no satisfaction in riches, and depriving himself of pleasure, without even having an heir for the fruit of his labors (4:8). This consideration of the futility apparent in labor and wealth foreshadows the most concentrated section on riches and poverty in the book of Ecclesiastes, stretching from 5:10 to 6:9.[62] In this section, Qoheleth strikes a middle path between wealth and poverty, confronting the temptation to idealize poverty on the one hand and to act indifferently towards wealth on the other.[63] Since Qoheleth identifies some amount of pleasure as key to enjoying life under the sun, abject poverty would make any pleasure in poverty unattainable and so some measure of wealth is essential (5:12–20), whether one lives in relative poverty (5:18) or wealth (5:19–20).[64]

<h2 style="text-align:center">JUSTICE AND INJUSTICE</h2>

Near the end of ch. 3, Qoheleth begins to explore the presence of injustice in his world, finding wickedness in the place of justice and righteousness (3:16). He consoles himself with the fact that there is a time when "God will judge both the righteous and the wicked" (3:17). In the chapters that follow, Qoheleth observes oppressive activity conducted "under the sun," seen in the uncomforted oppressed in subjection to the power of their oppressors (4:1). For Qoheleth, it would be better either to be dead or to have never existed than to see or experience such oppression (4:2–3). He observes that there is an element of oppression in all human labor, in that it is always related to rivalry between fellow humans (4:4). One can discern a progression in Qoheleth's treatment of the issue of oppression in the book. While in 4:1–3 Qoheleth appears surprised at the oppression he

62. On the cohesion of this section, see Seow, *Ecclesiastes*, 216–17; Fredericks and Estes, *Ecclesiastes*, 147–49; Bartholomew, *Ecclesiastes*, 216.

63. Krüger, *Qoheleth*, 122. Brown notes how "Qoheleth does not struggle with rectifying the systemic problem with economic disparity. The sage, admittedly, is no revolutionary. Yet he is far from endorsing the status quo and particularly the lifestyles of the rich and famous. To the contrary Qoheleth sees little gain from such hyperconsumption . . . Consumption, in short, does not render contentment; it simply leads to more consumption, a vicious cycle" (*Ecclesiastes*, 60).

64. Krüger, *Qoheleth*, 4: "Thus we see that human beings must have at their disposal a certain amount of personal property (and necessarily wealth) in order to have the possibility of becoming happy. To this 'portion' every person has a 'right'"; cf. ibid., 122.

observes, by 5:8–9 he instructs his audience not to be shocked at the sight of the oppression of the poor and denial of justice and righteousness. By 7:7, however, he reveals that oppression has the potential to ruin even the wise man.[65] For Qoheleth, oppression is a permanent feature of human experience that contributes to his conclusion that life under the sun is futile.

SUMMARY OF ECCLESIASTES ON WEALTH AND POVERTY AND JUSTICE

The strength of the book of Ecclesiastes is its honest descriptions of the sobering realities of life under the sun, especially in relation to economics and justice. The strategy of Qoheleth is first to recognize the futility of these realities.[66] Second, in relation to economics, Qoheleth encourages a *via media* between wealth and poverty so that one can enjoy the gifts of God, which include eating and drinking, while fearing God.[67] Third, in relation to justice, while Qoheleth encourages living in light of the assurance that God has a time to judge oppression, he also suggests it would be better to be dead than to face oppression.

Job

Like Ecclesiastes, the book of Job reflects on the established truths of the wisdom tradition, but takes this reflection in a different direction. An important dimension of the teaching of the book of Job is to challenge any hastily-made correlations between the stance of God toward a person and the experience of that person. Blameless Job is identified by God from the outset as his special servant and this is related by the narrative to the extraordinary blessing that Job experiences. The cursed condition that Job subsequently finds himself in is thus considered by the friends to be evidence of God's displeasure. Job's shock over his condition reveals that he assumes at the outset of the book the same hermeneutical grid as his friends. It appears then that within this hermeneutical tradition of wisdom, those who suffer, supposedly including the poor and needy, do so because of the displeasure of God. This is not, however, completely accurate as the

---

65. It is unclear, however, whether the verb used here refers to the wise man becoming mad at the sight of oppression or the wise man becoming foolish because of his participation in oppression. The latter is more likely because of the second part of 7:7, which speaks of the bribe corrupting the heart; cf. Fredericks and Estes, *Ecclesiastes*, 169.

66. See Bartholomew, *Ecclesiastes*, 192.

67. See further Boda, "Speaking into the Silence," for the message of Qoheleth and the relationship of this message to the final authoritative voice of the Sage in 12:9–14.

argument of the friends and Job progresses, since in their search for a sinful cause for Job's suffering and loss, both the friends and Job focus on the possibility of social injustice. While the friends refer to various socially unjust acts that could have prompted this divine punishment (5:15–16; 20:19; 22:4–11),[68] Job refutes these accusations by cataloguing his socially just behavior, which included caring for the needy and attacking the wicked who sought to abuse them (29:12–17; 30:25; 31:5–6, 13, 16–25).[69] In Job's speech in ch. 29, "Job presents his justice as his sole claim for honour in the community, in preference to his wealth or his ancestry."[70] Thus, one can discern within the traditional arguments of Job and his friends on the one side the view that suffering and loss by one who is rich are evidence of divine punishment, and on the other, the view that the poor may suffer due to the abuse of the rich and not divine displeasure.[71] While many have sought to pit the perspectives in the book of Job (even of traditional wisdom) over against the wisdom tradition found in the book of Proverbs, it is apparent from our presentation above that these two views have been encountered within Proverbs already. It is true, however, that there is greater emphasis in Job on the elite's need to enact social justice, even though one can discern at certain points the viewpoint that some deserve social estrangement and economic poverty (Job 30:1–8).

Ultimately, however, the book of Job critiques the key wisdom hermeneutic of retribution, that is, that suffering and loss are related to God's displeasure due to sin and folly, and that success and riches are related to God's blessing due to faithfulness and wisdom. The final shape of the book with its concluding narrative that mirrors the opening narrative by restoring to Job twofold what was lost at the outset, however, reveals that the principle is not entirely abandoned. What is challenged is the rigid application of the

68. Pleins, *Social Visions*, 500–501.

69. See esp. Houston, *Contending for Justice*, 128–29, who is careful to note, based on 30:1–5 that "in Job's moral world there are undeserving as well as deserving poor" and "to give *them* charity would be a breach of justice rather than an instance of it: they stand altogether outside the community in which justice is meaningful" (129).

70. Ibid., 128.

71. Pleins sees this as a key contrast between the vision of Proverbs (with its "standard wisdom explanation for poverty . . . that it results from laziness") and Job (which "focuses on poverty as the product of exploitation"). He treats this as "prophetic language" (*Social Visions*, 501). Bergant also highlights how assertions by the visitors and Job that "God intervenes on behalf of the poor (5:15–16) and punishes those who take advantage of them (20:19ff)" (cf. 24:2–12, 18–24), "contradicts the assumption that misfortune is the consequence of some kind of transgression" (*Israel's Wisdom Literature*, 39).

principle and especially the logical fallacy that if God blesses wise behavior with riches and curses foolish behavior with poverty, then the rich are by definition wise and the poor are by definition foolish.

The emphasis in the book of Job is definitely on the innocent sufferer—that is, one whose powerlessness and poverty are not due to foolish or wicked behavior, but rather to forces beyond his control. This emphasis is not lacking in the practical wisdom presented in Proverbs, even though there it is but one of many perspectives.

The consideration of the innocent sufferer in Job, however, raises some serious questions about Yahweh's role in social injustice. In ch. 24 this is expressed in Job's searching questions: "why are times not stored up by the Almighty, and why do those who know Him not see his days?" (v. 1). These questions ask about God's seeming inaction before the injustices that are then described in the verses that follow, a description that is interrupted by the phrase "yet God does not pay attention to folly" (v. 12c).[72] Elihu is incensed by Job's accusations, noting in 34:17, "shall one who hates justice rule? And will you condemn the righteous Mighty One?" and arguing that God does hear the cry of the poor and the afflicted (34:28) and shows no partiality to princes and the rich (34:19). However, the book casts great doubts over Elihu's defense. At the outset of the book Yahweh is presented as negotiating with another heavenly figure over the fate of helpless Job, a scenario that suggests the context of the elite lording over the lower classes. Throughout the book the figure Job increasingly highlights the injustice of his present predicament, suggesting God's involvement. This is illustrated poignantly in the persistent employment of legal motifs throughout the book.[73] Legal vocabulary, such as צדק (Qal), מִשְׁפָּט, שפט ענה רשע (Hiphil), תָּם (guiltless), עקש (Hiphil, declare guilty), נקה (Piel), דִין, עֵד, רִיב, תּוֹכַחַת, יכח, is found on the lips of most of the participants. A burning question throughout the book is "[how] can a person be declared in the right before God?," appearing on the lips of Eliphaz (4:17), Job (9:2–3), and Bildad (25:4). Job's strategy to contend with Yahweh in court can be seen as it develops with increasing passion from chs. 9–10 (see esp. 9:2–3, 14–16, 20–21, 28–29, 32–33; 10:3, 6–7, 14–15, 17), to ch. 13 (see esp. 13:3, 6–10, 15–19; cf. 16:19), to ch. 23 (see esp. vv. 3–7), and finally ch. 31 (see esp. v. 35). However, Eliphaz's question in 4:17, "Can a person be declared

72. See Houston, *Contending for Justice*, 130.

73. See Boda, *Severe Mercy*, 387–89; cf. Richter, *Studien zu Hiob*; Habel, *Book of Job*, 54–57.

in the right before God?" implicitly casts doubt from the outset over the likelihood that Job would have a successful trial. This is made explicit in Eliphaz's later statement in 15:5 that Job's mouth has already condemned him (רשע Hiphil) and his lips have testified (ענה) against him. Elihu's statements in chs. 34–35 make clear that Job's case is in serious jeopardy, since "the Almighty will not pervert justice" (34:12). In the end Job abandons his request for trial since he sees little hope of success because of God's control of the legal system, interestingly a concern often expressed over the unjust legal systems within the Old Testament.[74]

God finally does respond in chs. 38–41 in two phases (chs. 38–39, 40–41). While both speeches begin with the divine exhortation: "Now gird up your loins like a man; I will ask you, and you will inform me" (38:3; 40:7), the first speech begins with the rhetorical question, "Who is this that darkens counsel by words without knowledge?" (38:2), while the second speech begins with, "Will you really annul my judgment? Will you condemn me that you may be in the right?" (40:8).[75] These latter questions reveal that these speeches represent Yahweh's response to Job's longstanding request for a trial, but the former questions in 38:2 create a much broader context for the trial, that is, not the specific issue of justice (מִשְׁפָּט) in Job's case, but rather the much larger "counsel" (עֵצָה) of God. This "counsel of God" is first introduced into the book by Job himself in 12:13, when he declares that "with [God] are wisdom and might, to Him belong counsel (עֵצָה) and understanding," before tracking the variety of ways God is involved in the affairs of earth, both human and natural.[76] The purview of the counsel of God is made clear in the speeches that follow. Yahweh relentlessly pummels Job with a series of rhetorical questions that highlight the breadth of divine activity both past and present that has little to do with humanity, but is essential to the maintenance of the universe.

While some have treated God's answer here as merely "a power play designed to silence Job or, at least, to deflect attention from his suffering,"

---

74. Bergant, *Israel's Wisdom Literature*, 30: "The futility of this undertaking is obvious. God, who is the accused, is also the judge and the jury. There is no place to which Job can turn for justice."

75. See also the question that is placed after the first speech (40:2), separated by the introductory speech formula, "then Yahweh said to Job" (40:1), prior to Job's first response in 40:3–5, which is loaded with legal terminology: ריב, יכח (Hiphil), ענה.

76. See Habel, "In Defense of God," 34, who describes this as "God's design of the cosmos . . . the wisdom of God expressed in the plan of creation, as discrete from any history-oriented plan of salvation."

it appears that through it "God reconstructs the world that Job has decon-structed by his curse and contempt."[77] The purpose of these divine speeches, then, is to reveal that Job's plight must be seen on a much larger stage than merely human experience. Job is reduced to an ant as the camera pans back to reveal the Creator at work in all of creation, forming and sustaining it by his power as well as his love. In all this Yahweh never admits that Job has experienced an injustice. It is clear from the opening narrative that Job has experienced suffering unrelated to any evil or foolish behavior on his part, but to call this suffering unjust would mean to affirm the very rigid retribu-tion theory that the book seeks to undermine. Yahweh never answers this issue directly, although the expansion of the viewpoint seems to suggest that there are forces at work within the universe that Yahweh must attend to that are unknown to humans.[78] Thus, the attack by the Adversary on the honor of Yahweh and his servant in the opening chapter may have been considered a greater injustice to an ancient audience than our modern eyes will allow.[79]

77. Brown, "Introducing Job," 234. Many have struggled with the place of the divine speeches in the book of Job. Williams argues for the integrity of the book of Job (that is, these speeches are not later insertions) but simply concludes that: "In God's speeches he seems to ignore or evade the question of justice that Job poses. Contrary to the drift of recent Job interpretation, I would call this poor theology("God of Victims," 208)." Wil-liams's hermeneutic is made clear on p. 224: "The first obligation of the interpreter who stands in service to the biblical tradition of the disclosure of the innocent victim and the God of victims is not to the text as such but to the victim and the God of love and justice." (He also cites Girard, *Scapegoat*, 8: "one must either do violence to the text or let the text do violence to innocent victims.")

78. Note especially the link pointed out by Clifford, *Wisdom Literature*, 93–94, be-tween the beasts of ch. 40, Behemoth (40:15–24) and Leviathan (40:25—41:26), and the Adversary figure in chs. 1–2, something that does not appear to be lost on the writer of Revelation who links the beast (Rev 11:7; 13:1–4, 11–18, etc.), a Leviathan-like creature (12:3; 13:1; 17:3), and Satan / the devil (12:9, 12; 20:2, 10) together; cf. 2 Esdr 6:49–52; 2 Bar 29:4.

79. Often the conversation between Yahweh and the Adversary at the outset of the book is treated as significant only insofar as it reveals to the reader that Job's suffering is not just unrelated to any sin on his part, but is related directly to his obedience (because he was blameless he was picked out as a target by the Adversary). For most interpreters, the particulars of the debate between Yahweh and the Adversary are irrelevant. However, if one takes into account the speeches of Yahweh in chs. 38–41, it may well be that the particulars are important (see Murphy, *Tree of Life*, 36, who argues that the key issue is identified at the outset of the book by the interchange between Yahweh and the Adver-sary as human sincerity not divine caprice). The divine speeches remind Job that there is divine activity of which he knows nothing, but which is essential to the maintenance of a just and abundant universe. This may be what is at work in the heavenly realm, as the

What is then the purpose of these speeches? By ignoring the plight of the human Job and speaking instead of Yahweh's activity especially throughout the non-human world, Yahweh is showing Job, first, that he is indeed at work maintaining justice throughout his creation and, second, that Job's plight is not the center of the universe.[80] Habel summarizes well the first purpose:

> God offers a defense by challenging Job, and any who would listen, to discern God as the sage who designed a world of rhythms and paradoxes of balanced opposites and controlled extremes, of mysterious order and ever-changing patterns, of freedom and limits, of life and death. Within this complex universe God functions freely to monitor the intricacies of the system, to modulate its ebb and flow and to balance its conflicting needs.[81]

The second purpose challenges a tradition that celebrated the wonder that the creator God would take thought of and care for humanity (Ps 8:4). God's speeches here remind humanity that they are still created beings, and that the activity of the world does not revolve around them. The wisdom tradition of Job and his friends clearly displays sensitivity to a retribution theory that had taken on board what is often called the prophetic sensitivity (but is a part of the wisdom tradition) to justice for the poor and needy, but the speeches of God reveal that even this can easily slip into a focus on human need and conditions at the expense of the rest of creation.[82] The divine speeches remind humanity of its place within the cosmos and God's responsibility to all of creation. As Bergant notes:

Adversary attacks Job and Yahweh defends him, allowing the test to proceed in order to exonerate Job's integrity.

80. So also Clifford, *Wisdom Literature*, 94: "human beings cannot assume that they are the center of the universe . . . Job's preoccupation with his own case led him to narrow his focus and concentrate on the human race and on himself"; cf. Greenberg, "Job," 298, who notes how humankind (represented by Job) is "displaced from its center to a remote periphery"; and Levenson, *Creation*, 153–56, who notes that "creation is a wondrous and mysterious place that baffles human assumptions and expectations because it is not anthropocentric but theocentric. Humanity must learn to adjust to a world not designated for their benefit."

81. Habel, "In Defense of God," 38.

82. We all can call to mind those instances when we are heading out for a picnic and we see rain clouds approaching. We blame God, who in a biblical worldview is in charge of such operations, but we fail to take account of the fact that the farmers in the area may be in need of rain for their crops, and that the wild plants and bodies of water on which the local animal life depends need water.

Job's breathtaking experience of creation has catapulted him out of his narrow confines of anthropocentricism into the vast expanse of mystery. His encounter with the ineffable Creator-God has led him to the new and transformative insight that human history unfolds within the broader context of the natural world and not vice versa; the natural world does not merely serve the ends of human history.[83]

CONCLUSION

Our journey has revealed the theological and ethical resources of the wisdom tradition, which have the potential to shape our own response to contemporary injustices. The tradition speaks through the practical voice of Proverbs as well as the philosophical voices of Ecclesiastes and Job.

This study illustrates that the book of Proverbs understood and taught that justice should be practiced in all areas of life including the family unit (household), relationships with neighbors, the marketplace, the judicial system, and the ruling class including the king. All segments of the population were to experience justice in these contexts. The poor are singled out and represent one segment of the population that is in special need of help because they are particularly vulnerable to injustice in any sphere of life. Studies by Pleins, Malchow, and Houston overlook the inclusive nature of justice and instead only view (social) justice as pertaining to the poor. Specifically, Houston notes that charity and justice towards the poor are absent in Proverbs 1–9.[84] Though the poor are not specifically mentioned, justice/injustice is present within this section: a prohibition against robbing and injuring the innocent for the acquisition of possessions (1:10–14), an instruction to provide the needs of a neighbor immediately (3:27–28), a prohibition against falsely accusing one's neighbor (3:30), and a judgment that a false witness is an abomination to God.

Malchow identifies the presence of both charity and social justice towards the poor in Proverbs. The sages taught that people were to be both generous and open to the poor, helping to meet their immediate needs, actively defending their rights, and avoiding exploitation, violence, and oppression––all forms of injustice–– toward the poor. However, the term "charity," which Pleins, Malchow, and Houston use, is problematic, because it denotes that a person chooses both the nature of the charitable act (i.e.,

83. Bergant, *Israel's Wisdom Literature*, 44.
84. Houston, *Contending for Justice*, 118.

what is given and how much) and when it will be given. In contrast to charity, Proverbs teaches that generosity entails giving the poor what they require and when they require it (immediately).

Pleins's caricature that "the poor are considered a despised and lazy lot in the proverbial literature"[85] does not hold true in light of this analysis undertaken on Proverbs. Laziness is identified as one of the many causes of poverty presented in Proverbs alongside sinfulness, selfishness, failure to heed discipline, failure to plan, injustice and oppression, the pursuit of pleasure over work, and contractual obligations. Passages that instruct the audience about generosity and the just treatment of the poor do not address the causes of poverty, blame the poor for their circumstances, or portray the poor negatively.

Within the philosophical stream of wisdom, Ecclesiastes voices what we often feel about the oppressive circumstances we encounter: that under the sun human experience is futile. This is even as the book encourages us to pursue and provide the resources for all humans to enjoy God's gracious creational gifts in the fear of Yahweh, and finally reminds us of divine accountability in time. Job contributes to the wisdom tradition, affirming on the one side the important role that social justice played within traditional wisdom, while in the end challenging our notions of justice and the anthropocentric fixation of humanity. This study affirms the evaluations of Malchow and especially Houston, that emphases in Proverbs can be discerned in Ecclesiastes and Job. It challenges not only Pleins's juxtaposition of Proverbs over against Ecclesiastes and especially Job, but also Pleins's embrace of Job as a text that merely champions social justice.

It is interesting that two key Latin American theologians have drawn on this philosophical tradition of wisdom as resources for their vision of social justice. Liberation and feminist theologian Elsa Tamez, in her analysis of Ecclesiastes, recognizes the mysterious characterization of God in the book, a divine figure who appears to act arbitrarily (cf. 3:11; 6:2).[86] Yet she recognizes that Yahweh in Ecclesiastes is a gracious change agent who can transform situations, especially noting the dominant role played by 3:1–6:12, which she titles "Facing the Present with Trust in God's Grace."[87]

The great liberation theologian Gustavo Gutiérrez also drew on wisdom's philosophical tradition, using the book of Job to articulate his

---

85. Pleins, *Social Visions*, 470.

86. Tamez, *When the Horizons Close*, 87.

87. With thanks to Drewes, "Reading the Bible in Context," 130.

vision for social renewal. In Job he found two kinds of God-talk. First is the prophetic voice, with its demand to live an ethical life because of God's preferential love for the poor, a voice that denies any simplistic links between poverty and divine punishment. There is also a contemplative voice that seeks an encounter with God through complaint, bewilderment, and confrontation, and through which Job aligns himself with the poor and speaks to God regarding injustice. However, Gutiérrez is well aware that the speeches of God do not appear to embrace this voice of protest, so Gutiérrez seeks to incorporate this into his viewpoint:

> What is it that Job has understood? That justice does not reign in the world God has created? No. The truth that he has grasped and that has lifted him to the level of contemplation is that justice alone does not have the final say about how we are to speak of God. Only when we have come to realize that God's love is freely bestowed do we enter fully and definitively into the presence of the God of faith. Grace is not opposed to the quest of justice nor does it play it down; on the contrary, it gives it its full meaning. God's love, like all true love, operates in a world not of cause and effect but of freedom and gratuitousness.[88]

Gutiérrez is thus shaped by the text. Rather than ignoring the text or attacking the text, he is willing to side with a God whose

> special love does not have for its ultimate motive the virtues and merits of the poor but the goodness and freedom of God, a God who is not simply the guardian of a rigid moral order . . . There is indeed a contradiction between the free, gratuitous, and creative love of God and the doctrine of retribution that seeks to pigeonhole God.[89]

Thus, Gutiérrez bravely notes: "emphasis on the practice of justice and on solidarity with the poor must never become an obsession and prevent our seeing that this commitment reveals its value and ultimate meaning only within the vast and mysterious horizon of God's gratuitous love."[90]

88. Gutiérrez, *On Job*, 87.

89. Ibid., 88.

90. Ibid., 96. Bergant notes that Job presumes "that God is bound to the same law and order assigned to human society and, being negligent in this regard, God is guilty of injustice. Job has labored under the assumption that human society, the physical world, and the mystery of God itself are all subject to the moral laws that Job knows . . . He expects God to enforce the causal relationship between human behavior and life circumstances that retribution, as he understands it, demands. In this he has been wrong"

Job thus reminds those of us consumed by the pursuit of justice and tempted to build a deistic and humanistic utopia that there is far more at work in this universe than human activity and that our demand for attention to human need may not always be the preferred priority for the divine who carries the universe in his loving and powerful arms. This last point is humbling, but also may be freeing to those commissioned to enact justice in the world of humanity.

BIBLIOGRAPHY

Bartholomew, Craig G. *Ecclesiastes.* BCOTWP. Grand Rapids: Baker Academic, 2009.

Bartholomew, Craig G., and Ryan P. O'Dowd. *Old Testament Wisdom Literature: A Theological Introduction.* Downers Grove, IL: IVP Academic, 2011.

Bergant, Dianne. *Israel's Wisdom Literature: A Liberation-Critical Reading.* Minneapolis: Fortress, 1997.

Berry, Donald K. *An Introduction to Wisdom and Poetry of the Old Testament.* Nashville: Broadman & Holman, 1999.

Boda, Mark J. *A Severe Mercy: Sin and Its Remedy in the Old Testament.* Siphrut: Literature and Theology of the Hebrew Scriptures 1. Winona Lake, IN: Eisenbrauns, 2009.

———. "Speaking into the Silence: The Epilogue of Ecclesiastes." In *The Words of the Wise Are like Goads: Engaging Qoheleth in the 21st Century,* edited by Mark J. Boda, Tremper Longman, III, and Cristian G. Rata, 257–79. Winona Lake, IN: Eisenbrauns, 2013.

Brown, William P. *Ecclesiastes.* Interpretation. Louisville, KY: WestminsterJohn Knox, 2000.

———. "Introducing Job: A Journey of Transformation." *Int* 53 (1999) 228–38.

———. "The Pedagogy of Proverbs 10:1—31:9." In *Character and Scripture: Moral Formation, Community, and Biblical Interpretation,* edited by William P. Brown, 150–82. Grand Rapids: Eerdmans, 2002.

Clifford, Richard J. *The Wisdom Literature.* Interpreting Biblical Texts. Nashville: Abingdon, 1998.

Curtis, Edward M., and John J. Brugaletta. *Discovering the Way of Wisdom: Spirituality in the Wisdom Literature.* Grand Rapids: Kregel, 2004.

Davis, Ellen F. "Preserving Virtues: Renewing the Tradition of the Sages." In *Character and Scripture: Moral Formation, Community, and Biblical Interpretation,* edited by William P. Brown, 183–201. Grand Rapids: Eerdmans, 2002.

Drewes, Barend F. "Reading the Bible in Context: An Indonesian and a Mexican Commentary on Ecclesiastes: Contextual Interpretations." *Exchange* 34 (2005) 121–33.

Fredericks, Daniel C., and Daniel J. Estes. *Ecclesiastes and the Song of Songs.* Apollos Old Testament Commentary. Downers Grove, IL: Apollos, 2010.

Garrett, Duane A. *Proverbs, Ecclesiastes, Song of Songs: An Exegetical and Theological Exposition of Holy Scripture.* NAC 14. Nashville: Broadman, 1993.

Girard, René. *The Scapegoat.* Baltimore: Johns Hopkins University Press, 1986.

(*Israel's Wisdom Literature,* 33).

Greenberg, Moshe. "Job." In *The Literary Guide to the Bible*, edited by Robert Alter and Frank Kermode, 283–304. Cambridge, MA: Belknap Press of Harvard University Press, 1987.

Gutiérrez, Gustavo. *On Job: God-Talk and the Suffering of the Innocent*. Maryknoll, NY: Orbis, 1987.

Habel, Norman C. *The Book of Job: A Commentary*. OTL. Philadelphia: Westminster John Knox, 1985.

———. "In Defense of God the Sage." In *The Voice from the Whirlwind: Interpreting the Book of Job*, edited by Leo G. Perdue and W. Clark Gilpin, 21–38. Nashville: Abingdon, 1991.

Hatton, Peter T. H. *Contradiction in the Book of Proverbs: The Deep Waters of Counsel*. SOTSMS. Aldershot, England: Ashgate, 2008.

Houston, Walter. *Contending for Justice: The Ideologies and Theologies of Social Justice in the Old Testament*. LHBOTS 428. London: T. & T. Clark, 2006.

Koptak, Paul E. *Proverbs*. NIVAC. Grand Rapids: Zondervan, 2003.

Krüger, Thomas. *Qoheleth: A Commentary*. Hermeneia. Minneapolis: Fortress, 2004.

Levenson, Jon D. *Creation and the Persistence of Evil: The Jewish Drama of Divine Omnipotence*. San Francisco: Harper & Row, 1988.

Longman, Tremper, III. *Proverbs*. BCOTWP. Grand Rapids: Baker Academic, 2006.

Longman, Tremper, III, and David E. Garland. *Proverbs–Isaiah*. Expositor's Bible Commentary 6. Grand Rapids: Zondervan, 2008.

Malchow, Bruce V. "The Role of the Poor in Proverbs." In *Reading from Right to Left*, edited by J. C. Exum and H. G. M. Williamson, 229–40. Sheffield: Sheffield Academic, 2003.

———. *Social Justice in the Hebrew Bible*. Collegeville, MN: Michael Glazier / Liturgical, 1996.

McKane, William. *Proverbs: A New Approach*. OTL. Philadelphia: Westminster John Knox, 1970.

Murphy, Roland E. *Proverbs*. WBC 22. Nashville: Thomas Nelson, 1998.

———. *The Tree of Life: An Exploration of Biblical Wisdom Literature*. 2nd ed. Grand Rapids: Eerdmans, 1996.

Murphy, Roland E., and Elizabeth Huwiler. *Proverbs, Ecclesiastes, Song of Songs*. NIBCOT 12. Peabody, MA: Hendrickson, 1999.

Nardoni, Enrique. *Rise Up, O Judge: A Study of Justice in the Biblical World*. Translated by Seán Charles Martin. Peabody, MA: Hendrickson, 2004.

Perdue, Leo G. *Wisdom Literature: A Theological History*. Louisville, KY: Westminster John Knox, 2007.

Pleins, J. David. *The Social Visions of the Hebrew Bible: A Theological Introduction*. Louisville, KY: Westminster John Knox, 2001.

Richter, Heinz. *Studien zu Hiob: Der Aufbau des Hiobbuches, dargestellt an den Gattungen des Rechtslebens*. Theologische Arbeiten 11. Berlin: Evangelische Verlagsanstalt, 1959.

Seow, C. L. *Ecclesiastes: A New Translation with Introduction and Commentary*. AB. New York: Doubleday, 1997.

Tamez, Elsa. *When the Horizons Close: Rereading Ecclesiastes*. Maryknoll, NY: Orbis, 2000.

Waltke, Bruce K. *The Book of Proverbs: Chapters 1–15*. NICOT. Grand Rapids: Eerdmans, 2004.

———. *The Book of Proverbs: Chapters 15–31*. NICOT. Grand Rapids: Eerdmans, 2005.

Washington, Harold C. *Wealth and Poverty in the Instruction of Amenemope and the Hebrew Proverbs*. Atlanta: Scholars, 1994.

Whybray, R. N. *Proverbs*. NCBC. Grand Rapids: Eerdmans, 1994.

———. *Wealth and Poverty in the Book of Proverbs*. JSOTSup 99. Sheffield: JSOT, 1990.

Williams, James G. "Job and the God of Victims." In *The Voice from the Whirlwind: Interpreting the Book of Job*, edited by Leo G. Perdue and W. Clark Gilpin, 208–31. Nashville: Abingdon, 1991.

3

Seek Yahweh, Establish Justice

Probing Prophetic Ethics. An Orientation from Amos 5:1–17

M. Daniel Carroll R.

INTRODUCTION

"JUSTICE!" HAS BEEN THE human cry throughout the centuries. The concept has been variously understood across cultures and eras in terms of its content, motivations, and sanctions, but the condemnation of mistreatment of the vulnerable and the deep longing for the removal of oppression and for ordered, peaceful flourishing mark all of history. One can hear the anger and this yearning from the frustrated despair in ancient Egypt's *The Eloquent Peasant* and *Prophecy of Neferti* to the sophisticated arguments of the philosophical treatises of Plato and Aristotle to social movements around the globe in the past and today. Of course, justice is a central theme of the Bible.

The prophetic literature and office in particular have been a key resource to which Christians have appealed to understand the divine demand for justice and to bring attention to human suffering caused by its rejection. Sometimes this turn to the biblical material can be spotty, but its impact is undeniable. The term "jeremiad," an eponym drawn from the name of the prophet Jeremiah, was coined years ago to refer to any bitter denunciation of a society's ills.[1] In many circles, the adjective "prophetic" is taken to be a reference to someone or something that is critical of the status quo. A "prophetic voice" or a "prophetic church" is a person or ecclesial body

---

1. Bercovitch, *American Jeremiad.*

that proclaims a message censuring inequity and works to change existing social structures.

The prophetic literature has also been the cornerstone of several recent movements. One example is Latin American Liberation Theology.[2] Motivated by a "preferential option for the poor," these theologians, church leaders, and activists grounded much of the substance of their radical critique of society and of their hope for a transformed world in these books. There, too, they mined a philosophy of history and established criteria for evaluating Christian praxis, teaching, and liturgy. Another example comes from South Africa. During the struggle to overturn apartheid, church leaders crafted *The Kairos Document*, which distinguished a "prophetic theology" from "state" and "Church" theologies. The last two were said to be compromised and unwilling to speak out against institutionalized and cultural wrongs.[3]

Recently, however, some question whether the prophets should serve, in whole or in part, as ethical guides. Cyril Rodd says that in the modern world it is no longer possible to believe people who claim that they, as prophets, reveal God's displeasure with the world and can announce that he will intervene in the future. Anyway, Rodd claims, the prophets were less interested in injustice and the fate of the poor than is commonly supposed.[4] A growing group of voices protest that the violence of the judgment of God in prophetic texts is culturally conditioned and not acceptable,[5] an issue to which we will return below. The horrors of the last century, such as the Holocaust, or Shoah, raise the profile of this challenge as never before,[6] but I suspect the contemporary penchant for an amicable deity of blessing and happiness also cringes at the thought of the "dark side of God."

In this essay, the prophetic literature is taken as part of the Christian Scripture. As such—and in contradistinction to some of these dissenting opinions—I hold that it is relevant for ethics today. Our attention will be on the canonical shape, or final form, of the text, instead of on theoretical

---

2. E.g., Miranda, *Marx and the Bible*; Rigol, *Misión profética de la iglesia*; Gutiérrez, *On Job*, 19–49; Ellacuría, "Utopia and Prophecy"; cf. Carroll R., *Contexts for Amos*, 109–20, 289–306, 312–19; Carroll R., *Amos*, 53–72.

3. *Kairos Document*.

4. Rodd, *Glimpses of a Strange Land*, 170–74, 296.

5. See below, n 19.

6. Sweeney, *Reading the Hebrew Bible after the Shoah*.

redactional layers.[7] We will not try to establish the possible socio-economic and political context of mid-eighth century BCE Israel that fuels the prophet Amos's condemnation. Those debates are valuable, but they lie beyond my purview here. Suffice it to say that I believe that this book's message is set within a largely agrarian peasant world,[8] which is experiencing the breakdown of its traditional patronage system. The poor suffer injustice perpetrated by the monarchy and other government officials, merchants, and religious leaders in both rural and growing urban areas, even as the entire nation celebrates a patriotic ideology of blessing and victory.[9] This, broadly speaking, is the deplorable state of affairs that prompts the ethical calls that permeate other prophets, not just Amos (e.g., Isa 1:16–17; Jer 7:5–6; 22:3, 16; Ezek 18:5–18; 22:7, 29; Mic 6:8; Zech 7:9–10; Mal 3:5).[10] The emphatic defense of the vulnerable by Israel's prophets is unique among prophets in the ancient Near East, where references to justice are rare.[11]

This essay will concentrate on the book of Amos. Amos is perhaps best known for the pronouncement of 5:24: "Let justice roll on like a river, righteousness like a never failing stream!"[12] Martin Luther King, Jr., for instance, quoted these words in his landmark "I Have a Dream" speech at the Lincoln Memorial in August 1963. Amos is characterized by the mandate for justice in multiple spheres and is representative of the prophetic commitment to justice, so it can serve our purposes well.

7. See Carroll R., "Ethics and the Old Testament." In any case, I take the book of Amos to reflect substantially the eighth century, in contrast to those who propose subsequent redactional layers in the later pre-exilic period or in the exile, or who postulate the book's production in post-exilic Yehud.

8. For the agricultural lens of Amos, note E. F. Davis, *Scripture, Culture, and Agriculture*, 120–38; Marlow, *Biblical Prophets*, 120–57.

9. The following works are helpful, though I do not subscribe to aspects of their socio-historical reconstructions: Domeris, *Touching the Heart of God*; Houston, *Contending for Justice*; Coomber, *Re-reading the Prophets*; Knight, *Law, Power, and Justice*, 115–224; Dever, *Lives of Ordinary People*, 106–248.

10. I have dealt with the ethics of the prophetic literature more generally in "Failing the Vulnerable" and "Ethics."

11. Examples are found in letters from Nur-Sin in Aleppo to King Zimri-Lim of Mari (A. 1121 + A. 2731; A. 1968). See Nissinen, *Prophets and Prophecy in the Ancient Near East*, 17–22.

12. All citations are from NIV 2011, unless stated otherwise.

YAHWEH AND JUSTICE IN AMOS 5:1–17

Instead of surveying the ethical message of the entire book,[13] this study instead focuses on Amos 5:1–17. There we find the constitutive elements of the message of justice in the prophetic literature. The passage is structured chiastically. Chiasms, or inverted structures, move progressively through their corresponding pairs of passages toward the emphasis in the middle. The book of Amos has several chiasms (with varying levels of probability), and these range in length from one verse to larger passages.[14] Several scholars even propose that the entire book is in the form of a chiasm, though this idea is not widely embraced.[15] Amos 5:1–17 is its best known chiasm,[16] and its climatic center proclaims, "The Lord [Yahweh] is his name" (v. 8). The person of Yahweh himself is at the core of prophetic ethics. My exposition will follow the flow of the passage and use each section to highlight matters relevant to our topic.

The Cost of Injustice (Amos 5:1–3, 16–17)

We begin with perhaps the most difficult issue related to justice in the Bible, one that, as stated earlier, is receiving a lot of attention: the violence of God and the suffering that it brings. It is one thing to make the claim that God *demands* justice of all humanity, especially of his people, and that he *sides with* those who suffer injustice; it is quite another to probe *how* God *responds* to injustice and its perpetrators *with punishment* in history. I read and hear much about the former point, but almost nothing about the latter. What do we do with the judgment of Yahweh, who sits enthroned as the judge of the nations of the earth (Gen 18:25; Ps 82:8; 96:13; Isa 2:4; Jer 9:24; Joel 3:12)? This is an exceedingly complex—and I contend, inescapable—topic for those of us committed to seeing justice made manifest in

13. In addition to the sources listed above in n 9, note, e.g., Fendler, "Zur Sozialkritik des Amos"; Fleischer, *Von Menschenverkäufern*; Bohlen, "Zur Socialkritik des Propheten Amos."

14. Some scholars rightly warn against seeing too many chiasms in the biblical text (e.g., Boda, "Chiasmus in Ubiquity"). The chiasm of Amos 5:1–17, however, is well established.

15. Smalley, "Recursion Patterns and the Sectioning of Amos"; Dorsey, "Literary Architecture and Aural Techniques in Amos"; Dorsey, *Literary Structure of the Old Testament*, 285–86; Rotzoll, *Studien zur Redaktion und Komposition des Amosbuchs*, 1–7.

16. De Waard, "The Chiastic Structure of Amos V 1–17." This structure is recognized by many commentators. For a literary reading of 5:1–17, see Carroll R., *Contexts for Amos*, 221–40.

our world. Here I set forth several preliminary textual observations to orient some initial reflections on the issue.[17]

In the passage preceding 5:1–3, God rehearses his repeated, but spurned, attempts to bring the nation to repentance (4:6–11). That series climaxes with the first of the three hymns in the book (4:12–13; cf. 5:8–9; 9:5–6), which announces Israel's imminent encounter with the Lord God Almighty (*Yhwh 'elohê ṣᵉ'bā'ōt*), an epithet with military overtones of Yahweh as warrior.[18] In the literary context, this dreadful meeting leads to death, a fate worse than the litany of catastrophes of 4:6–11. Hence the lament (v. 1): the nation has fallen in battle (v. 2), its armies decimated (v. 3). This divine epithet reappears in the matching verses of the chiasm (vv. 16–17), where we hear ubiquitous wailing at this terrible loss. Anguish at the horrors of war is heard throughout the land.[19] God passes through Israel, but not as its champion as he did so many years before against the Egyptians (Exod 12:12; 14:13–14; 15:1–18). Instead, Yahweh judges the nation, which has become the oppressor of its own people and does not fulfill its calling before him. They, more than any other nation, are without excuse (cf. Amos 3:1–2).

What are we to do with judgment scenes like these? For some, that violence is decreed at all by God is problematic.[20] This flat reading of the text, however, is ethically and theologically inadequate. First, the language of such passages needs to be set against its *contextual background*. To do so is to recognize that many of the expressions of judgment are stereotypical, utilizing vocabulary that is found throughout the ancient Near East.[21] These are hyperbolic, highly emotive, sometimes contradictory, messages that are designed to generate fear and obedience in a people towards their sovereign—here, Israel towards Yahweh—via the threat of disaster. This information is helpful, in that it explains the source and significance of certain vocabulary. Thus, the interpreter can avoid imposing twenty-first-century sensibilities on these texts with an overly literal reading.

17. I develop the ideas of this section more extensively in "I will send fire."

18. Paas, *Creation and Judgement*, 231–44.

19. Note Eph'al, *City Besieged*.

20. E.g., Dempsey, *Hope amid the Ruins*, 90–100; Davies, *Double Standards in Isaiah*; O'Brien, *Challenging Prophetic Metaphor*, 101–24; cf. Seibert, *Disturbing Divine Behavior*; Seibert, *Violence of Scripture*.

21. Fensham, "Common Trends in Treaty Curses"; Sandy, *Plowshares and Pruning Hooks*, 75–102.

While this information can put the issue into cultural perspective, however, admittedly it does not eliminate the moral challenge of divine punishment. In Amos, God sends destruction by war on surrounding nations (1:4–5, 7–8, 10, 12, 14–15), Judah (2:5), and Israel (2:14–16; 3:11–4:3; 4:10; 5:1–6, 27; 6:7–11, 14; 7:7–9, 17; 8:3; 9:1–4, 8–10). Defeat in war leaves but a remnant (3:12; 5:3, 15–17; 6:8–11; 8:3; 9:8) and is coupled with exile (1:5, 15; 4:2; 5:27; 6:7; 7:17; 9:4, 9). The judgment includes an earthquake (1:1; 8:8; 9:5)[22]—one so powerful that it would be called to mind centuries later (Zech 14:5). The mourning of the people is understandable.

Second, such observations lead to questions about *the person of God* that require a careful, integrated reading of the text. Images of the divine judge should not be sharply separated from, and placed over against, images of him as the One who watches over the defenseless. This, for example, is Walter Brueggemann's approach. He categorizes judgment texts as part of Israel's "counter-testimony"—those disturbing, ambiguous, and negative Old Testament portrayals of God, which he juxtaposes without co-mingling and resolution to the "core testimony" of Israel.[23] The latter are the "characteristic" ways of talking about Yahweh, the sovereign God who is in a committed relationship of gracious solidarity with his people. These two tracks are different ways of comprehending and experiencing God, he says, and to mix them would be to betray the theological tension that is fundamental to the faith of the Old Testament. For his part, Eric Seibert differentiates between what he sees as the "disturbing behavior" of the God of the Old Testament text and the actual God we follow, who is revealed by Jesus.[24] This approach, he argues, produces discerning and ethically responsible readings.

In contrast, a more fully canonical treatment of the biblical text appreciates that the anger and judgment of Yahweh are grounded in his *pathos.* These arise from deep within his being, and God, who brings chastisement to bear, does so with sorrow.[25] Heschel rightly says: "It is because God is

22. Some verses listed here for war have been taken as allusions to the earthquake: 2:13; 3:14–15; 4:11, 13; 6:9–11; 9:1, 5.

23. Brueggemann, *Theology of the Old Testament,* 373–99. This approach also appears in other works.

24. Seibert, *Disturbing Divine Behavior,* 169–240; Seibert, *Violence of Scripture,* 61–92.

25. See the comments by Fretheim, "Some Reflections on Brueggemann's God." Also note his *Suffering of God* and *God and World in the Old Testament,* 157–98. On occasion, however, I believe that Fretheim distances God too much from direct involvement in

the source of justice that His pathos is ethical; and it is because God is absolutely personal . . . that this ethos is full of pathos."[26] Yahweh is deeply invested in justice (in discreet behaviors and in the character of nations) and cares for the victims of injustice. He is rightly moved to anger at contexts of oppression and at those who disregard human dignity and life,[27] but he also mourns the cost of righteous punishment. Note that 5:1–3 is a lament (*qînâ*) that God himself lifts up!

Laments are usually an expression of grief over the death of a loved one or friend (2 Sam 1:17–27; 3:31–35), but, in the prophets, occasionally they can be an ironic taunt over a people deserving of judgment (e.g., Ezek 26:17; 28:11–19; cf. Isa 14:4–23). These opening lines to Amos 5, however, express divine pain and disappointment at what Israel experiences and mirror the wailing of the people in 5:16–17. Yahweh takes no joy in their affliction.[28] To neatly distill God's commitment to justice, his punishment, and his sorrow in those judgments into separate theological strands is to misrepresent and limit God's engagement with his people and the world.

Amos makes clear that God's judgments are not haphazard; they are not arbitrary or hasty. The history of his people began in grace (2:9–12). God periodically and patiently attempted to push his people to recognize their rebellious ways (4:6–11) and for a time responded to the intercession of the prophet and was willing to hold his hand of judgment (7:1–6). That is, patience and incremental discipline precede the announcement of a more definitive wrath (2:14–16; 7:7–10; 8:1–3; 9:1–4). Even the Oracles against the Nations (chs. 1–2) demonstrate divine tolerance. "For three, no four" suggests a pattern of sin, in which one more transgression finally forces God to send judgment.[29] In addition, and very importantly for this discussion, punishment is not his final word. Amos calls for his people to choose life and ends with a promise of peace and restoration, aspects that will be dealt with in the next section.

---

nature and history and minimizes divine foreknowledge.

26. Heschel, *Prophets*, 290. For his comments on Amos, see 32–46.

27. I do not go here into the basis for his judgments. In the Old Testament, for all of humanity these are grounded in the natural moral order; his people have the added responsibility of Abrahamic and Mosaic covenant obligations.

28. In other passages it is clear that God in his mercy is willing to override decrees of judgment (e.g., Jer 18:5–10; Jonah 3:9—4:2). The key is human repentance, something that Israel in the book of Amos is not willing to contemplate.

29. There are several options in Amos research about the meaning of "for three sins . . . even for four." See Paul, *Amos*, 27–30.

God's emotional engagement with the cause of justice and his punishment for its violation are fundamental to our own involvement in issues of justice. Righteous anger at injustice is grounded in the person of God. This should not be surprising. Humans are made in the image of God, so indignation within our own beings at the absence of justice is to be expected. For the people of God, to this general human impulse must be added the ethical demands of God's revelation—another item to be considered in a later section. As in the case of God, human disapproval of wrong should find expression in deterrents and systems of penalties locally, nationally, and internationally in order to safeguard social justice as best we can, within our human limitations.

A third issue, in addition to the usefulness of cultural background to understand the language of judgment and the appropriateness of wrath properly conceived in relation to the person of God, concerns the *scope of judgment*. Throughout the prophetic literature the punishment often mirrors the crime (*lex talionis*). Nations are turned over to the very violations in which they have participated. Accordingly, in the first two chapters of Amos, the nations' cruelty in war yields defeat in war. Similarly, those who immorally acquire luxury forfeit that lifestyle and are singled out for their transgressions (3:15—4:1; 5:11; 6:4–7). Nevertheless, it appears that the net of those who suffer from judgment is cast wider than the perpetrators of injustice. Both the earthquake and the invasion by a foreign army would impact everyone indiscriminately, including those who were not the targets of the prophet's accusations. How just then is the justice of Yahweh?

Different solutions have been offered to this theological and moral quandary. One alternative is to reject the prophetic message for this very reason. The judgments, it is said, are evidence of God's irrational unfairness or of an unacceptable worldview.[30] Another option is to interpret the totalizing passages in light of others that make distinctions within the nation (7:9; 9:8–10) in order to contend that the actual victims of God's judgment are limited to the monarchy, its collaborators, and other oppressors.[31] Of course, the problem with this idea is that war and earthquakes are not selective in their casualties. For others, the answer to the complication of coupling the defence of the victims of injustice with the descriptions of sweeping destruction lies in sorting out the redaction history of

---

30. See the sources listed above in n 19; cf. Houston, *Contending for Justice*, 71–73.

31. Reimer, *Richtet auf des Recht*, 16–17, 22–27, *passim*; Möller, *A Prophet in Debate*, 139–41.

the production of the book. Coote argues that the original version of the prophet's message did single out those who had committed social and economic crimes as the specific targets of divine wrath; their doom was certain and irrevocable. According to his reconstruction, later additions to the text broadened that message by including religious violations to the list of transgressions. The entire nation was made guilty, thereby weakening the impact of Amos's attack against injustice.[32] The problem with this solution is twofold. On the one hand, these proposed steps in the book's production and their accompanying moral stances are hypothetical and cannot be proved. On the other hand, this solution evades the text that we actually do possess that presents the theological and moral challenge.

A dimension that none of these attempts consider is that the entire nation indeed was sinful, even as its leadership was engaged in particular transgressions that the prophets emphasized.[33] The nature of sin (whether religious, ideological, racial, socioeconomic, or political) perhaps is much more complex than scholars realize, with different levels of complicity and participation by the wider population. Examples in our era could include the involvement of the German people in the horrific acts of genocide of the Nazi regime and the involvement of different groups in the state terrorism of the dictatorial regimes of the Middle East that have resisted the changes sought by the so-called Arab Spring, which began in December 2010. In both cases, support was sought in the religious convictions of these societies. No one is innocent, although there are those who must be held most responsible. They make the decisions and lifestyle choices that affect everyone in the short and long term. This socio-political, economic, and cultural fact explains why in the Bible nations are judged, while certain individuals and select groups are singled out for special censure. Such judgments, whether in the form of armed conflict or natural disasters, are messy and heart-wrenching. This is why God grieves.

In sum, to speak about justice in the Bible requires that we seriously grapple with how injustice is punished. What is often lacking in justice

32. Coote, *Amos among the Prophets*, 16–19, 22–24, 46–53, 62–65. Houston contends that the post-exilic educated patron class that he believes produced the book maintained its social conscience and sense of responsibility, but also saw the fate of the nation as of one piece (*Contending for Justice*, 58–61, 71–73, 93–98). For a recent study that seeks to decipher the social criticism of each redactional layer, see Hamborg, *Still Selling the Righteous*.

33. Houston disagrees with me on this point (*Contending for Justice*, 55, 60), although here the argument has additional points not mentioned in earlier publications.

discussions is *a theology of historical judgment* on societies and nation states that can take us beyond simply an awareness of God's commitment to justice to the thornier matters of judgment for its violation. This section has suggested some of the elements that would need to be part of such reflections: the cultural context, the nature of the person of God, and the scope of divine judgment. What cannot be denied is that God does punish injustice. Much work remains to be done to integrate that conviction properly into prophetic theology and ethics. Perhaps these comments will help move those challenging discussions forward.

Religious Practice and Justice (Amos 5:4–6, 14–15)

The next pair of verses in this chiasm provides the platform for dealing with three other components of the prophetic engagement with social justice. These are, in turn, the relationship between religion and justice, the call for virtue, and the significance of a future hope of global justice.

First, the cult. The prophets very obviously were critics of the religious life of Israel. In the nineteenth century some scholars believed that the classical prophets of the eighth century BCE decried ritual altogether and campaigned for an "ethical monotheism" devoid of ceremony, guided by a pure concern for the needy. Of course, in the ancient world a religion without sanctuaries, priests, offerings, and holy days would have made no sense. This interpretation represents more the view of certain segments of the Protestantism of those scholars' time than it does that of the prophets of Israel.

The prophetic denunciation of the religious life is undeniable but, if not ethical monotheism, what triggered that condemnation? The problem in the book of Amos is that the official religion of the nation had become compromised.[34] The confrontation between the prophet and the chief priest at Bethel makes this clear (7:10–17). Bethel was the principal temple of Israel; in Amaziah's words, it was "the king's sanctuary and the temple of the kingdom" (7:13). There the national ideology of the divine legitimization of Jeroboam II's regime was propagated and celebrated, a religious perspective common in the ancient world where the lives and rule of the

---

34. It is possible that popular religion was connected to oppressive practices, if passages like 2:8 refer to popular religious practices. See Carroll R., *Contexts for Amos*, 48–122, 273–77; Carrol R., "Can the Prophets Shed Light on Our Worship Wars?"; Carroll R.,"Imagining the Unthinkable." For the distinction between official and popular religion, see Carroll R.,"For so you love to do."

gods and the king were intertwined.[35] To proclaim the king's demise was both treason and blasphemy, conspiracy against the crown and a denial of the religion of the monarchy (7:9–11). This is why Amaziah ordered Amos, a foreigner from Tekoa in Judah, to leave Israel and return to his own country (7:12).

The book offers several clues as to the thought and practices of this state religion. The sanctuaries were abuzz with religious activity (4:4–5; 5:21–23), but the focus largely was on celebrating, with thanksgiving, the blessings of God. The common conviction was that Yahweh was Israel's provider and protector. There could be strong confidence of victory in wartime (a day of the Lord), and recent success had confirmed that sentiment (6:13). The entire populace would have participated in this religion of national assurance and pride. The sanctuaries and the religious personnel (especially Bethel) would have risen in stature and benefitted financially from this belief,[36] while the king would have been honored as the people's benefactor and triumphant leader. This was a feel-good and triumphant religion that the people "loved to do" (4:5).

Brueggemann uses the term "prophetic imagination" to communicate that the prophet had a very different lens through which to perceive and evaluate reality.[37] Whereas the nation commemorated triumph and blessing in its self-serving and self-congratulating religion, the prophet revealed cancerous corruption and cruelty, unscrupulous leaders, and imminent defeat. The rhetoric of the book of Amos puts the lie to the false consciousness of the people. Recent history had been characterized by disasters of many kinds, demonstrating that their theology was divorced from reality. There was no reason to thank God; repentance would have been the appropriate response (4:4–11). The future was more ominous. The capital city Samaria, along with its citadels, was going to be destroyed (3:9—4:2; 6:8–11; 7:7–8) and the armies of Israel put to flight (2:14–16; 6:14). The shouts of victory over taking Lo-Debar (lit. "no-thing") were a hollow celebration of an

35. There were also the wider connections between earthly temples and cosmic realities. For a helpful introduction, see Walton, *Ancient Near Eastern Thought*, 113–34, 275–86.

36. For the socio-economic role of temples, see Stevens, *Temples, Tithes, and Taxes*, 82–173.

37. Brueggemann, *Prophetic Imagination*, 1–57; cf. more recently, Brueggemann, *Journey to the Common Good*; and Breuggemann, "Prophetic Ministry in the National Security State," in *Disruptive Grace*, 129–54.

insignificant battle. Utter darkness, not light—that is, defeat and exile (4:3; 5:18–20, 27)—are what awaited Israel on that day of the Lord.

The national ideology did not acknowledge that social justice was part of the essence of true religion in the sight of Yahweh (5:24), a stance echoed in other prophets (e.g., Isa 1:10–20; 58:1–14; Jer 7:1–29; Hos 6:4–6; Mic 6:6–8). To engage in religious activity without practicing justice was to misconceive what acceptable worship of God was about. To ignore the demands of mercy and compassion rendered rituals useless and a stench before Yahweh (5:21–23).[38] The national ideology had blinded the nation to its social responsibilities, and their commitment to those beliefs silenced contrary voices. Why question the glories of Israel? Yet more insidious was that the very victims of oppression would have joined in the throngs at the sanctuaries to cheer the government and their god, that very socio-religious social construction of reality that exploited them.[39] This was a brutal irony that justified the divine displeasure even more.

Yahweh will not tolerate a distorted view of his person, who is presented as supporting the arrogance of a political scheme and as indifferent to injustice. This intolerable view of God and society emanated from the historic sanctuaries of Gilgal and especially Bethel, and there judgment would begin. The altars of Bethel would be destroyed (3:14), its sanctuary "reduced to nothing" (5:5), and the high priest sent out of the land (7:17). Yahweh himself would stand by its altar and bring down its pillars (9:1). Their idea of God himself was at stake in the prophetic vehement exposé of Israel's faith.

Second, Amos 5:4–6 challenges the Israelites to "seek me and live." The meaning of what it means to seek Yahweh in this context is found in the parallel verses of 5:14–15. It is to "seek good" and to "hate evil, love good." These phrases are paralleled with "maintain justice in the courts" (lit. "in the gate"). The next section of the chiasm will define these matters more concretely, but what needs to be appreciated here is that the prophet is appealing to the moral disposition ("love," "hate") to do good (cf. "the right," 3:10). Said another way, what is required of Israel is that they be a people of virtue,[40] a people who share life in community in accordance with the good revealed in their traditions (their history and law). A truly just society is one that not only functions equitably but is inhabited by just persons.

38. Note the emotive nature of the verbs in this passage.

39. For the "social construction of reality," see Carroll R., *Contexts for Amos*, 49–76.

40. Carroll R., "Seeking the Virtues among the Prophets."

The just follow the lead of moral exemplars that embody the good and, in the case of a religious people, engage in worship as a practice. From the perspective of virtue ethics, to configure worship as a practice is to frame it as the time and place to educate people in justice and to nurture it (and other virtues, like peace).

Yahweh was Israel's greatest exemplar, but their religious life misrepresented his person. Their rituals of celebration made a mockery of the virtue of justice and disconnected Yahweh from social realities. The prophets and Nazirites could also have served as models, but they were commanded not to speak and urged to violate their vows, respectively (2:10–11; 7:13). The ethical norms of the covenant were not respected, and the history that should have prompted obedience was not heeded (2:9–10; 3:2). On every count, Israel failed to pursue or incarnate justice.

Justice in the prophets is inseparable from satisfactory religion and is to be inculcated as a virtue; it also is, third, characterized by hope. Amos 5:4 and 5:6 offer life for seeking God and the good. Scholars debate how genuine this possibility might be (and to what "life" refers), if inescapable judgment has already been decreed. Was there any expectation that the nation would turn from its sinful and destructive ways, or that at least some individuals would respond to the call? It seems more likely that the prophet desired that at least some might choose life with God and the good over Israel's deluded march to death. These individuals "perhaps" could experience the mercy of Yahweh and be the remnant with which he would restore the nation (5:15). To choose justice was potentially to choose survival.

The prophetic hope was also corporate. That future would be a time of renewed urban and rural dwellings, a setting of abundance, where the people would be rooted once more in the land of promise (9:11–15). In addition, "David's fallen tent" was to be restored. That is, the future government was to be centered in the south, in Judah. All of these features are connected to the injustices of the prophet's own context. The future would be the reversal of what many in Israel were suffering and what all would experience in the judgment. In the future, there would be food and drink, unlike the recent hunger and drought that the general population endured (4:6–9), while the well-to-do enjoyed the bounty of its resources (6:4–6); the return to the land would negate the poor's descent into debt slavery (2:6; 8:6) and the exile of the nation (5:27; cf. 4:3; 6:7); and armed conflict and the earthquake would be in the past, as the people rebuilt the ruins in peace. Finally, Jeroboam's regime, which had permitted so much injustice and had made the disastrous decisions that led to divine judgment, would be replaced by a king of the Davidic line. What is more, the sanctuary at Bethel could no longer propagate its destructive ideology. The assumption is that worship would be on Zion, the place from which Yahweh roars at the beginning of the book (1:2). That roar alerts the reader that, from the opening chapter, the government of Jeroboam II, its servile religious establishment, and the society that their temple extolled were illegitimate and doomed.

Justice must reign in the present, and in the future we can trust that it will. Those who seek justice must believe that one day Yahweh will establish it on the earth through Messiah (cf. Isa 11:1–11; 42:1–9). With that hope, the just today, as in ancient Israel, can persevere in doing the right, promoting and protecting it in this fallen world.[41]

Defining Social Justice (Amos 5:7, 10–13)

The next set of passages describes the abuse of justice in Israel. In the Old Testament the concepts of "justice" and "righteousness" are rich and complex.[42] Nevertheless, justice is never defined in the prophetic literature. These books do make clear, however, what justice and injustice entail in the world. It is not uncommon that "justice" and "righteousness" appear together, as they do in 5:7 (cf. 5:24; 6:12). In broad terms, justice in the book of Amos is connected to legal matters that should conform to the standards of Israel's Torah. It also can refer to a moral principle for the proper functioning of society. While the former is more grounded in the particulars of that ancient context, the latter endures.

The first thing to notice in Amos 5:7 is Israel's negative and dismissive attitude toward justice (cf. 6:12). What is right is turned into "bitterness" and thrust to the ground. While one might assume that this description fits the elite, the nearest referent is the "house of Joseph" in 5:6, and 5:1–17 has the whole nation in view. While the matching verses, 5:10–13, do detail transgressions of the powerful, a literary reading suggests that this

41. German theologian Jürgen Moltmann has emphasized the ethical power of hope. However one may evaluate his views on eschatology, it is undeniable that he has captured the impact that the future can have in the present. See most recently his *Ethics of Hope*; cf. Moltmann, *Broad Place*, 97–118. Also note Brueggemann, *Prophetic Imagination*, 59–79; *Theology of the Old Testament*, 643–49; "Every City a Holy City," in *Disruptive Grace*, 112–28.

42. See C. J. H. Wright, *Old Testament Ethics for the People of God*, 253–80; Birch, "Justice." For more technical studies, see Johnson, "*mishpat*"; Schultz, "Justice."

is a national trait that is evident at the higher levels of society as well. Its compelling imagery of injustice is complemented by those in other verses: "trample" (2:7; 8:4), "unrest" and "oppression" (3:9), "hoard plunder and loot" (3:10), "crush" (4:1), "oppress" (4:1; 5:12), and "poison" (6:12)—all of which require some level of violence, whether individual or structural. This language should elicit moral revulsion,[43] and it communicates Yahweh's concern to protect the victims of injustice.

Amos 5:10–13 makes explicit the metaphor in 5:7. These verses cite intimidation in legal proceedings, probably motivated by special interests, and unfair taxation of the poor in order to fund a comfortable, but oppressive, lifestyle in a context of material need (cf. 3:15—4:1; 6:4–7). Other passages in the book allude to the corrupt legal system (2:7) and unjust fines (2:8), to which can be added debt slavery (2:6; 8:6), taking advantage of young maidens (2:7), and dishonest business measures (8:4–5). Each of these violations of the poor is in some way referred to in Old Testament legislation.[44]

Justice is an ethical demand, and its violation, then and now, becomes reality in the legal and economic spheres and in the attitudes of disdain toward the defenseless. This fact has not changed over the centuries. The mechanisms and means of oppression of eighth-century Israel are not ours, but the moral principle of justice remains pertinent, as does the reality of the violence of injustice. A literary feature in Amos that facilitates appropriation of this prophetic word to contemporary society is the anonymity of both the perpetrators of injustice and its victims (2:6–8; 3:10; 4:1; 5:7, 10–12; 6:1, 3–7; 8:4–6). They are nameless in the text, but can find their counterparts today. We can supply the missing names and put faces on these characteristic behaviors. The abusers and the abused live among us.

Yahweh the Guarantor of Justice (Amos 5:8–9)

The center of the chiasm is found at the last line of 5:8, "Yahweh is his name." This declaration underscores that important truth that justice in the end is grounded in the person of God. His absolute sovereignty is communicated literarily in this passage by a progression from the constellations in the sky to the daily rhythm of day and night in v. 8 to his intervention in the human sphere in v. 9 to destroy the fortresses that serve the regime's ideological

43. For the vocabulary of oppression, see Tamez, *Bible of the Oppressed*; Jaramillo Rivas, *La injusticia y la opresión en el lenguaje figurado de los profetas*.

44. See Baker, *Tight Fists*.

pretensions. The verb "turns" in v. 8 is the same verb used in the previous verse (5:7), a juxtaposition that highlights the contrast between humanity's character and actions and Yahweh's. Israel works to change the justice of God into what it is not for its own goals, while the God of justice controls all of nature to punish transgressions and establish universal equity.

This is the second of the three doxologies in the book (the others are 4:13; 9:5–6). Each describes the incomparable power of the Creator,[45] but what can be missed is that they reveal that the morality of the human social order is connected to the cosmic and natural order. If justice comes from the person of God, then it follows that to disturb that ethical principle is to affect the wider scheme of things, which he has fashioned. Thus the land mourns (as will Israel) at Yahweh's roar of judgment in Amos 1:2 (cf. Hos 4:1–3), and the nation's agricultural environment suffers because of its rebellion (4:6–9), even as the land later is renewed supernaturally (9:13–15).

An impressive picture of God is fundamental to justice in the prophetic literature. Only an omnipotent deity can demand justice of all of humanity and one day establish it globally. For justice to have a consistent essence and be free from machinations and manipulation, it must come from the holy transcendent One. For justice to be meaningful for the victims of oppression and not be an abstract idea, it must touch the heart of God. A lesser god than Yahweh would yield a relative sense of justice, a diminishing of the weight of its universal imperative under the divine threat of judgment, and the hopeless despair that evil's reign has no end. Without the God of the prophets, we labor in vain for justice.

CONCLUSION

This essay has presented various elements of the prophetic message of justice, using Amos 5:1–17 as an exemplary passage. Following the unfolding of the chiastic structure of these verses, we learn the following:

- Amos 5:1–3, 16–17: It is important to not limit discussion of justice in the prophets to identifying passages that require it of the people of God. The Bible teaches that God is just and that as the divine judge he will punish the violation of justice. This judgment must be read against the backdrop of the cultural context of that time. Yahweh's patience and pain in judgment must be recognized, and the ample scope of judgment cannot be minimized. A commitment to justice needs a developed theology of judgment.

- Amos 5:4–6, 14–15: Acceptable religion before Yahweh cannot be divorced from justice. In fact, God desires his people to exhibit the virtue of justice, and their religious life should cultivate that. In the future, beyond judgment, God will establish justice in all the earth, and this hope should be a prime motivator to pursue justice.

- Amos 5:7, 10–13: Justice is tied to legal measures and is as well a moral principle. Although precisely how justice is abused is context-specific, the principle transcends all cultures and settings.

- Amos 5:8–9: Justice is grounded in the person of Yahweh, the incomparable Creator and sovereign God.

I close with an additional point that supplements and fulfills this survey of justice in the prophetic books. It must not be forgotten that Jesus was the greatest prophet.[46] Jesus demonstrates prophetic characteristics in his message: the woes of Matthew 23 echo prophetic concerns; he predicts the destruction of Jerusalem and the Temple; he speaks the words of the Father; and he calls the nation to turn to God. Jesus' ministry reflects prophetic patterns: he is sent by God, performs miraculous deeds, and suffers as a prophet. He exhibits anger at wrongs, divine pathos in the face of hypocrisy and injustice (e.g., Matt 12:22–37; 15:1–20; 22:15–22, par.). Jesus was recognized as a prophet by the masses (Luke 7:16–17; 9:18–19, par.), his enemies (Luke 22:63–65, par.), and the disciples (Luke 24:18–21, par.; Acts 3:22–23).

To take seriously the prophetic demand for justice ultimately means to follow the example of Jesus in word and deed and to become his disciple. There is no greater calling in the way of justice.

BIBLIOGRAPHY

Baker, David L. *Tight Fists or Open Hands: Wealth and Poverty in Old Testament Law.* Grand Rapids: Eerdmans, 2009.

Bercovitch, Sacvan. *The American Jeremiad.* Madison: University of Wisconsin Press, 1978.

Birch, Bruce C. "Justice." In *Dictionary of Scripture and Ethics*, edited by Joel B. Green, 433–37. Grand Rapids: Baker Academic, 2011.

46. Of course, one of the major sources for this theme is N. T. Wright, *Jesus and the Victory of God*, 145–474. Also note that Stassen and Gushee connect the ethics of Jesus (specifically the Sermon on the Mount) with the prophet Isaiah, in *Kingdom Ethics*.

Boda, Mark J. "Chiasmus in Ubiquity: Symmetrical Images in Nehemiah." *JSOT* 71 (1996) 55–70.

Bohlen, Reinhold. "Zur Socialkritik des Propheten Amos." *TTZ* 95 (1996) 282–301.

Brueggemann, Walter. *Disruptive Grace: Reflections on God, Scripture, and the Church*, edited by C. J. Sharp. Minneapolis: Fortress, 2011.

———. *Journey to the Common Good*. Louisville, KY: Westminster John Knox, 2010.

———. *The Prophetic Imagination*. 2nd ed. Minneapolis: Fortress, 2001.

———. *Theology of the Old Testament*. Minneapolis: Fortress, 1997.

Carroll R., M. Daniel. *Amos—the Prophet and His Oracles: Research on the Book of Amos*. Louisville, KY: Westminster John Knox, 2002.

———. "Can the Prophets Shed Light on Our Worship Wars? How Amos Evaluates Religious Ritual." *Stone-Campbell Journal* 8, no. 2 (2005) 215–27.

———. *Contexts for Amos: Prophetic Poetics in Latin American Perspective*. JSOTSup 132. Sheffield: Sheffield Academic, 1992.

———. "Ethics." In *Dictionary of the Old Testament: Prophets*, edited by M. Boda and J. G. McConville, 185–93. Downers Grove, IL: InterVarsity, 2012.

———. "Ethics and the Old Testament." In *Hearing the Old Testament*, edited by Craig Bartholomew and David Beldman, 204–27. Grand Rapids: Eerdmans, 2012.

———. "Failing the Vulnerable: The Prophets and Social Care." In *Transforming the World: The Gospel and Social Theology*, edited by D. Hughes and J. A. Grant, 35–50. Nottingham: Apollos, 2009.

———. "'For so you love to do': Probing Popular Religion in the Book of Amos." In *Rethinking Contexts, Rereading Texts: Contributions from the Social Sciences to Biblical Interpretation*, edited by M. D. Carroll R., 168–89. JSOTSup 299. Sheffield: Sheffield Academic, 2000.

———. "'I will send fire': Reflections on the Violence of God in Amos." In *Wrestling with the Violence of God: Soundings in the Old Testament*, edited by M. D. Carroll R. and J. Blair Wilgus, 113–32. Winona Lake, IN: Eisenbrauns, 2015.

———. "Imagining the Unthinkable: Exposing the Idolatry of National Security in Amos." *Ex Auditu* 24 (2008) 37–54.

———. "Seeking the Virtues among the Prophets: The Book of Amos as a Test Case." *Ex Auditu* 17 (2001) 77–96.

Coomber, Matthew J. M. *Re-reading the Prophets through Corporate Globalization: A Cultural-Evolutionary Approach to Understanding Economic Injustice in the Hebrew Bible*. Biblical Intersections 4. Piscataway, NJ: Georgias, 2010.

Coote, Robert B. *Amos among the Prophets: Composition and Theology*. Philadelphia: Fortress, 1981.

Davies, Andrew. *Double Standards in Isaiah: Re-evaluating Prophetic Ethics and Divine Justice*. BibInt 46; Leiden: Brill, 2000.

Davis, Ellen F. *Scripture, Culture, and Agriculture: An Agrarian Reading of the Bible*. Cambridge: Cambridge University Press, 2009.

Dempsey, Carol J. *Hope amid the Ruins: The Ethics of Israel's Prophets*. St. Louis: Chalice, 2000.

Dever, William G. *The Lives of Ordinary People in Ancient Israel: Where Archaeology and the Bible Intersect*. Grand Rapids: Eerdmans, 2012.

De Waard, J. "The Chiastic Structure of Amos V 1–17." *VT* 27 no. 2 (1977) 170–77.

Domeris, William Robert. *Touching the Heart of God: The Social Construction of Poverty among Biblical Peasants*. LHBOTS 446. New York: T. & T. Clark, 2007.

Dorsey, D. A. "Literary Architecture and Aural Techniques in Amos." *Bib* 73 no. 3 (1992) 305–30.

———. *The Literary Structure of the Old Testament: A Commentary on Genesis–Malachi.* Grand Rapids: Baker, 1999.

Ellacuría, Ignacio. "Utopia and Prophecy in Latin America." In *Mysterium liberationis: Fundamental Concepts of Liberation Theology*, edited by I. Ellacuría and J. Sobrino, 289–328. Translated by J. R. Brockman. Maryknoll, NY: Orbis, 1993.

Eph'al, Israel. *The City Besieged.* CHANE 36. Leiden: Brill, 2009.

Fendler, Marlene. "Zur Sozialkritik des Amos: Versuch einer wirtschafts- und sozialgeschichtlichen Interpretation alttestamentlicher Texte." *EvT* 33 no. 1 (1973) 32–53.

Fensham, F. Charles. "Common Trends in Treaty Curses of the Near Eastern Treaties and *KUDUR-RU*-Inscriptions Compared with the Maledictions of Amos and Isaiah." *ZAW* 2 (1963) 155–75.

Fleischer, Gunther. *Von Menschenverkäufern, Baschankühen und Rechtsverkehrern: Die Sozialkritik des Amosbuches in historisch-kritischer, sozialgeschichtlicher und archäologischer Perspektive.* BBB 74. Frankfurt am Main: Athenäum, 1989.

Fretheim, Terence E. *God and World in the Old Testament: A Relational Theology of Creation.* Nashville: Abingdon, 2005.

———. "Some Reflections on Brueggemann's God." In *God in the Fray: A Tribute to Walter Brueggemann*, edited by T. Linafelt and T. K. Beal, 24–37. Minneapolis: Fortress, 1998.

———. *The Suffering of God: An Old Testament Perspective.* OBT. Philadelphia: Fortress, 1984.

Gutiérrez, Gustavo. *On Job: God-Talk and the Suffering of the Innocent.* Translated by M. J. O'Connell. Maryknoll, NY: Orbis, 1987.

Hamborg, Graham R. *Still Selling the Righteous: A Redactional-Critical Investigation of Reasons for Judgment in Amos 2.6–16.* LHBOTS 555. London: T. & T. Clark, 2012.

Heschel, Abraham. *The Prophets.* 1962. Reprint, New York: Perennial Classics, 2001.

Houston, Walter J. *Contending for Justice: Ideologies and Theologies of Social Justice in the Old Testament.* Rev. ed. London: T. & T. Clark, 2008.

Jaramillo Rivas, Pedro. *La injusticia y la opresión en el lenguaje figurado de los profetas.* Estella: Verbo Divino, 1992.

Johnson, B. "*mishpat.*" In *TDOT*, 9:86–98.

The Kairos Document. Challenge to the Church: A Theological Comment on the Political Crisis in South Africa. 2nd ed. Grand Rapids: Eerdmans, 1986.

Knight, Douglas A. *Law, Power, and Justice in Ancient Israel.* Library of Ancient Israel. Louisville, KY: Westminster John Knox, 2011.

Marlow, Hillary. *Biblical Prophets and Contemporary Environmental Ethics: Re-reading Amos, Hosea, and First Isaiah.* Oxford: Oxford University Press, 2009.

Miranda, José Porfirio. *Marx and the Bible: A Critique of the Philosophy of Oppression.* Translated by J. Eagleson. Maryknoll, NY: Orbis, 1974.

Möller, Karl. *A Prophet in Debate: The Rhetoric of Persuasion in the Book of Amos.* JSOTSup 372; Sheffield: Sheffield Academic, 2003.

Moltmann, Jürgen. *A Broad Place: An Autobiography.* Translated by M. Kohl. Minneapolis: Fortress, 2008.

———. *Ethics of Hope.* Translated by M. Kohl. Minneapolis: Fortress, 2012.

Nissinen, Martti. *Prophets and Prophecy in the Ancient Near East.* Writings from the Ancient World 12. Atlanta: SBL, 2003.

O'Brien, Julia M. *Challenging Prophetic Metaphor: Theology and Ideology in the Prophets.* Louisville, KY: Westminster John Knox, 2008.

Paas, Stefan. *Creation and Judgement: Creation Texts in Some Eighth Century Prophets.* OTS 47. Leiden: Brill, 2003.

Paul, Shalom. *Amos.* Hermeneia. Minneapolis: Fortress, 1991.

Reimer, Harold. *Richtet auf des Recht! Studien zur Botschaft des Amos.* Stuttgarter Bibel-Studien 149. Stuttgart: Verlag Katholisches Bibelwerk, 1992.

Rigol, P. N., et al. *Misión profética de la iglesia.* Mexico: CUPSA, 1981.

Rodd, Cyril S. *Glimpses of a Strange Land: Studies in Old Testament Ethics.* OTS. Edinburgh: T. & T. Clark, 2001.

Rotzoll, Dirk U. *Studien zur Redaktion und Komposition des Amosbuchs.* BZAW 243. Berlin: Walter de Gruyter, 1996.

Sandy, D. Brent. *Plowshares and Pruning Hooks: Rethinking the Language of Biblical Prophecy and Apocalyptic.* Downers Grove, IL: InterVarsity, 2002.

Schultz, Richard. "Justice." In *NIDOTTE* 4:837–46.

Seibert, Eric A. *Disturbing Divine Behavior: Troubling Old Testament Images of God.* Minneapolis: Fortress, 2009.

———. *The Violence of Scripture: Overcoming the Old Testament's Troubling Legacy.* Minneapolis: Fortress, 2012.

Smalley, W. A. "Recursion Patterns and the Sectioning of Amos." *BT* 30, no. 1 (1979) 118–27.

Stassen, Glen H., and David O. Gushee. *Kingdom Ethics: Following Jesus in Contemporary Context.* Downers Grove, IL: InterVarsity, 2003.

Stevens, Marty E. *Temples, Tithes, and Taxes: The Temple and the Economic Life of Ancient Israel.* Peabody, MA: Hendrickson, 2006.

Sweeney, Marvin A. *Reading the Hebrew Bible after the Shoah: Engaging Holocaust Theology.* Minneapolis: Fortress, 2008.

Tamez, Elsa. *The Bible of the Oppressed.* Translated by M. J. O'Connell. Maryknoll, NY: Orbis, 1982.

Walton, John H. *Ancient Near Eastern Thought and the Old Testament: Introducing the Conceptual World of the Hebrew Bible.* Grand Rapids: Baker Academic, 2006.

Wright, Christopher J. H. *Old Testament Ethics for the People of God.* Downers Grove, IL: InterVarsity, 2004.

Wright, N. T. *Jesus and the Victory of God.* Minneapolis: Fortress, 1996.

4

Social Justice or Personal Righteousness?
What Jesus Has to Say in Matthew and Mark

CRAIG A. EVANS

ACCORDING TO THE KING James Version the Psalmist declares (Ps 103:6):

> The Lord executeth righteousness
> And judgment for all that are oppressed.

Similarly the American Standard Version reads:

> Jehovah executeth righteous acts,
> And judgments for all that are oppressed.

The New English Bible reads somewhat differently:

> The Lord gives righteousness
> And justice to all who are treated unfairly.

The Revised Standard Version reads even more differently:

> The Lord works vindication
> And justice for all who are oppressed.

Similarly the New International Version reads:

> The Lord works righteousness
> And justice for all the oppressed.

The New American Standard Bible reads still more differently:

> The Lord performs righteous deeds,
> And judgments for all who are oppressed.

The New English Translation reads in very contemporary idiom:

> The Lord does what is fair,
> And executes justice for all the oppressed.

The seven English versions above are based on the Hebrew text (i.e., the MT). The English translation of the Greek version (i.e., Ps 102:6) reads:

> He who does merciful deeds is the Lord
> And (does) judgment for all who are being wronged.

Why the differences? Are there variant readings in the original texts? Other uncertainties? Not really. The Hebrew, Greek, and Latin (also Ps 102:6) texts read as follows:

עֹשֵׂה צְדָקוֹת יְהוָה וּמִשְׁפָּטִים לְכָל־עֲשׁוּקִים

ποιῶν ἐλεημοσύνας ὁ κύριος
καὶ κρίμα πᾶσι τοῖς ἀδικουμένοις.

faciens iustitias Dominus
et iudicia cunctis qui calumniam sustinent.[1] (Vulgata)

faciens misericordes Dominus
et iudicium omnibus iniuriam patientibus.[2] (Biblia Sacra Vulgata)

faciens iustitias Dominus
et iudicium omnibus iniuriam patientibus.[3] (neo-Vulgata)

There are no significant variants in the Hebrew and the Greek.[4] The variants in the Latin translation do not attest variants in the Hebrew or the Greek;

1. "The Lord performs justice and (gives) judgment for all who sustain false accusation." The meaning of the Latin *iustitia*, from which we derive our English word "justice," is not so much *justice* as it is *duty*, at least as it was understood in the time of Jesus. One thinks of Cicero's assertions, *est enim pietas iustitia adversum deos* "for piety is duty directed toward the gods" (*Nat. d.* 1.116), and *iustitia dicitur, eaque erga deos, religio, erga parentes, pietas* "duty toward the gods is called religion, toward our parents, piety" (*Part. or.* 22.78).
2. "The Lord performs mercies and (gives) judgment for all who endure injury." This form of the Latin appears to be influenced by the LXX.
3. "The Lord performs justice and (gives) judgment for all who endure injury." On the meaning of "justice" in Latin, see n 1 above.
4. There is a slight variant in the vowel pointing of the first word in the Hebrew text and, in a very few mss, a different preposition at the beginning of the second line. See Alt, *Biblia Hebraica Stuttgartensia, ad loc.* Apart from spelling, there are no variants in the Psalms scrolls from Qumran (cf. 2Q14 frag. 1, line 3; 4Q84 frag. 14, col. iv, lines

they attest the range of semantic possibilities for the words involved. The language of the Hebrew, Greek, and Latin versions is not especially difficult. So how do we account for the variations in the English translations? In the first line should we translate "righteousness" (so the KJV, NEB, and NIV) or "vindication" (as in the RSV) or "righteous deeds" (as in the NASB), "righteous acts" (as in the ASV), or "what is fair" (as in the NET)? And why does the Greek translator use ἐλεημοσύνη to translate צדקה? In the second line of Ps 103:6 we have "judgment" (in the KJV), "justice" (in the NEB, RSV, and NET), and "judgments" (in the NASB). The Greek translator's rendering of the second line is pretty much what we would expect. We encounter no surprises in the Latin.

I have provided a sampling of translations of a single verse in the Bible to illustrate how difficult it is to pin down the nuance of words like צדקה (in the first line) and משפט (in the second line). This problem also applies to the cognates of these words. Invariably translators (English or Greek or Latin!) must decide primarily on the basis of what is perceived to be the context and meaning of the passage in question.[5]

δικαιοσύνη and its cognates are semantically tricky.[6] Often it is not clear if the meaning is *righteousness* in the sense of personal piety or if it is *justice* in the sense of duty. δικαιοσύνη can refer to a *gift* (in the sense of God's grace) or it can refer to a *requirement* (in the sense of God's law). These distinctions are very important, as we see, for example, in the ongoing discussion of Paul's understanding of justification. But they are important too in the exegesis of the Gospels. Most of the occurrences of δίκαιος and its cognates are outside of the Gospels, but these words are very important for interpretation of Matthew and Luke. δίκαιος occurs seventy-nine times

---

5–6). With regard to the LXX no variants are cited in Rahlfs, *Septuaginta, ad loc*. For the Vulgate, see Weber, *Biblia sacra iuxta vulgatam versionem*, 1:898.

5. Some of the linguistic and interpretive problems in Psalm 103 are explored in O'Kennedy, "Relationship between Justice and Forgiveness."

6. For studies concerned with the semantic range and usage of δικαιοσύνη and its cognates, as well as the Hebrew equivalents, in biblical literature, see Baird, *Justice of God*; Quell and Schrenk, "δίκη, δίκαιος, δικαιοσύνη, κτλ"; Spicq, "δίκαιος, δικαιοσύνη, δικαιόω, κτλ"; Lang, "Gesetz und Gerechtigkeit Gottes"; Reumann, "Righteousness (Early Judaism)"; Scullion, "Righteousness (OT)"; Reumann, "Righteousness (NT)"; Weinfeld, "Justice and Righteousness"; Jackson, "'Law' and 'Justice'"; Reumann, "Justification and Justice"; Vincent, "Un regard sur la 'justice'"; Sacchi, "From Righteousness to Justification"; Leonhardt-Balzer, "Righteousness in Early Jewish Literature"; Soards, "Righteousness in the NT"; Declaissé-Walford, "Righteousness in the OT"; Schwartz, "Revelation and Revolution"; Hayes, "Justice, Righteousness."

in the New Testament, with thirty-three of these occurrences in the Gospels. δικαιοσύνη occurs ninety-two times in the New Testament, with ten of these occurrences in the Gospels. The verb δικαιόω occurs thirty-nine times in the New Testament, with seven in the Gospels. In all, these words occur about fifty times in the Gospels, with half of these occurrences in the Gospel of Matthew.

My task is to assess this language and its meaning in Matthew and Mark, especially as it relates to the teaching of Jesus. I begin with Mark.

JUSTICE AND RIGHTEOUSNESS IN MARK

Words from the δίκαιος family occur only twice in Mark, once as a description of John the Baptizer and once on the lips of Jesus. Of John it is said: "Herod feared John, knowing that he was a righteous and holy man (ἄνδρα δίκαιον καὶ ἅγιον)" (Mark 6:20). Explaining his association with sinners and tax collectors, Jesus says, "Those who are well have no need of a physician, but those who are sick; I came not to call the righteous, but sinners (δικαίους ἀλλὰ ἁμαρτωλούς)" (Mark 2:17).

These two passages give us little to go on. There is no doubt that Jesus himself would have concurred with the evangelist's comment that John was a "righteous and holy man." The fuller tradition of John's teaching in Luke 3:10–14, where he instructs the people "what to do," is consistent with the description in Mark. John commands the people to share with those in need, tax collectors to take only what is appointed, and soldiers not to extort or steal but to be content with their wages. Josephus says John was a "good man," who commanded the Jewish people to "practice virtue" toward one another and toward God and to undergo baptism to indicate that the soul had been "purified beforehand by righteousness" (*Ant.* 18.117). The δίκαιος of John, as described by Mark, Luke, and Josephus, seems to apply to personal righteousness and social justice.

Jesus' declaration that he "came not to call the righteous, but sinners" is helpful in defining these categories. The contrast is obvious: righteous persons and sinful persons are opposites as are the healthy who need no physician and the sick who do. But in what sense are the "sinners" sinful? Do they fall short in personal piety or righteousness or are they unjust? The context seems to allow for both meanings of δίκαιος. The "sinners" as such could refer to both, but the reference to "tax collectors" likely would make first-century people think of injustice, of being cheated and oppressed (where the use of the word ἀδικέω would be expected), which coheres with the instructions John gave the tax collectors who came to him. Thus, Jesus' fellowship with "sinners and tax collectors" probably implies a mission to those who were unrighteous, in terms of personal piety, and to those who were unjust, in terms of their unfair and oppressive actions toward others. In other words, these were people who, until they encountered Jesus, had not practiced virtue toward one another and toward God.

It is interesting that Mark 2:17 is the only passage in that Gospel where Jesus employs the explicit language of righteousness or justice. Nonetheless, there are a few passages in Mark where righteousness and justice may be implied. In Mark, Jesus' teaching begins with his proclamation of the kingdom of God: "The time is fulfilled, and the kingdom of God is at hand; repent, and believe in the gospel" (1:15). The announcement of the arrival of God's kingdom would likely have stirred thoughts of justice and righteousness. Dozens of times in biblical literature God is said to be righteous. He is "a faithful God, and there is no injustice [ἀδικία], a righteous and holy Lord [δίκαιος καὶ ὅσιος κύριος]" (LXX Deut 32:4). In her song of praise the grateful Hannah, mother of Samuel, exalts God, "because there is none holy like the Lord, and there is none righteous [δίκαιος] like our God" (1 Sam 2:2; see also Isa 41:10; 45:21). Many more times in the Bible God is linked to righteousness. To cite one example: "But the Lord of hosts shall be exalted in judgment [ἐν κρίματι], and the Holy God shall be glorified in righteousness [ἐν δικαιοσύνῃ]" (Isa 5:16).

Biblical literature also speaks of God as a righteous king: "Mighty King [מֶלֶךְ / βασιλέως], lover of justice, you have established equity; you have executed justice and righteousness [מִשְׁפָּט וּצְדָקָה / κρίσιν καὶ δικαιοσύνην] in Jacob" (Ps 99[8]:4); "O Lord, Lord God, Creator of all things, you are awe-inspiring and strong and just [δίκαιος] and merciful; you alone are king [βασιλεύς]" (2 Macc 1:24); God "is a great and righteous king [βασιλεὺς καὶ δίκαιος]" (Pss. Sol. 2:32). Passages that were probably understood in an eschatological sense, if not a messianic sense as well, envisioned the rise of a righteous king (see Isa 9:7 [= Messiah in the Targum]; 11:1–5 [= Messiah in the Targum]; 16:5 [= Messiah in the Targum]; 49:1–4 [= Messiah in the Targum]; 52:13—53:12 [= Messiah in the Targum]; Jer 23:5 [= Messiah in the Targum]; Ps 45:3–8 [= Messiah in the Targum]; 72:1–3 [= Messiah in the Targum]).

In view of this scriptural and interpretive backdrop, I think it is likely that Jesus' announcement of the in-breaking kingdom of God would have brought to mind ideas of justice and with it the need to embrace personal righteousness. Indeed, these were the very things John's preaching and baptizing evidently called for. In this sense John truly prepared Israel for Jesus' preaching and ministry.

There are other passages in Mark that would have called to mind the theme of justice and righteousness. When his disciples were accused of eating with unwashed hands and therefore becoming defiled, Jesus criticized the oral traditions of the scribes and Pharisees, which in effect nullified the written law (Mark 7:1–13). Jesus pointed out that their practice of *corban*, whereby one's wherewithal was dedicated to the Temple, resulted in the unlawful failure to care for one's parents. Such a practice surely would have struck his sympathizers as a case of gross neglect, if not injustice.[7] But this can only be inferred. Likewise when Jesus taught his disciples that what comes out of the heart of a person is what really defiles (e.g., "evil thoughts, fornication, theft, murder, adultery, coveting, wickedness, deceit," etc.), hearers and readers would in all probability think of unrighteousness. Implicit in the entire exchange is a debate over what constitutes true justice and righteousness and what does not.

The matter of justice and righteousness is surely part of Jesus' angry denunciation of temple polity in his well-known demonstration in the temple precincts. The implications of his appeal to Isa 56:7 and Jer 7:11 would have been hard to miss: "Is it not written, 'My house shall be called a house of prayer for all the nations'? But you have made it a 'cave of robbers'" (Mark 11:17). Under the administration of the priestly family of Annas, the temple has failed to live up to Isaiah's grand vision (Isa 56:1–8), itself based on King Solomon's prayer of dedication (see 1 Kgs 8:41–43). Instead of becoming a spiritual beacon, a place where all peoples could gather and pray, the temple precincts had become a gathering place for oppressive criminal activity. As in the days of Jeremiah, so in the days of Jesus the temple establishment promoted injustice and villainy, not justice and righteousness.

A number of passages in Mark 12 reflect the theme of justice and righteousness. The well-known parable of the Wicked Vineyard Tenants (12:1–12) portrayed the ruling priests as thieves and murderers, whose day of reckoning was not too far off. The exchange with the scribe who inquired of Jesus which commandment was greatest (12:28–34) ended on a more positive note, with the scribe acknowledging "You are right, Teacher; you have truly said that he is one, and there is no other but he; and to love him with all the heart, and with all the understanding, and with all the strength,

---

7. Recall Cicero's definition (noted above) of what constituted justice and piety.

and to love one's neighbor as oneself, is much more than all whole burnt offerings and sacrifices" (vv. 32–33). The scribe's declaration is fully consistent with Jesus' earlier teaching, whether concerning what really defiles or concerning the temple establishment's failings. Justice and righteousness trump religiosity and cultic activity.[8]

Mark 12 concludes with two short vignettes that again presuppose justice and righteousness, even if this language does not appear. Both of these passages make the point that religious show cannot compensate for injustice. In vv. 38–40 Jesus warns of the "scribes, who like to go about in long robes, and to have salutations in the market places and the best seats in the synagogues and the places of honor at feasts, who devour widows' houses . . ." For all their religiosity and ostentation, Jesus tells his disciples, "They will receive the greater condemnation." Immediately following, probably as an illustration of the warning regarding the avaricious scribes, the evangelist narrates the story of the poor widow who gave the temple her last penny (vv. 41–44). Observing her, Jesus says to his disciples, "Truly, I say to you, this poor widow has put in more than all those who are contributing to the treasury. For they all contributed out of their abundance; but she out of her poverty has put in everything she had, her whole living" (vv. 43–44). This is no word of praise; it is a lament. Instead of being assisted by the temple establishment, as the Law of Moses commands, the poor widow has been exploited by the temple establishment and reduced to abject poverty.

Finally, we find in Mark 15 the theme of justice and righteousness presupposed in the condemnation, crucifixion, and death of Jesus. After examining Jesus, Pontius Pilate asks the crowd what he should do. When they call for crucifixion, Pilate asks, "Why, what evil has he done?" (v. 14). Pilate's question implies that there is no evidence that Jesus has done anything deserving crucifixion. Nevertheless, the crowd demands that he be crucified and Pilate acquiesces (vv. 14–15). The implied innocence of Jesus is intensified in the mockery of the ruling priests: "He saved others; he cannot save himself" (v. 31). Even if these words do not imply innocence, they at least acknowledge that Jesus was a doer of good (see Mark 3:4). The innocence of Jesus is implied too in the centurion's confession, uttered when Jesus dies: "Truly this man was the Son of God" (v. 39). It is probable that anyone recognized in such lofty terms would be viewed as just and as

---

8. Sänger, "Recht und Gerechtigkeit." Sänger discusses the meaning of מִשְׁפָּט ("justice") and צדקה ("righteousness") in Hebrew Scripture, which then forms the backdrop of his study of Mark 10:17–22 and 12:28–34.

righteous in the sight of God. This is why Luke is able to rephrase the centurion's words: "Certainly this man was innocent [δίκαιος]" (Luke 23:47). This cursory review of the Gospel of Mark shows that, in both the teaching of Jesus and the narrative itself, the evangelist, had he wished to do so, could have made the theme of justice and righteousness more explicit. It seems he was content to let the implications of Jesus' teaching and actions speak for themselves.

JUSTICE AND RIGHTEOUSNESS IN MATTHEW

Whereas the theme of justice and righteousness is implicit in the Gospel of Mark, it is quite explicit and emphasized in the Gospel of Matthew. In contrast to two appearances of δίκαιος in Mark, there are twenty-eight appearances of δίκαιος and cognates in Matthew. Most of these words have been inserted into material Matthew inherited from Mark and Q and in material that is special to Matthew. I shall survey this material and then suggest what δίκαιος and δικαιοσύνη mean in Matthew.[9]

Righteousness in Material Inherited from Mark

Matthew 3:15: In Mark's version of Jesus' baptism (Mark 1:9–11) there is no exchange between John and Jesus. But in Matthew's version John protests: "I need to be baptized by you" (Matt 3:14). To this protest Jesus replies, "Let it be so now; for thus it is fitting for us to fulfill all righteousness [πληρῶσαι πᾶσαν δικαιοσύνην]" (v. 15). Part of the purpose of this expansion is to mitigate the potential awkwardness of having Jesus submit to John's baptism "for the forgiveness of sins" (Mark 1:5). It is also in keeping with Matthew's interest in fulfillment. What the "righteousness" means here will be considered later.

Matthew 9:13: In rewriting Mark's account of the criticism leveled against Jesus for eating with "sinners and tax collectors" (Mark 2:15–17), Matthew expands Jesus' reply: "Go and learn what this means, 'I desire mercy, and not sacrifice.' For I came not to call the righteous, but sinners [δικαίους ἀλλὰ ἁμαρτωλούς]" (Matt 9:13; compare Mark 2:17). Matthew's

---

9. For studies concerned with righteousness in Matthew, see Lambrecht, "Righteousness in the Bible"; Bratcher, "'Righteousness' in Matthew"; Popkes, "Die Gerechtigkeitstradition"; Hagner, "Righteousness in Matthew's Theology"; Kampen, "'Righteousness' in Matthew"; Grassi, "Matthew's Gospel of Justice"; Chouinard, "Kingdom of God"; Combrink, "Overflowing Righteousness"; Deines, "Not the Law"; Evans, "Fulfilling the Law."

"I desire mercy, and not sacrifice" is taken from Hos 6:6 (according to the LXX, not the Hebrew, which reads "I desire steadfast love and not sacrifice"). Matthew will again use this verse from Hosea in Matt 12:7.

Matthew 10:41: The saying reads: "He who receives a prophet because he is a prophet shall receive a prophet's reward, and he who receives a righteous man because he is a righteous man [ὁ δεχόμενος δίκαιον εἰς ὄνομα δικαίου, literally: "he who receives a righteous man in the name of a righteous man"] shall receive a righteous man's reward [μισθὸν δικαίου]." It is difficult to tell, but Matthew's saying seems to be a reworking of Mark 9:37 ("Whoever receives one such child in my name receives me") and 9:41 ("whoever gives you a cup of water to drink . . . will by no means lose his reward").

Matthew 21:32: To Mark's account of the question by what authority Jesus acts as he does (Mark 11:27–33) the Evangelist Matthew appends the parable of the Two Sons (Matt 21:28–31a) and then a pronouncement: "Truly, I say to you, the tax collectors and the harlots go into the kingdom of God before you. For John came to you in the way of righteousness [ἐν ὁδῷ δικαιοσύνης], and you did not believe him, but the tax collectors and the harlots believed him" (vv. 31b–32).

Matthew 27:19: Elaborating on Mark's account of Pilate's offer of a Passover pardon (Mark 15:6–15), the Evangelist Matthew tells us that the governor's wife warned him, "Have nothing to do with that righteous man [τῷ δικαίῳ ἐκείνῳ], for I have suffered much over him today in a dream."

Righteousness in Material Inherited from Q

Matthew 5:6: Luke's version of the beatitude reads: "Blessed are you who hunger now, for you shall be satisfied" (Luke 6:21a). Matthew expands the beatitude to read: "Blessed are those who hunger and thirst for righteousness, for they shall be satisfied." The combination of hunger and thirst was probably suggested by Scripture (see LXX Ps 106:5–6; Isa 49:10; Jer 38:25 [= MT 31:15]).

Matthew 5:10: Perhaps inspired by the beatitude in v. 11 ("Blessed are you when people revile you and persecute you" = Luke 6:22) Matthew adds a second beatitude that once again brings the theme of righteousness into play: "Blessed are those who are persecuted for righteousness' sake, for theirs is the kingdom of heaven."

Matthew 6:33: Luke's version of the saying reads: "Seek his kingdom, and these things shall be yours" (Luke 12:31). Matthew's expanded version reads: "Seek first his kingdom and his righteousness [καὶ τὴν δικαιοσύνην αὐτοῦ] and all these things shall be yours as well."

Matthew 11:19: In the parallel at Luke 7:35 the verb δικαιόω appears, so this is not a case where the evangelist Matthew has added the word. What strikes me is the change elsewhere in the saying. Luke's reading probably reflects the original wording in Q: "Yet wisdom is justified by all her children [ἐδικαιώθη ἡ σοφία ἀπὸ πάντων τῶν τέκνων αὐτῆς]" (Luke 7:35). Matthew reads: "Yet wisdom is justified by her works [ἐδικαιώθη ἡ σοφία ἀπὸ τῶν ἔργων αὐτῆς]" (Matt 11:19). Matthew may be saying that rather than being justified by her children (probably meaning John and Jesus), wisdom is justified by her works, that is, her righteous works (as seen in the righteous works of John and Jesus).[10] Understood this way the saying coheres well with Matthew's theology.

Matthew 12:37: This verse appears to be part of some reworked Q material, which in places overlaps with Mark 3:20–30. Matthew 12:22–30 parallels Luke 11:14–23 + 12:10 and Matt 12:33–37 parallels Luke 6:43–45. The Evangelist Matthew augments the warning in Matt 12:34, "For out of the abundance of the heart the mouth speaks" (= Luke 6:45), with additional sayings in Matt 12:35–37, the last part of which reads: "by your words you will be justified [δικαιωθήσῃ], and by your words you will be condemned [καταδικασθήσῃ]."

Matthew 13:17: Expanding on Mark's material concerned with the meaning of parables (see Mark 4:10–12, 25), Matthew draws on Q, adding a beatitude and an "amen" saying (compare Matt 13:16–17 with Luke 10:23–24). In Luke the saying reads: "For I tell you that many prophets and kings desired to see what you see, and did not see it, and to hear what you hear, and did not hear it." However, in Matthew the saying reads: "Truly, I say to you, many prophets and righteous men [δίκαιοι] longed to see what you see, and did not see it."

Matthew 23:28: Portions of Matthew's diatribe against the scribes and Pharisees are drawn from Q, especially Matt 23:13–36, which parallels Luke 11:37–54. In the analogy with whitewashed tombs, which appear beautiful on the outside but inside are full of human bones and corruption (Matt 23:27–28), Jesus applies the lesson to his religious critics: "So you also outwardly appear righteous [δίκαιοι] to people, but within you are full of hypocrisy and iniquity."

---

10. France, *Gospel of Matthew*, 434–35.

Matthew 23:29: In the succeeding woe against the scribes and Pharisees, Jesus asserts, that they "build the tombs of the prophets and adorn the monuments of the righteous [τὰ μνημεῖα τῶν δικαίων]." The Evangelist Matthew seems to have expanded the original woe. The parallel in Luke 11:47 reads: "Woe to you! For you build the tombs of the prophets whom your fathers killed."

Matthew 23:35: Matthew has again expanded the Q tradition, in part so reference could be made to righteousness. The parallel in Luke reads: "from the blood of Abel to the blood of Zechariah, who perished between the altar and the sanctuary" (Luke 11:51a). In Matthew the charge reads: "all the righteous blood [πᾶν αἷμα δίκαιον] shed on earth, from the blood of innocent Abel [Αβελ τοῦ δικαίου] to the blood of Zechariah the son of Barachiah, whom you murdered between the sanctuary and the altar."

Righteousness in Material Inherited from Matthew's Special Material

Matthew 5:20: At the conclusion of his "thesis statement" in the Sermon on the Mount, where Jesus makes clear his view of the Law of Moses (Matt 5:17–20), he warns his disciples: "For I tell you, unless your righteousness [ὑμῶν ἡ δικαιοσύνη] exceeds that of the scribes and Pharisees, you will never enter the kingdom of heaven." In the so-called antitheses that follow (Matt 5:21–48) Jesus clarifies in what ways the righteousness he requires exceeds that of his religious rivals.[11]

Matthew 13:43: Only Matthew presents the parable of the Wheat and Weeds (Matt 13:24–30) and, later, an explanation of the parable (13:36–43). At the conclusion of the explanation Jesus declares that evildoers will be cast into the "furnace of fire" and the "righteous [οἱ δίκαιοι] will shine like the sun in the kingdom of their Father" (v. 43). The latter part of the saying appears to be based on Dan 12:3. Whereas the standard LXX text reads "And those who are intelligent will light up like the luminaries of heaven, and those who strengthen my words will be as the stars of heaven forever and ever," the text of Theodotion reads "And those who are intelligent will shine like the splendor of the firmament, and some of the many righteous [ἀπὸ τῶν δικαίων τῶν πολλῶν], like the stars forever and ever," which more

---

11. In recent years a number of important studies have treated Matt 5:20. See Eckstein, "Die 'bessere Gerechtigkeit'"; Charles, "Garnishing with the 'Greater Righteousness'"; Mukasa, "Righteousness"; Garlington, "The 'Better Righteousness.'" For a major study on the passage and its relevance for Matthean theology and Christology, see Deines, *Die Gerechtigkeit*.

closely approximates the Hebrew text, which reads "And those who are wise shall shine like the brightness of the firmament; and those who turn many to righteousness [וּמַצְדִּיקֵי הָרַבִּים], like the stars for ever and ever." The Hebrew text and Theodotion's text are not identical (though it is not hard to see how an unpointed Hebrew text could be rendered the way it is in Theodotion), but they do have in common reference to the righteous.[12]

Matthew 13:49: The lesson appended to the parable of the Fishnet makes the same point: "The angels will come out and separate the evil from the righteous [ἐκ μέσου τῶν δικαίων], and throw them into the furnace of fire" (vv. 49–50).

Matthew 20:4: In Matthew's parable of the Workers in the Vineyard (Matt 20:1–16) the manager promises to those whom he has hired, "You go into the vineyard too, and whatever is right [δίκαιον] I will give you." That is, the manager will pay a just or fair wage.

Matthew 20:13: At the end of the parable, those who labored the full day complain that they have been paid the same as those who worked only part of the day. To one of these grumblers the manager replies, "Friend, I am doing you no wrong [οὐκ ἀδικῶ σε]; did you not agree with me for a denarius?"

Matthew 25:37: In eschatological material found only in Matthew (25:31–46), we are told that "the righteous [οἱ δίκαιοι] will answer him, 'Lord, when did we see you hungry and feed you, or thirsty and give you drink?'"

Matthew 25:46: Matthew's special eschatological material concludes with the prophetic announcement that the wicked "will go away into eternal punishment, but the righteous [οἱ δὲ δίκαιοι] into eternal life."

Analysis of Matthew's Use of Tradition

More than three decades ago Canadian New Testament scholar Benno Przybylski cautioned that we not define Matthew's use of δίκαιος and δικαιοσύνη in a Pauline sense.[13] Whereas Paul employed this language to speak of God's grace, freely given, Matthew employed this language to speak of ethical requirements, focused on fulfilling the Law. (Przybylski speaks of "gift" versus "demand.") Some have faulted Przybylski's work for limiting

12. For helpful discussion of this difficult text, see Collins, *Daniel*, 393–94.

13. Przybylski, *Righteousness in Matthew*. In his analysis Przybylski also included ἐλεημοσύνη (Matt 6:2–4). Przybylski's principal Hebrew terminology included צדיק, צדק, and צדקה.

the literature used for comparison to the Dead Sea Scrolls and early rabbinic writings,[14] while others think the differences between Matthean and Pauline use of these words have been exaggerated.[15]

I do not think there is much doubt that most occurrences of δίκαιος and δικαιοσύνη in Matthew are in reference to ethical requirements, things that God and/or Jesus expect his people to do, but some of them may be in reference to the grace of God, to God's own righteousness. With this possibility in mind let us take another look at some of the texts that have just been surveyed. First, let us consider the passages where the righteous and righteousness language probably is in reference to ethical requirements.

Those who are persecuted for righteousness (Matt 5:10) are persecuted for doing what is right (see 1 Pet 3:14). The prophets and righteous who long to see what the disciples see (Matt 13:17) are probably just persons. The manager in the parable of the Workers in the Vineyard is a just man who pays his workers what is "just" (20:4); he has "wronged" no one (v. 13). Those commended in the final judgment are just persons, for they took pity on the hungry and thirsty, giving them food and drink (25:37). We should understand the advice of the worried wife of Pilate in the same sense. She tells her husband to have nothing to do with the righteous or just Jesus (27:19). He is a man the prefect should not punish; he is innocent.

That the scribes and Pharisees outwardly appear "righteous" to people (Matt 23:28) probably means that they appear as "just" persons, but in reality they are full of hypocrisy and iniquity. The denunciation coheres with the warning regarding the scribes who make a show of religiosity but in the end devour the substance of the poor (Mark 12:41–44). Matthew's context of the denunciation coheres with the woe pronounced on the scribes and Pharisees who build the tombs of the prophets whom their fathers have murdered (Matt 23:29). By "fathers" it is probably meant masters, teachers, exemplars. In a sense the Pharisees and scribes of Jesus' day are the spiritual descendants of those who persecuted the prophets.

---

14. For example, see Waetjen's Review. Among other things, Waetjen faults Przybylski for treating the two bodies of literature (i.e., the scrolls and early rabbinic literature) as more or less homogeneous. Not only is there a range of nuance in these bodies of literature, there is also a range of nuance in the usage of δίκαιος and δικαιοσύνη in Matthew and the Pauline letters. I observe that the relevant vocabulary occurs hundreds of times in the Pseudepigrapha. This literature, it seems to me, is every bit as relevant to Matthean and Pauline study as the Dead Sea Scrolls and early rabbinic literature.

15. Mohrlang, *Matthew and Paul*.

Now let us consider those passages in Matthew where "righteousness" does not seem to reference ethical requirements and obligations, but seems to reference the righteousness or justice of God. Those who "hunger and thirst for righteousness" (Matt 5:6) are those who desire justice. But the justice they long for here is not of their doing. They are not hungering and thirsting for the opportunity to be righteous, or to do the will of God, or to act in a just manner toward their neighbor. No, they are longing for *God to act*, for God to fill the earth with his justice.[16] One thinks of the prophetic hope expressed by Isaiah long ago: "He will not fail or be discouraged till he has established justice in the earth; and the coastlands wait for his law" (Isa 42:4). Even more poetically the prophet proclaims: "My righteousness [ἡ δικαιοσύνη μου] draws near swiftly; my salvation [τὸ σωτήριόν μου] will go out, and the nations will hope in my arm; the islands will wait for me and hope in my arm . . . my righteousness [ἡ δὲ δικαιοσύνη μου] will not fail . . . my righteousness [ἡ δὲ δικαιοσύνη μου] will be forever" (Isa 51:5–6, 8). It is for God's righteousness that God's people hunger and thirst.

Another passage in Matthew in which "righteousness" does not seem to refer to ethical demands is 6:33, where Jesus enjoins his disciples to seek God's "kingdom and his righteousness." The most natural meaning of δικαιοσύνη in this context seems to be "justice," that is, God's people are to seek the kingdom, or rule, of God and along with it they are to seek God's righteous judgment, the kind of justice one would expect to prevail under the rule of God. Jesus is not asking his disciples to establish *their* righteousness but to seek *God's* righteousness.

The final two passages that I want to consider both concern John. When Jesus tells John that it is fitting to "fulfill all righteousness" (Matt 3:15), it is possible to understand this utterance in the sense of fulfilling ethical requirements or fulfilling the Law, much as is meant in Matt 5:17, where Jesus declares that he has not come to abolish the law and the prophets but to fulfill them. But the statement may have a very different meaning.[17] When Jesus says that it is "fitting for us to fulfill all righteousness," instead of "for me," he has included John. What John the forerunner inaugurates, Jesus the Savior (Matt 1:23) completes. Together they fulfill "all" of God's righteous, saving work.[18]

---

16. For support of this interpretation and the citation of a number of relevant prophetic passages, see Hagner, "Righteousness in Matthew's Theology," 112–13.

17. On the range of meanings, see Eissfeldt, "πληρῶσαι πᾶσαν δικαιοσύνην."

18. See Hagner, *Matthew 1–13*, 56–57.

When Jesus admonishes the religious leaders in the temple precincts, saying that "John came to you in the way of righteousness" (Matt 21:32), he may have deliberately echoed Isa 40:3, which enjoined Israel to "Prepare the way of the Lord." John came in the way of God's righteousness, the way of salvation.[19] Recall that Isaiah 40 goes on to declare that "all flesh will see the salvation of God" (Isa 40:5; cited in Luke 3:4–6). Is the "way of righteousness" in reference to what we must do or is it in reference to what God will do? The context seems to indicate the latter. Jesus reproaches the religious teachers because although John came to them in the way of righteousness, they "did not believe him." Jesus does not say they did not adopt John's piety or adopt his understanding of the Law; he accuses them of not *believing* John's message, namely, that God was preparing Israel's salvation. In contrast to the unbelieving response of the ruling priests and elders (Matt 21:23), the "tax collectors and the harlots believed" John. Even then, after seeing people such as these express faith in John's message, the religious rulers "did not afterward repent and believe him." They thus play the part of the son in the parable of the Two Sons (Matt 21:28–32) who says "yes" but then does nothing, and so does not fulfill the will of his father.

I end my discussion of Matthew with a comment regarding the well-known observation that δικαιοσύνη occurs seven times in Matthew, five times in the Sermon on the Mount and twice in the two passages concerned with John. Only Jesus as Israel's Messiah and as God's Son can fulfill the Law and the Prophets and so establish a righteousness that exceeds that of the scribes and Pharisees.[20] It is in this "way of righteousness" that John appeared (Matt 21:32), preparing for Jesus' appearance, so that together with Jesus he might "fulfill all righteousness" (3:15). There is little doubt that for the Evangelist Matthew, the meaning of "righteousness" and the Hebrew and Aramaic vocabulary that lies behind the Greek vocabulary are defined in the Sermon on the Mount. Both concepts—that righteousness entails ethical obligations, and righteousness describes the nature of God and his saving, redemptive work—seem to be expressed in the Sermon. Appropriately, both of these concepts also seem to underlie the ministry of John, the forerunner of the Messiah.

19. See Nolland, *Gospel of Matthew*, 864: "'John came to you in [the] way of righteousness' points generally to John's role in the fulfillment of this project."

20. Deines, *Die Gerechtigkeit*, 257–87. Jesus' understanding of righteousness is especially seen in the antitheses. On this point, see Cuvillier, "Torah Observance," 148–49.

CONCLUDING COMMENTS

My brief assessment of the language of justice and righteousness in the Gospels of Mark and Matthew has tried to show how fluid and contextual this terminology was in the Jewish world in late antiquity. Even the absence of this language (as in Mark) does not necessarily mean the absence of the concepts. And of course the frequency of the language (as in Matthew) does not always guarantee clarity or consistency.

Ongoing research into this important vocabulary and the significant theological concepts to which it gives expression must carefully assess the meaning of every occurrence, taking care not to lapse into the assumption that a given author uses the vocabulary in a consistent, unvarying manner. The complexity we face in the study of the Gospel of Matthew should be obvious, and I have only touched on some of the possible meanings of the vocabulary of justice and righteousness.

There is little doubt that the Jesus portrayed in the Gospels of Matthew and Mark called for personal righteousness and social justice, especially in view of the appearance of the kingdom of God. The New Testament Gospels provide us with invaluable insight into Jesus' teaching on righteousness and justice, but his teaching is not limited to the Gospels. It comes to further expression and creative applications in the book of Acts and several letters of the New Testament. This is hardly surprising, given the semantic range of this important vocabulary.

BIBLIOGRAPHY

Alt, A., et al. *Biblia Hebraica Stuttgartensia.* Stuttgart: Deutsche Bibelgesellschaft, 1983.

Baird, J. Arthur. *The Justice of God in the Teaching of Jesus.* Philadelphia: Westminster, 1963.

Bratcher, R. G. "'Righteousness' in Matthew." *BT* 40 (1989) 228–35.

Charles, J. Daryl. "Garnishing with the 'Greater Righteousness': The Disciple's Relationship to the Law (Matthew 5:17–20)." *BBR* 12 (2002) 1–15.

Chouinard, Larry. "The Kingdom of God and the Pursuit of Justice in Matthew." *Restoration Quarterly* 45 (2003) 229–42.

Collins, J. J. *Daniel: A Commentary on the Book of Daniel.* Hermeneia. Minneapolis: Fortress, 1993.

Combrink, H. J. B. "The Challenge of Overflowing Righteousness: To Learn to Live the Story of the Gospel of Matthew." In *Identity, Ethics, and Ethos in the New Testament,* edited J. G. Van der Watt, 23–48. BZNW 141. Berlin: de Gruyter, 2006.

Cuvillier, Élian. "Torah Observance and Radicalization in the First Gospel: Matthew and First-Century Judaism." *NTS* 55 (2009) 144–59.

Declaissé-Walford, N. "Righteousness in the OT." In *NIDB* 4:818–23.

Deines, Roland. *Die Gerechtigkeit der Tora im Reich des Messias: Mt 5,13–20 als Schlüsseltext der matthäischen Theologie.* WUNT 177. Tübingen: Mohr Siebeck, 2004.

———. "Not the Law but the Messiah: Law and Righteousness in the Gospel of Matthew: An Ongoing Debate." In *Built upon the Rock: Studies in the Gospel of Matthew*, edited by D. M. Gurtner and J. Nolland, 53–84. Grand Rapids: Eerdmans, 2008.

Eckstein, Hans-Joachim. "Die 'bessere Gerechtigkeit': Zur Ethik Jesu nach dem Matthäusevangelium." *Theologische Beiträge* 32 (2001) 299–316.

Eissfeldt, O. "πληρῶσαι πᾶσαν δικαιοσύνην in Matthäus 3,15." *ZNW* 61 (1970) 209–15.

Evans, Craig A. "Fulfilling the Law and Seeking Righteousness in Matthew and in the Dead Sea Scrolls." In *Jesus, Matthew's Gospel and Early Christianity: Studies in Memory of Graham N. Stanton*, edited by D. M. Gurtner, J. Willitts, and R. A. Burridge, 102–14. LNTS 435. London: T. & T. Clark, 2011.

France, R. T. *The Gospel of Matthew.* NICNT. Grand Rapids: Eerdmans, 2007.

Garlington, Don. "The 'Better Righteousness': Matthew 5:20." *BBR* 10 (2010) 479–502.

Grassi, Joseph A. "Matthew's Gospel of Justice." *Bible Today* 38 (2000) 234–38.

Hagner, Donald A. *Matthew 1–13.* WBC 33A. Dallas: Word, 1993.

———. "Righteousness in Matthew's Theology." In *Worship, Theology and Ministry in the Early Church*, edited by M. J. Wilkins and T. Paige, 101–20. JSNTSup 87. Sheffield: JSOT Press, 1992.

Hayes, E. R. "Justice, Righteousness." In *DOTP* 466–72.

Jackson, B. S. "'Law' and 'Justice' in the Bible." *JJS* 49 (1998) 218–29.

Kampen, J. "'Righteousness' in Matthew and the Legal Texts from Qumran." In *Legal Texts and Legal Issues: Proceedings of the Second Meeting of the International Organization for Qumran Studies, Cambridge, 1995, Published in Honour of Joseph M. Baumgarten*, edited by M. Bernstein, F. García Martínez, and J. Kampen, 461–87. STDJ 23. Leiden: Brill, 1997.

Lambrecht, Jan. "Righteousness in the Bible and Justice in the World." *Theologica Evangelica* 21 (1988) 6–13.

Lang, F. "Gesetz und Gerechtigkeit Gottes in biblisch-theologischer Sicht." *Theologische Beiträge* 22 (1991) 195–207.

Leonhardt-Balzer, J. "Righteousness in Early Jewish Literature." In *NIDB* 4:807–13.

Mohrlang, Roger. *Matthew and Paul: A Comparison of Ethical Perspectives.* SNTSMS 48. Cambridge: Cambridge University Press, 1984.

Mukasa, E. "A Righteousness Greater than That of the Scribes and Pharisees (Mt 5:20): Righteousness for the Kingdom of God." *Hekima Review* 37 (2007) 55–66.

Nolland, John. *The Gospel of Matthew.* NIGTC. Grand Rapids: Eerdmans, 2005.

O'Kennedy, D. F. "The Relationship between Justice and Forgiveness in Psalm 103." *Scriptura* 65 (1998) 109–21.

Popkes, W. "Die Gerechtigkeitstradition im Matthäus-Evangelium." *ZNW* 80 (1989) 1–23.

Przybylski, Benno. *Righteousness in Matthew and His World of Thought.* SNTSMS 41. Cambridge: Cambridge University Press, 1980.

Quell, G. and G. Schrenk, "δίκη, δίκαιος, δικαιοσύνη, κ.τ.λ." In *TDNT* 2:174–225.

Rahlfs, A. *Septuaginta.* 2 vols. 3rd ed. Stuttgart: Wüttembergische Bibelanstalt, 1935, 1947.

Reumann, J. "Justification and Justice in the New Testament." *HBT* 21 (1999) 26–45.

———. "Righteousness (Early Judaism)." In *ABD* 5:736–45.

———. "Righteousness (NT)." In *ABD* 5:745–73.

Sacchi, P. "From Righteousness to Justification in the Period of Hellenistic Judaism," *Henoch* 23 (2001) 1–26.

Sänger, D. "Recht und Gerechtigkeit in der Verkündigung Jesu: Erwägungen zu Mk 10,17–22 und 12,28–34." *Biblische Zeitschrift* 36 (1992) 179–94.

Schwartz, R. M. "Revelation and Revolution: Law, Justice, and Politics in the Hebrew Bible." In *Sacred Tropes: Tanakh, New Testament, and Qur'an as Literature and Culture*, edited by R. S. Sabbath, 485–92. BibInt 98. Leiden: Brill, 2010.

Scullion, J. J. "Righteousness (OT)." In *ABD* 5:724–36.

Soards, M. L. "Righteousness in the NT." In *NIDB* 4:813–18.

Spicq, C. "δίκαιος, δικαιοσύνη, δικαιόω, κ.τ.λ." In *TLNT* 2:318–47.

Vincent, J. M. "Un regard sur la 'justice' dans l'Ancien Testament." *Etudes théologiques et religieuses* 74 (1999) 321–33.

Waetjen, H. C. Review of *Righteousness in Matthew and His World of Thought* by Benno Przybylski. *Int* 36 (1982) 318–20.

Weber, R., *Biblia sacra iuxta vulgatam versionem*. 2 vols. 3rd ed. Stuttgart: Deutsche Bibelgesellschaft, 1985.

Weinfeld, M. "'Justice and Righteousness'—מִשְׁפָּט וּצְדָקָה—The Expression and Its Meaning." In *Justice and Righteousness: Biblical Themes and Their Influence*, edited by H. G. Reventlow and Y. Hoffman, 228–46. JSOTSup 137. Sheffield: JSOT Press, 1992.

5

Good News to the Poor

Social Upheaval, Strong Warnings, and Sincere Giving in Luke–Acts

BRYAN R. DYER

INTRODUCTION

LUKE'S TWO-VOLUME WORK IS among the richest in the New Testament regarding issues of social justice—concern for the poor and marginalized, an emphasis on equality and solidarity, and putting wrongs to right. In fact, Luke has been referred to as the "Gospel of the Good News for the Poor" as many scholars identify these persistent themes.[1] When one compares Luke's Gospel to the other Gospels—regardless of what one makes of Luke's use of sources—there is unique material that demonstrates the author's intentional emphasis on justice and caring for the poor and oppressed. This continues into the Acts of the Apostles as Luke presents the earliest church in Jerusalem as one where "there was not a needy person among them" (Acts 4:34).[2]

That this theme in Luke–Acts is well known is both a blessing and a curse for my purposes here. It is a blessing because of the vast scholarship that has been devoted to this issue and the many helpful studies that assist in navigating these waters.[3] However, it is a curse for that very same reason:

---

1. Evans, *Luke*, 12.

2. Scripture passages, unless noted otherwise, are taken from the NRSV version.

3. See C. M. Hays, *Luke's Wealth Ethics*; Johnson, *Sharing Possessions*; Pilgrim, *Good News to the Poor*; Kim, *Stewardship and Almsgiving*.

what is left to say about Luke's concern for justice and the poor that has not already been said? My purpose in this paper is two-fold. First, I wish to be faithful to Luke's texts and through the course of this study to present an overview of his concern for social justice.[4] Second, I will highlight how Luke draws upon Old Testament prophetic literature—particularly Isaiah—for his understanding of *justice* and its role in the ministry of Jesus and his earliest followers. This is seen in a variety of ways in Luke's Gospel: direct quotations, allusions, borrowed terminology and themes, and other general appeals to the prophetic tradition.[5] In Acts, direct appeals to the prophetic literature are scarce, yet Luke presents a community motivated by the ideals presented in the life and teaching of Jesus. It is clear that this prophetic concept of justice is a significant concern for Luke as he highlights its role in the ministry and mission of Jesus and the early church.

JUSTICE IN THE OLD TESTAMENT PROPHETIC LITERATURE

Before moving into our examination of Luke–Acts, we must first look at some preliminary issues. "Social justice" has been defined in a variety of ways—particularly in American political discourse.[6] I do not wish to use the term in any way that clouds its definition by imposing political or polemical attachments that it can be given in contemporary society. Rather, a major component in this paper is that the concept of *justice* in Luke's presentation of Jesus' ministry and that of the early church has its source in the prophetic literature. Thus, we will briefly examine how justice was understood in that literature before showing how it is played out in Luke's writings. After this, we will look closely at key passages from Luke–Acts that engage with issues of social justice.

That the Old Testament was significant for Luke's writing is evidenced by the numerous quotations and allusions to Scripture throughout his two volumes.[7] C. K. Barrett considered the influence of the Old Testament upon

4. I will often engage with particular scholarly views within the body of this paper but reserve much of this to the footnotes.

5. For a discussion on what constitutes a quotation, allusion, or other appeal to the Old Testament in the New, see Porter, "Further Comments."

6. On the history and challenges of the term, see Novak, "Defining Social Justice."

7. UBS4 counts twenty-five explicit quotations in Luke's Gospel (also Fitzmyer, *To Advance the Gospel*, 297; Moyise, *Old Testament in the New*, 45) and forty in Acts. This is in addition to the countless allusions, echoes, and paraphrases of the Old Testament ("An analytical count of the instances of the use of the OT in Acts is impossible because of the variety of types of usage and the difficulty of assigning uses to specific categories"

Luke–Acts as "profound and pervasive" and noted that "it is safe to say that there is no major concept in the two books that does not to some extent reflect the beliefs and theological vocabulary of the OT."[8] For his concept of justice, Luke draws heavily from Isaiah and other prophetic literature.[9] The significance of Isaiah for the New Testament writers is apparent in that it is quoted or alluded to more than any other Old Testament book.[10] Its importance for Luke is seen not only in that it is often referenced, but that it is evoked at significant points in his writing (Isa 61:1–2 and 58:6 in Luke 4:18–19; numerous allusions in Luke 7:22; Isa 53:7–8 in Acts 8:32–33; Isa 6:9–10 in Acts 28:26–27).

Justice is a major theme in the prophetic literature and is often mentioned using the Hebrew term מִשְׁפָּט, frequently meaning "justice," but also "judgment" or "ordinance."[11] As J. Daniel Hays has shown, when carrying the meaning of "justice," מִשְׁפָּט is used in certain contexts by the prophets: as a characteristic of Yahweh (Isa 5:16; 30:18; 61:8; Jer 9:24; Hos 2:19), a quality that Yahweh expects his people to live by (Isa 1:21–23; 5:1–7; 56:1; Jer 5:5; Mic 6:8; Amos 5:15), and as an aspect of the eschatological restoration by Yahweh (Isa 16:5; 42:1–4; Jer 23:5; Ezek 34:16).[12] Justice is often closely connected with righteousness (צֶדֶק; Isa 1:21; 5:16; 56:1)[13] and humility (Isa 58:1–8; Mic 6:8; Zeph 2:3). It is also commonly contrasted with empty religious ritual (Amos 5:21–24; Isa 58:1–8) and taking advantage of the lowly (Isa 1:21–23; 5:1–7; Jer 22:13–16).

Two elements of justice found in Isaiah and the other prophets will be particularly important as we turn to Luke–Acts. First, social justice is a standard that Yahweh holds his people to. Throughout the prophets, how a nation or ruler upholds justice—often seen in how they care for the

[Marshall, "Acts," 513]).

8. Barrett, "Luke/Acts," 231. For a recent overview of scholarly opinion on the use of Scripture in Luke–Acts, see Litwak, *Echoes of Scripture in Luke–Acts*, 1–30.

9. An article by J. D. Hays ("Sell Everything You Have") has made this very point. I am indebted to his work for this section. See also the paper by M. Daniel Carroll R. in this volume.

10. Sanders, "Isaiah in Luke," 14.

11. "מִשְׁפָּט," BDB, 4941.

12. J. D. Hays, "Sell Everything You Have," 45–46. Hays actually cites four contexts, but his second and fourth overlap in considering Yahweh's expectation that his people live by מִשְׁפָּט.

13. See McKnight, "Justice, Righteousness."

needy—is the measure by which Yahweh judges them.[14] This notion of social justice did not originate with the prophets; it is a theme throughout the Hebrew Bible, particularly Deuteronomy (10:17–19; 15:1–11; 26:12–13). The prophets merely point back to this standard of social justice and call for repentance from the injustices in their time and place.[15] This standard is seen in Isa 56:1: "Thus says the Lord: Maintain justice, and do what is right." Also Micah 6:8:

> He has told you, O mortal, what is good;
>   and what does the Lord require of you
> but to do justice, and to love kindness,
>   and to walk humbly with your God?

Jeremiah 5:27–28 is an example of Yahweh's standard of justice being broken:

> They [the rulers] have become great and rich,
>   they have grown fat and sleek.
> They know no limits in deeds of wickedness;
>   they do not judge with justice the cause of the orphan, to make
>   it prosper,
>   and they do not defend the rights of the needy.

The concept of social justice is important for the theology of the prophets. While it did not originate there, the prophetic literature upholds Yahweh's standard of justice—pointing out its neglect and abuse.

Second, justice is closely connected with caring for the orphan, widow, oppressed, and poor (Isa 41:17; 61:1; Jer 5:28). Isaiah 1:17 states, "Learn to do good; seek justice, rescue the oppressed, defend the orphan, plead for the widow." Of Yahweh, Isa 25:4 says, "You have been a refuge to the poor, a refuge to the needy in their distress." The prophet Zechariah writes, "Do not oppress the widow, the orphan, the alien, or the poor; and do not devise evil in your hearts against one another" (7:10). These groups (poor, orphans, widows, oppressed, aliens) are commonly linked together in the prophetic literature and share certain features that connect them. On these groups, Donald Gowan writes, "The worst problem, that which these groups have in common, is powerlessness and its consequences: lack of status, lack of respect, making one an easy mark for the powerful and

---

14. See J. D. Hays, "Sell Everything You Have," 45–46.

15. See Fretheim, "Prophets and Social Justice."

unscrupulous."[16] The prophetic literature not only speaks of justice for the poor and marginalized, but also contains strong warnings against those who inflict such injustices. For example, Isa 10:1–3:

> Ah, you who make iniquitous decrees,
>> who write oppressive statutes,
> to turn aside the needy from justice
>> and to rob the poor of my people of their right,
> that widows may be your spoil,
>> and that you may make the orphans your prey!
> What will you do on the day of punishment,
>> in the calamity that will come from far away?
> To whom will you flee for help,
>> and where will you leave your wealth?

The instruction to care for and support the poor and marginalized found in the notion of justice in the prophets is followed closely by harsh words of condemnation for those responsible for injustice.

SOCIAL JUSTICE IN LUKE–ACTS

Luke's portrayal of the ministry of Jesus and his earliest followers incorporates the language and themes of social justice from Isaiah and the other prophets. In some places he draws directly upon notions of justice from Deuteronomy and other parts of the Hebrew Bible. Yet, as we will see, Luke presents Isaiah as foundational for how Jesus viewed his ministry—an example followed by his disciples.

Luke 4:18–19

We begin our examination of Luke–Acts with a passage that marks the beginning of Jesus' public ministry and is commonly understood as a paradigm for his teaching and vocation.[17] Luke 4:16–30 tells of Jesus teaching at a Nazareth synagogue, when Jesus places his ministry within the context of Jewish Scripture and is ultimately run out of his home town by an angry crowd. Similar accounts are given in Matthew and Mark's Gospels (Matt 13:53–58; Mark 6:1–6), but Luke's account is unique in that it is located at

---

16. Gowan, "Wealth and Poverty in the Old Testament," 344.

17. "Luke has deliberately put this story (4:16–30) at the beginning of the public ministry to encapsulate the entire ministry of Jesus and the reaction to it" (Fitzmyer, *Luke*, 529). See also Bock, *Luke*, 1:394; Marshall, *Luke*, 179; Talbert, *Reading Luke*, 57; Johnson, *Gospel of Luke*, 81; Green, *Gospel of Luke*, 207.

the beginning of Jesus' ministry and provides the content of his teaching. According to Luke, Jesus entered the synagogue in Nazareth and read from the prophet Isaiah:

> The Spirit of the Lord is upon me
>> because he has anointed me;
> He has sent me to proclaim good news to the poor:
>> to proclaim release to the captives
>> and recovery of sight to the blind
>> to let the oppressed go free,
>> to proclaim the year of the Lord's favor.[18]

Following this, Jesus closes the scroll, sits down, and tells those in the synagogue, "Today this scripture has been fulfilled in your hearing" (Luke 4:20).

The quotation is from Isa 61:1–2 with a line from Isa 58:7 inserted. The punctuation of this Old Testament quotation is disputed,[19] as is its construction.[20] First, as is often noted, the quotation omits words of judgment from the second half of Isa 61:2.[21] It could be that Luke, or Jesus (if

---

18. My own translation, to emphasize the grammar.

19. Some place a stop after πτωχοῖς so that εὐαγγελίσασθαι is dependent upon ἔχρισεν ("he has anointed me to bring good news") (So the KJV, ESV, NRSV, NIV, and NASB). Others place a stop after με so that εὐαγγελίσασθαι is dependent upon ἀπέσταλκεν ("he has sent me to bring good news") (So the CEB translation and NEB text). The latter view is to be preferred since it more closely parallels the MT and LXX and finds support in Jesus' words in 4:43, "I must proclaim the good news . . . because that is why I was sent" (so Marshall, *Luke*, 183). Joel Green argues not only for this construction, but also that "proclaim[ing] good news to the poor" becomes Jesus' primary mission and the following three infinitives are understood as subordinate clauses that amplify this mission (Green, "Good News to Whom," 73). Green further supports this punctuation by noting the structure of the quotation: the first three lines in Greek end with "me," repeating the pronoun at the end; the three following infinitives appear in parallel and emphasize "release." If this grammatical construction is correct—and I believe it is—then Green's argument would be supported by noting that ἀπέσταλκεν ("he has sent") is in the perfect tense, and as such it rises to a greater level of prominence than the following aorist infinitives. Whether or not the Lukan author intended the proclamation of good news to the poor as Jesus' primary mission, it serves as the starting point on this list of the elements of divine favor taken from Isaiah 61.

20. The quotation is from Isa 61:1–2 and contains two omissions ("to bind up the brokenhearted" and "[to proclaim] the day of vengeance of our God; to comfort all who mourn") and adds a line from Isa 58:6 ("to let the oppressed go free") at the end of 4:18. On possible reasons for these omissions and additions, see Bock, *Luke*, 1:404–11.

21. The NRSV of Isaiah reads: "[To proclaim] the day of vengeance of our God; to comfort all who mourn."

the construction of this quotation originated with him),[22] intentionally left out the words of vengeance in order to downplay the theme of judgment.[23] However, given the association of vengeance with this passage—as seen at Qumran (11QMelch)[24]—judgment may simply be assumed in Jesus' appeal to these verses. Yet, the effect of ending Jesus' quotation before the mention of vengeance places the focus on the good news to the poor and release of the oppressed. From a literary point of view, the end of the quotation emphasizes the proclamation of the year of the Lord's favor. Second, the insertion of a line from Isa 58:6 ("to let the oppressed go free") is often explained by the connection of this verse to Isaiah 61 around the word ἄφεσις ("forgiveness" or "release").[25] As such, some kind of midrashic technique may be in play in the combination of these two texts in Luke 4.[26]

This raises the question of who "the poor" (πτωχός) are in Luke's writings. This question has not been lost on biblical scholars and many commentaries and monographs have addressed it in some way or another.[27] Most scholars acknowledge that to some extent "the poor" refers to those of low economic means—while often allowing for some flexibility in this meaning.[28] Other scholars emphasize the spiritual dimension of "the poor"—sometimes to the neglect of any literal understanding of the term. Darrell Bock, for example, considers the term a "soteriological generalization"—that is, "the poor" refers to those who "most often responded to Jesus" and who are "open to God."[29] Similarly, in reference to Luke 4:18, I. Howard Marshall understands the poor as "the people who are most in need of divine help and who wait upon God to hear his words."[30]

To understand what Luke means when he writes of "the poor," we must first begin by examining how the term is used within its linguistic co-text. That is to say that the meaning of πτωχός in a given use will be dependent upon the other words that appear around it—essentially constraining how

22. On this, see Porter, "Scripture Justifies Mission," 116–17.

23. Fitzmyer, *Luke*, 533.

24. See Miller, "Function of Isa 61:1–2"; also, Strauss, *Davidic Messiah*, 220; Porter, "Scripture Justifies Mission," 111–12.

25. Evans, *Luke*, 74–75; also Koet, *Five Studies*, 30.

26. Porter, "Scripture Justifies Mission," 112.

27. Pilgrim, *Good News to the Poor*; Stegemann, *Gospel and the Poor*, 22–31.

28. Fitzmyer, *Luke*, 248; Davids, "Rich and Poor."

29. Bock, *Luke*, 1:408.

30. Marshall, *Luke*, 183.

it is being used and what it means.[31] Particularly enlightening is that seven of ten uses of πτωχός by Luke come within lists of descriptive terms of low status or physical destitution.

Below is a table of the places where πτωχός appears in Luke in a list of descriptive terms.[32]

Luke 4:18	6:20	7:22	14:13	14:21	16:20, 22
poor captive blind oppressed	poor hungry mournful persecuted	blind lame leper deaf dead poor	poor maimed lame blind	poor maimed blind lame	poor ulcerated hungry

We will look more closely at several of these passages, but we can make some determinations about the referents of "the poor" in Luke's writing. First, apart from 7:22—where πτωχός is placed at the end of the list (possibly for emphatic reasons)—"poor" stands at the beginning of each list. "As such it interprets and is amplified by the others."[33] Second, the other terms describe physical ailment or pain, oppression, and abuse. All of these terms have referents to people who were typically of low status and with little honor. The inclusion of "the poor" in these lists connects the term to a group of those marginalized and defined by a lack of social status.[34] As Fitzmyer points out, the poor "represent generically the neglected mass of humanity."[35]

The other three uses of πτωχός are in reference to persons in need and of low economic status. Two of the uses come within the context of selling one's possessions and giving the money to the poor (Luke 18:22; 19:8). The third use, in Luke 21:3, is a description of the poor widow whose offering at the Temple was of more value than the large contributions of the rich. Here again, πτωχός is connected with a person of low status. Within this same pericope is another term meaning "poor" that is in the same semantic

31. Here I am following Malina, "Wealth and Poverty," esp. 355–58; Green, "Good News for Whom," 66–69.

32. This list comes from Green, "Good News for Whom," 68.

33. Ibid.

34. Malina would say that "the poor" are those unable to maintain their inherent status ("Wealth and Poverty," 357).

35. Fitzmyer, *Luke*, 250.

domain as πτωχός and only appears here in the New Testament.[36] In Luke 21:2, the widow is also described using the adjective πενιχρός—a term meaning "poor" or "needy" that is virtually synonymous to πτωχός. In the same semantic domain is ἐνδεής (meaning "poor" or "needy") found in the New Testament only in Acts 4:34—Luke's description of the early church in Jerusalem: "There was not a needy person among them."[37] Thus, it is apparent that in Luke–Acts, references to "the poor" signify persons with economic and/or physical need. Further, the common association of "the poor" with other terms of low status and marginalization significantly connects them as a group to those on the outside of the social order. Joel Green argues that "the poor" should be understood as an inclusive term that includes any person of low status and on the fringe of society.[38] At the very least, "the poor" are closely tied to such persons and themselves represent those overlooked and often excluded from community. This is in line with what we saw in the prophetic literature—the poor were often understood in a literal sense and closely connected to other marginalized groups.

We can understand Jesus' proclamation of "good news to the poor" in Luke 4:18–19 as a dedication of his ministry—at least to some degree—to those on the outskirts of society. The rest of Jesus' quotation from Isaiah extends his ministry to the captive, the oppressed, and the blind. It is clear that in Luke this quotation from Isaiah is significant for Jesus' ministry. It is essentially, as Bruce Longenecker states, "the Isaianic narrative of divine triumph" and Jesus, in Luke's Gospel, places his actions and teaching squarely within this narrative.[39] This is supported by the fact that Jesus associates his ministry with that of Elijah and Elisha in vv. 24–28, specifically in their ministries to widows and lepers.[40]

Two other features of Jesus' application of these passages from Isaiah to his own ministry are worth noting. First, the quotation emphatically ends with an appeal to the "year of the Lord's favor"—that is, the Year of Jubilee. In Isaiah 61, the prophet had converted the levitical law of Jubilee

---

36. See Louw and Nida, *Greek-English Lexicon*, 564, domain 57.49. πενιχρός is used in the LXX (translating the Hebrew עני and דל) in reference to the poor or afflicted in Exod 22:24, Prov 28:15 and 29:7.

37. Louw and Nida, *Greek-English Lexicon*, domain 57.51.

38. Green, "Good News to Whom," 74.

39. Longenecker, *Remember the Poor*, 118.

40. C. M. Hays, *Luke's Wealth Ethics*, 111; Tannehill, *Narrative Unity*, 1:71.

into a divine promise of liberation.[41] There is no sense in Jesus' quotation, nor in the audience's reaction, that Jesus is reinstating the Year of Jubilee as described in Leviticus 25.[42] Rather, Jesus incorporates the themes of Jubilee in order to emphasize the "liberating character of the kingdom he was announcing and bringing into action."[43] Second, Jesus' illustrations of Elijah and Elisha in 4:25–27 hint at the extension of Jesus' ministry to the poor beyond Israel, to the Gentiles. While the point of these examples seems to be that Israel has a history of rejecting God's messengers,[44] it also points to the pattern of that messenger doing ministry outside of Israel. According to Jesus in Luke 4, Elijah was not sent to help the widows of Israel but only a Gentile widow—similarly, Elisha was not sent to heal the lepers of Israel but rather a Syrian. These allusions at least hint at the universal scope of Jesus' mission and the extension beyond Jewish borders of the liberating power of the kingdom of God. This extension of Jesus' ministry to the Gentile world was taken up by the early church and is portrayed in greater detail in Luke's second volume.[45]

Luke 7:18–23

An interesting parallel passage is Luke 7:18–23, in which John the Baptist sends his disciples to ask whether Jesus is in fact the Christ.[46] Jesus' reply is that they must report to John what they have seen: the blind are receiving sight, the crippled are walking, those with leprosy are clean, the deaf hear, the dead are raised, and good news is proclaimed to the poor (v. 22). Matthew's Gospel also tells of this interaction (Matt 11:2–6), but Luke alone includes the context of Jesus performing healings and exorcisms within the hour of John's disciples' question. Thus, Luke connects Jesus' words to his concrete deeds for those in need. "It is plain that the sick and the poor are not vague metaphors or spiritualized concepts. Rather, they represent per-

---

41. Nardoni, *Rise Up, O Judge*, 243–44.

42. Contra Yoder, *Politics of Jesus*, 34–36.

43. Nardoni, *Rise Up, O Judge*, 244–45. See also Sloan, *Favorable Year*, 28–110. For an opposing view, see O'Brien, "Comparison." O'Brien argues against any clear motifs or references to the Jubilee Year in Luke's Gospel. Further, he argues against a "Jubilary reading of Luke 4," saying that such readings "involve the commentator reading in his own theological schema into the text rather than being derived from it" (439).

44. Pao and Schnabel, "Luke," 291.

45. Nardoni, *Rise Up, O Judge*, 245.

46. On the historicity of this event, see Meier, *Marginal Jew*, 2:130–37.

sons in definite situations of need, who find their needs met by the power and presence of the one who is to come."[47]

As is clear from John's question, this passage is about the identity of Jesus—particularly, is Jesus the eschatological redeemer promised in Scripture?[48] In his response in Luke 7:22, Jesus again places his ministry within the context of Isaiah and the "narrative of divine triumph." Each part of Jesus' response corresponds to the eschatological liberation performed by a divine figure described in Isaiah:

- the blind receive sight (Isa 29:18; 35:5; 42:7, 18; 61:1)
- the crippled walk (Isa 35:6)
- the deaf hear (Isa 29:18–19; 35:5)
- the dead are raised (Isa 26:19)
- the poor have the good news proclaimed to them (Isa 61:1)

The only exception is the reference to lepers being made clean—although this may find support in Isaiah's words that the coming one carries our sickness (Isa 53:4).[49]

Jesus' inclusion of good news being proclaimed to the poor seems out of place within this list of miracles and healings. While it may seem anticlimactic to place proclamation to the poor as the culmination of the dramatic and miraculous, its placement actually stresses the importance of this feature in Jesus' ministry. As Longenecker points out, "Jesus' reply depicts a world in which healing blindness, curing disease, restoring hearing and raising the dead were as exceptional as encouraging the poor."[50] As we saw, πτωχός usually appears first in such lists; here it is placed in the final, emphatic position as the capstone.

Luke 6:20–26

Luke's version of the Beatitudes in Luke 6:20–23 further confirms this picture of Jesus' mission having a focus on the poor, interpreted in the light

47. Pilgrim, *Good News to the Poor*, 72.

48. For more on this, see Bird, *Are You the One*, esp. 101–4.

49. The LXX uses ὀδυνάω, "to suffer greatly," to translate the Hebrew חלי, which is closer to "sickness" or "disease." Dunn argues that the reference to lepers has no foundation in Isaiah but was included simply because it was commonly known that Jesus healed lepers (Dunn, *Jesus Remembered*, 450).

50. Longenecker, *Remember the Poor*, 120.

of Isaiah. Many scholars have recognized the influence of Isa 61:1–2 on both the Matthean and Lukan beatitudes.[51] However, Luke is noticeably lacking Matthew's mention that "those who mourn" (οἱ πενθοῦντες) "will be comforted" (παρακληθήσονται)—verbs found in Isa 61:2 (LXX). This led Hans Dieter Betz to argue against Isaiah 61 as an influence behind Luke's beatitudes.[52] In response to Betz, we can offer two points of contention. First, the terms that Luke does use, "those who weep" (κλαίοντες) and "will laugh" (γελάσετε), are closely tied semantically to their Matthew/Isaiah counterparts and can be seen as variations on the terms.[53] Second, Luke does include the very terms for "mourn" and "comfort" from Isa 61:2 in his woes just a few verses later (6:24, 25).

In this passage we again see "the poor" among other terms of low status and oppression—the hungry, the hated, the persecuted.[54] Of importance is the language of exclusion that accompanies these terms. This is clear in the fourth beatitude (6:22–23), which mentions those "excluded" (ἀφορίζω) and "insulted" (ἐκβάλλω, which often has the sense of one being taken or driven out). That such exclusion is a result of association with Jesus is clear from the end of v. 22 (as well as v. 20). As such, the promise of v. 23 points to a restoration of community "in heaven" and camaraderie with the prophets.

Verses 24–26 contain woes to the rich, well-fed, and highly esteemed—serving as a parallel to the beatitudes in the earlier verses. The rich (v. 24) parallel the poor in v. 20; the well-fed (v. 25a) parallel the hungry in v. 21a; those laughing (v.25b) parallel those weeping in v. 21b; those highly esteemed (v. 26) parallel those hated and excluded in v. 22. As we saw above, "the poor" refers not only to those of low economic status but to them as representatives of those marginalized in the larger culture. Similarly, "the rich" designates not only an economic class, but is "related fundamentally to issues of power and privilege, social location as an insider, and arrogant

51. "This sermon calls for the implementation of those ideals contained in Isa. 61:1–2, the passage which Jesus quoted at the beginning of the Nazareth sermon" (Evans, *Luke*, 107). See also, Stassen and Gushee, *Kingdom Ethics*, 32–54, esp. 33–37.

52. Betz, *Sermon on the Mount*, 576.

53. Pao and Schnabel, "Luke," 295.

54. "Unlike Matthew's version, the Lucan sermon is referring to those who suffer from real poverty and hunger, not to those who are 'poor in spirit' (Matt. 5:3) or who 'hunger and thirst after righteousness' (Matt. 5:6). The Lucan form of the sermon reflects and contributes to Luke's overall concern with poverty and wealth" (Evans, *Luke*, 108).

self-security apart from God."[55] These notions that certain people are "inside" while others are "outside" are the societal norms that Jesus wished to overturn in his proclamation of the kingdom of God.[56]

As we have seen, the language used by Luke here mirrors that of Isa 61:2 (LXX). These verses can also be seen as a continuation of the harsh words in the prophetic literature to those who bring about injustice—or who fail to respond correctly to injustice.[57] The rich and the well-fed are similar to the rich and the fat mentioned in Jer 5:27–28. Jesus does not accuse these groups of directly bringing about great injustice, but the parallels connecting the woes to Jesus' beatitudes indicts them for failing to respond properly to injustice. Instead, Jesus warns them that the comfort they enjoy in this age—at the expense of those in need—will be reversed in the age to come.

Luke 11:37–54

As in 6:24–26, Luke includes a lengthy set of woes in ch. 11—this time directed at the Pharisees and experts in the law. In this passage, Jesus continues the prophetic tradition of calling out rulers for their empty rituals and lack of justice. Both Matthew (chs. 15, 23) and Mark (ch. 7) contain similar passages. While there are parallels between these accounts, Luke does not seem to follow either Gospel or organize his material in a similar way.[58] This section contains four woes on the Pharisees (vv. 39–44) and three on the experts in the law (vv. 46–52). Jesus accuses them of having the appearance of being religious, but "neglecting justice and the love of God" (v. 42). They load people with heavy burdens yet fail to carry such burdens themselves (v. 47). Further, Jesus connects them to those who killed the prophets—citing Zechariah specifically[59]—saying that they consent

---

55. Green, *Gospel of Luke*, 267. See Pilgrim, *Good News to the Poor*, 103–4: "[Luke 4:24–26] describes a privileged social and economic status. The woes only state with striking certainty that the future will bring about a complete reversal of conditions, in which the present status of the wealthy will be taken away" (104).

56. See Luke 1:51–53 where Mary sings, "[God] has shown strength with his arm; he has scattered the proud in the thoughts of their hearts. He has brought down the powerful from their thrones, and lifted up the lowly; he has filled the hungry with good things, and sent the rich away empty."

57. Note also the places where blessings and curses appear side by side: Isa 3:10–11; 65:12–16.

58. See Bock, *Luke*, 2:1105–8.

59. Whether this is the Old Testament prophet is unclear. The mention of Abel

(συνευδοκέω) to those deeds and are ultimately responsible for them (vv. 47–51).

The term οὐαί itself connects Jesus' words to the prophetic tradition (Isa 1:4; 3:11; 5:18; 28:1). The reference to justice (κρίσις—often used in the LXX for מִשְׁפָּט: Isa 56:1; 59:15; Jer 5:4) makes this connection clearer—as do Jesus' words that the Pharisees should give alms (ἐλεημοσύνη) to the needy in 11:41. The reference to justice and love in v. 42 may echo Mic 6:8 ("Do justice, love kindness, and walk humbly with your God")—although only vaguely so.[60] Jesus' condemnation of the Pharisees' and scribes' attention to religious ritual and external matters while ignoring their internal state and those needy around them is thematically linked to the condemnation of empty rituals in the prophetic literature.

In this passage Jesus points to the standard of justice set by God throughout the Hebrew Bible and emphasized by the prophets. The leaders have failed to uphold justice and they do not care for the poor. They are interested in empty rituals and having a religious appearance, but they ignore the important things of God. Jesus' rebuke calls for them to instead give alms to the needy and practice justice and love.

Luke 18:18–30

Chapter 18 of Luke's Gospel contains several parables and encounters with Jesus that continue the theme of justice. In fact, it has recently been argued that the prophetic theme of justice is the connecting motif through this chapter as well as the encounter with Zacchaeus in 19:1–10.[61] In the middle of this section is Jesus' interaction with a ruler in vv. 18–30 about the dangers of wealth. Matthew (19:16–30) and Mark (10:17–31) both contain similar accounts, and Luke's Gospel parallels them fairly closely.[62] However, Luke's account is unique in several ways—including the fact that he alone identifies the man as a ruler (ἄρχων). Luke uses this term nearly a dozen times in his Gospel and Acts in reference to the leadership in opposition to

---

broadens Jesus' use of "prophets" beyond those behind the prophetic literature. Fitzmyer points out that Abel and Zechariah are "the first and last person[s] murdered in the first and last books of the Hebrew canon of the OT" (*Luke*, 946).

60. Elsewhere in the prophets, "love" and "justice" appear together (Isa 16:5; 61:8; Jer 9:24; Hos 2:19; 12:6; Amos 5:15).

61. J. D. Hays, "Sell Everything You Have."

62. See Bock, *Luke*, 2:1473–74.

Jesus.[63] By comparison, Matthew uses the term five times and Mark once—both without the referent being one opposed to Jesus' ministry.[64] Ἄρχων has a very general sense of one who rules or exerts authority and is used over five hundred times in the LXX in a variety of ways. It should be noted, however, that in the prophetic literature it is often the *rulers* (ἄρχοντες) who are called out for bringing injustice and oppression (Isa 1:10, 23; 3:14; 22:3; 28:14; 40:23; Jer 1:28; 2:26; 4:9; 8:1; Ezek 7:27; 19:1; Hos 5:10; 7:3; 13:10).[65] Isaiah 1:23 (LXX) says, "Your rulers (ἄρχοντες) are rebels and companions of thieves . . . They do not defend the orphan, and the widow's cause does not come before them." Jesus' words to the ruler are not as hostile as those from Isaiah, however, Luke's account does set up this exchange as a rebuke. First, Luke does not lighten Jesus' remarks, as Mark does, by including a reference to his love toward the ruler (Mark 10:21). Second, Luke alone describes the man not only as a "ruler" but also as "rich" (πλούσιος)—the same term used by Jesus in the woes of ch. 6 and elsewhere. Third, while both Matthew and Mark have the man leave right after Jesus tells him to sell his possessions and give to the poor, Luke has him present to hear the strong words against wealth in the following verses.[66] In fact, Luke has Jesus

63. Luke 8:41; 14:1; 23:13, 35; 24:20; Acts 3:17; 4:5, 8, 26; 13:27; 14:5. It is also used in reference to a leader of demons (Luke 11:15) and to leaders in a general sense (Acts 16:19; 23:5).

64. Mark's use comes from a shared tradition of the religious leaders accusing Jesus of casting out demons by the power of Beelzebul, the ruler (ἄρχων) of demons (Mark 3:22). Two of Matthew's five uses of ἄρχων share the same referent (Matt 9:34; 12:24). Matthew's other uses are of a leader of the synagogue who asks for Jesus' help after his daughter dies (Matt 9:18, 23) and to the rulers of the Gentiles in an illustration of those who seek to be great (20:25).

65. J. D. Hays, "Sell Everything You Have," 56.

66. It is often pointed out that Jesus' command to sell everything and follow him is not a one-size-fits-all requirement for discipleship. While Jesus does require this of his disciples and others (Luke 5:11, 28; 14:23; 18:22, 28), he also tells some people to share their possessions and provide hospitality (9:53; 10:5–12; 24:28–32). If one sells everything, how can they share or have a home to welcome people into? Further, Zacchaeus gives half of his possessions and this is acceptable to Jesus (19:8–9). Schottroff and Stegemann have argued that the renunciation of all possessions should be limited to the disciples during the time of Jesus (*Jesus and the Hope of the Poor*, 80–86). However, it is better to understand Luke as being concerned with the right use of possessions than with the necessary renunciation of all possessions in every case (Kim, *Stewardship and Almsgiving*, 109).

look directly at him while saying, "How hard it is for those who have wealth to enter the kingdom of God!" (18:24).[67]

Concern for social justice is seen in many other places in Luke's Gospel. This theme is seen in the parables of the Good Samaritan who cares for a stranger in need at great risk to himself (10:25–37), the rich man who, unlike poor Lazarus, ends up in Hades for his failure to meet the needs of those around him (16:19–31), and of the Great Banquet where the poor, crippled, blind, and lame are invited once the original guests snub their invitation (14:15–24). It is also present in the teaching of John the Baptist, "Those who have two shirts, share with the one who has none; those with food should do likewise" (3:11) and the words of Mary in the Magnificat, "[The Lord] has lifted up the humble; he has filled the hungry with good things" (1:52–53). The theme is present in the story of Zacchaeus who gives away half of his possessions to the poor and promises to repay those he cheated by four times the amount (19:1–10). Finally, a concern for justice is emphasized in the parable of the widow—a member of another marginalized group—who persistently demands justice from a judge (18:1–8). Jesus concludes this parable by saying that, unlike the judge, God will quickly grant justice when his people cry out to him (18:7–8).

Acts 2:42–47 and 4:32–37

It is not just in Luke's Gospel where concern for social justice is prominent; this theme continues into the Acts of the Apostles. Admittedly, direct appeals to the prophetic concept of justice are noticeably lacking in Luke's second volume. In Acts, there is a stronger emphasis on how the early church wrestled with and lived out the teaching from Jesus on justice. The best examples come in the descriptions of the early church in Acts 2:42–47 and 4:32–37. Luke is not shy at other places in Acts about sharing the shortcomings of the early church in Jerusalem (5:1–11; possibly also 6:1–6),[68] but here he holds up this congregation as a model of harmony and community. The group's example of sharing possessions and caring for those in need is of particular importance for Luke. In Acts 2:45 he writes that the com-

---

67. The rich ruler is also contrasted with the children whom Jesus greets in the preceding pericope (Luke 18:15–17). Jesus' words there ("Whoever does not receive the kingdom of God like a child shall not enter it" v. 17) are in contrast to his words to the rich ruler ("How hard it is for those who have wealth to enter the kingdom of God"). See Green, *Gospel of Luke*, 653.

68. See Green, *Practicing Theological Interpretation*, 56–69.

munity members sold property and possessions—giving all the proceeds to those who had need. In 4:34–35, the author explains a similar dynamic, while noting that there was not a needy person in the community.

Scholars have pointed out that these utopia-like descriptions in Acts fulfill a Hellenistic ideal of friendship and sharing (cf. Ovid, *Metamorphoses*, 1:88–111; Plato, *Republic*, 420C–422B).[69] It does not detract from the historicity of the early church's joy and unity to understand that Luke idealized these summaries in his writing.[70] Certainly, the way Luke describes the early church's sharing of possessions and care for the needy would have been enticing to a Hellenistic reader. Yet, Luke does not simply appeal to this ideal of friendship. In Hellenistic society, friendship—like reciprocity—was a tool for the wealthy and people of high status. Its benefits were allocated among those of the same status or it expected reciprocal clientage from those of lower status. However, Luke appeals to friendship across social class and encourages those with possessions to provide help for the poor—without the expectation of goods or obedience in return. As such, Luke redefines the ideal of friendship as a means for helping the poor in a community.[71]

At the same time, these descriptions of the early Jerusalem church appeal not only to Hellenistic ideals but also the standard of justice set by Yahweh. That there "was not a needy person among them" (Acts 4:34) alludes to Deut 15:4 LXX (both using ἐνδεής).[72] As we saw in the prophetic literature, a community that takes care of its needy is a standard of justice set by Yahweh. Repeatedly in the prophetic literature, the rulers of the people were evaluated by how well they cared for the lowliest among them. What the prophets condemned unjust rulers for neglecting—caring for the poor, orphans, and widows—was a priority in the early church.[73] Here in the early chapters of Acts, Luke has presented the Christian community as one that met the ideals of Hellenistic culture and the standards of Yahweh.

69. Johnson, *Acts*, 62. For an examination of friendship language in Hellenistic literature, see Hume, *Early Christian Community*, 44–77.

70. Similarly, Peterson, *Acts*, 158–59; See Capper, "Jesus, Virtuoso Religion," 77–78. Capper writes that utopian stylizing in Acts "does not undermine the historical value of the accounts."

71. Mitchell, "Social Function of Friendship."

72. Peterson, *Acts*, 205; Parsons, *Acts*, 73; Bock, *Acts*, 214–15.

73. Elsewhere in Acts, care for widows in seen in the creation of the deacon role in 6:1–6. There is also the account of Peter raising Tabitha from the dead in front of widows whom she had helped (9:36–42).

Almsgiving in Acts

The last set of passages that I wish to explore are the references to almsgiving in Acts.[74] In his Gospel, Luke uses the term for giving alms (ἐλεημοσύνη) twice: in Jesus' woes on the Pharisees in 11:41 and as a command to his disciples in 12:33. It appears eight times in Acts and its usage is rare outside of Luke's writings.[75] The term appears around fifty times in the LXX—the majority of uses are in Tobit and Sirach.[76] Tobit 4:10–11 states: "For almsgiving delivers from death and keeps you from going in the Darkness. Indeed, almsgiving, for all who practice it, is an excellent offering in the presence of the Most High." In Isaiah, the LXX uses the word three times to translate צְדָקָה ("righteousness": Isa 1:27; 28:17; 59:16).[77] Two of these uses link the term to justice (κρίσις). Isaiah 1:27, for example, states: "Zion shall be redeemed by justice (κρίματος), and those in her who repent, by ἐλεημοσύνης." The concept of almsgiving has a continued presence in rabbinic literature, as it became the ideal way to respond to the poor in Israel.[78] As Luke Timothy Johnson has pointed out, in early Judaism almsgiving had become an important expression of "doing justice."[79]

So what exactly is almsgiving? The references in the New Testament connect the term to good works and acts of charity. Yet, almsgiving involves more than simple, one-time monetary gifts to the poor. Joel Green writes that almsgiving is "an expression of genuine social solidarity—that is, of caring for and embracing those in need as if they were members of one's own kin group."[80] The act of giving alms, while embraced in early Judaism, ran counter to the Roman culture that emphasized patronage and reciprocity—both of which favored the wealthy and expected something of those

---

74. When this paper was presented, it was helpfully pointed out by M. Daniel Carroll R. that charity is often not understood as "social justice." In response, I wish to emphasize the social aspect of almsgiving in this section, in particular how the giving of alms was a direct challenge to certain first-century customs and social orders. In this sense, almsgiving often served to undermine the societal system that perpetuated injustice.

75. Matthew uses the word three times in Jesus' teaching on how to give to the poor in 6:2–4.

76. These two books account for 36 occurrences of the word in the LXX.

77. The term is also used in Isa 38:18 to translate אֱמֶת ("truth").

78. See Johnson, *Sharing Possessions*, 132–38.

79. Johnson, *Acts*, 65.

80. Green, "Almsgiving."

receiving gifts or benefits.[81] Almsgiving, by contrast, expects nothing in return. This is reflected in Jesus' words in Luke 14:12–14:

> When you give a luncheon or a dinner, do not invite your friends or your brothers or your relatives or rich neighbors, in case they may invite you in return, and you would be repaid. But when you give a banquet, invite the poor, the crippled, the lame, and the blind. And you will be blessed, because they cannot repay you, for you will be repaid at the resurrection of the righteous.

This type of giving moves beyond a brief monetary gift or loan to those in need. This action—demonstrated in almsgiving—involves solidarity with the poor and sincere giving without the expectation of being repaid or receiving a benefit. In fact, getting a return or receiving repayment goes against the very essence of giving alms.

Almsgiving is first mentioned in Acts 3:1–10 when Peter and John come across a man lame from birth begging for alms. That the man is begging outside the temple coheres well with the notion that almsgiving was an important practice in early Judaism. Paradoxically however, needing to beg for alms was considered shameful and carried a stigma with it.[82] That the man was lame from birth emphasizes his plight and establishes him as someone on the margins of society. Peter replies that he has no gold or silver and instead heals the man in the name of Jesus. While Peter does not actually provide alms in the traditional sense, this is still an example of meeting a person's immediate needs. It is an example of how the expansion of the Kingdom of God brings justice to those in need. As Marshall has pointed out, this account should not be understood as a prohibition of meeting material needs nor as encouragement to meet only spiritual needs.[83] That Peter did not have alms to give fits with the situation of the Jerusalem community described immediately before this pericope in 2:42–47. With no money to give, Peter responds to the man's request for almsgiving by giving what he can—the healing power of Jesus Christ.

Almsgiving is used twice in Acts as a positive description of an individual's service. In 9:36, Tabitha from Joppa is introduced by stating that she was "full of good works and acts of charity that she was doing" (ἦν πλήρης ἔργων ἀγαθῶν καὶ ἐλεημοσυνῶν ὧν ἐποίει). We know little about Tabitha outside of this description, although she is the only woman in the

81. For more on this, see Moxnes, "Patron–Client Relations."

82. Keener, *Acts*, 2:1059–60.

83. Marshall, *Acts*, 88.

New Testament referred to as a disciple (μαθήτρια). Acts 10 introduces Cornelius, a centurion who, along with his family, feared God. The description in 10:1 includes that Cornelius gave many alms to the people (ποιῶν ἐλεημοσύνας πολλὰς τῷ λαῷ). His almsgiving is emphasized in v. 4 when in a vision an angel of the Lord tells Cornelius that his prayers and alms (αἱ ἐλεημοσύναι) have ascended before God as a memorial. Clearly Cornelius's alms were pleasing the Lord.[84] This is emphasized as Cornelius retells his vision to Peter in Acts 10:31. The last reference to almsgiving in Acts comes from the mouth of Paul as he provides a defense before Felix. In describing his arrest at the Jerusalem temple, Paul states that he had come to Jerusalem simply to give alms and to present offerings (24:17).

The references to almsgiving in Acts present giving to the needy as something highly esteemed and well-established in Jewish culture. The healing of the man born lame points to the reality of the need for almsgiving while also showing the continuation by the apostles of Jesus' ministry to the marginalized. That Paul—the obvious hero of the latter half of Acts—practiced almsgiving places it in good favor, while also suggesting that the practice was a common element of worship in the temple. The descriptions of Tabitha and Cornelius as godly people who were defined by giving alms further present the practice as something valued in the early church. Further, that Cornelius's alms ascended to Yahweh as would a temple offering establishes the practice as one that is pleasing to God. In short, to borrow Johnson's term, giving alms is seen in Acts as a way of "doing justice."

CONCLUSION

Social justice is a clear and prevalent theme throughout Luke's two volumes on the life and ministry of Jesus and his earliest followers. That Luke drew from the prophetic literature and its notion of justice is apparent from the numerous appeals to the prophets—especially Isaiah. Particularly intriguing is Jesus' quotation from Isaiah at the beginning of his public ministry that orients this ministry as one focused on "good news for the poor." This is modeled throughout his life and teaching and continued by the early church in Acts.

By way of conclusion, I wish to highlight three things that were emphasized in Luke–Acts. First, caring for the poor and marginalized was

---

84. This corresponds well to the reference in Tobit that alms are an "excellent offering in the presence of the Most High" (Tob 4:11). Witherington refers to this as a sacrifice that God honors outside the temple (Witherington, *Acts*, 348).

a defining motif in the prophetic view of justice and a priority for Jesus. Jesus appealed to this prophetic theme not only in Luke 4:18–19, but also in 6:20–25, 7:22, and elsewhere. Second, care for the poor and other marginalized groups must be understood—in some capacity—to involve caring for their physical and not just their spiritual needs. I do not wish to ignore the spiritual aspect of the ministry of Jesus and the early church, however I must stress that—particularly in Luke–Acts—caring for the poor involves caring for their physical needs. Third, how someone was concerned for justice—often understood by how they cared for the poor and marginalized—was a criterion in the prophetic literature by which Yahweh judged a person. This continues into Luke–Acts as Luke presents several positive (Tabitha, Cornelius) and negative (Pharisees, rich ruler) examples of using this standard in character descriptions. It is interesting how often in Luke's writing a person is defined by how well they cared for the poor through almsgiving or other means. By way of application, maybe this is the question we should be asking ourselves today: How well am I defined by "doing justice" and caring for the poor?

BIBLIOGRAPHY

Barrett, C. K. "Luke/Acts." In *It Is Written: Scripture Citing Scripture: Essays in Honour of Barnabas Lindars, SSF*, edited by D. A. Carson and H. G. M. Williamson, 231–44. Cambridge: Cambridge University Press, 1988.

Betz, Hans Dieter. *The Sermon on the Mount: A Commentary on the Sermon on the Mount, Including the Sermon on the Plain (Matthew 5:3—7:27 and Luke 6:20–49).* Minneapolis: Fortress, 1995.

Bird, Michael F. *Are You the One Who Is to Come? The Historical Jesus and the Messianic Question.* Grand Rapids: Baker Academic, 2009.

Bock, Darrell L. *Acts.* BECNT. Grand Rapids: Baker Academic, 2007.

———. *Luke.* 2 vols. BECNT. Grand Rapids: Baker Academic, 1994–96.

Capper, Brian. "Jesus, Virtuoso Religion, and the Community of Goods." In *Engaging Economics: New Testament Scenarios and Early Christian Reception*, edited by Bruce W. Longenecker and Kelly Liebengood, 60–80. Grand Rapids: Eerdmans, 2009.

Davids, Peter H. "Rich and Poor." In *Dictionary of Jesus and the Gospels*, edited by Joel B. Green, Scot McKnight, and I. Howard Marshall, 701–10. Downers Grove, IL: InterVarsity, 1992.

Dunn, James D. G. *Christianity in the Making.* Vol. 1, *Jesus Remembered*. Grand Rapids: Eerdmans, 2003.

Evans, Craig A. *Luke.* Peabody, MA: Hendrickson, 1990; reprinted Grand Rapids: Baker Books, 2011.

Fitzmyer, Joseph A. *The Gospel according to Luke: Introduction, Translation, and Notes.* AB. Garden City, NY: Doubleday, 1981–85.

———. *To Advance the Gospel: New Testament Studies.* 2nd ed. Grand Rapids: Eerdmans, 1998.

Fretheim, Terence E. "The Prophets and Social Justice: A Conservative Agenda." *Word & World* 28 (2008) 159–68.

Gowan, Donald E. "Wealth and Poverty in the Old Testament: The Case of the Widow, the Orphan, and the Sojourner." *Int* 41 (1987) 342–53.

Green, Joel B. "Almsgiving." In *Dictionary of Scripture and Ethics*, edited by Joel B. Green, 58–59. Grand Rapids: Baker Academic, 2011.

———. "Good News to Whom? Jesus and the 'Poor' in the Gospel of Luke." In *Jesus of Nazareth*, edited by Joel B. Green and Max Turner, 59–74. Grand Rapids: Eerdmans, 1994.

———. *The Gospel of Luke*. NICNT. Grand Rapids: Eerdmans, 1997.

———. *Practicing Theological Interpretation: Engaging Biblical Texts for Faith and Formation*. Grand Rapids: Baker Academic, 2011.

Hays, Christopher M. *Luke's Wealth Ethics: A Study in Their Coherence and Character*. WUNT 2nd ser., 275. Tübingen: Mohr Siebeck, 2010.

Hays, J. Daniel. "'Sell Everything You Have and Give to the Poor': The Old Testament Prophetic Theme of Justice as the Connecting Motif of Luke 18:1—19:10." *JETS* 55 (2012) 43–63.

Hume, Douglas A. *The Early Christian Community: A Narrative Analysis of Acts 2:41–47 and 4:32–35*. WUNT 2nd ser., 298. Tübingen: Mohr Siebeck, 2011.

Johnson, Luke Timothy. *The Acts of the Apostles*. Collegeville, MN: Liturgical, 1992.

———. *The Gospel of Luke*. Collegeville, MN: Liturgical, 1991.

———. *Sharing Possessions: Mandate and Symbol of Faith*. Philadelphia: Fortress, 1981.

Keener, Craig S. *Acts: An Exegetical Commentary*. 4 vols. Grand Rapids: Baker Academic, 2012–15.

Kim, Kyoung-Jin. *Stewardship and Almsgiving in Luke's Theology*. Sheffield: Sheffield Academic, 1998.

Koet, Bart J. *Five Studies on Interpretation of Scripture in Luke–Acts*. SNTA 14. Leuven: Leuven University Press, 1989.

Litwak, Kenneth Duncan. *Echoes of Scripture in Luke–Acts: Telling the History of God's People Intertextually*. London: T. & T. Clark, 2005.

Longenecker, Bruce W. *Remember the Poor: Paul, Poverty, and the Greco-Roman World*. Grand Rapids: Eerdmans, 2010.

Louw, J. P., and E. A. Nida. *Greek-English Lexicon of the New Testament Based on Semantic Domains*. 2 vols. 2nd ed. New York: United Bible Societies, 1989.

Malina, Bruce. "Wealth and Poverty in the New Testament and Its World." *Int* 41 (1987) 354–67.

Marshall, I. Howard. *Acts*. TNTC. Grand Rapids: Eerdmans, 1980.

———. "Acts." In *Commentary on the New Testament Use of the Old Testament*, edited by G. K. Beale and D. A. Carson, 513–606. Grand Rapids: Baker Academic, 2007.

———. *The Gospel of Luke: A Commentary on the Greek Text*. NIGTC. Grand Rapids: Eerdmans, 1978.

McKnight, Scot. "Justice, Righteousness." In *Dictionary of Jesus and the Gospels*, edited by Joel B. Green, Scot McKnight, and I. Howard Marshall, 413–14. Downers Grove, IL: InterVarsity, 1992.

Meier, John P. *A Marginal Jew: Rethinking the Historical Jesus*. Vol. 2, *Mentor, Message, and Miracles*. ABRL. New York: Doubleday, 1994.

Miller, Merrill P. "The Function of Isa 61:1–2 in 11Q Melchizedek." *JBL* 88 (1969) 467–69.

Mitchell, Alan C. "The Social Function of Friendship in Acts 2:44–47 and 4:32–37." *JBL* 111 (1992) 255–72.

Moyise, Steve. *The Old Testament in the New: An Introduction*. London: Continuum, 2001.

Moxnes, Halvor. "Patron–Client Relations and the New Community in Luke-Acts." In *The Social World of Luke-Acts*, edited by Jerome H. Neyrey, 241–68. Peabody, MA: Hendrickson, 1991.

Nardoni, Enrique. *Rise Up, O Judge: A Study of Justice in the Biblical World*. Translated by Seán Charles Martin. Peabody, MA: Hendrickson, 2004.

Novak, Michael. "Defining Social Justice." *First Things* 108 (2000) 11–13.

O'Brien, D. P. "A Comparison between Early Jewish and Early Christian Interpretation of the Jubilee Year." In *Papers Presented at the Thirteenth International Conference on Patristic Studies Held at Oxford, 1999*. Vol. 1, *Historica, Biblica, Theologica et Philosophica*, edited by M. F. Wiles, E. Yarnold, and P. M. Parvis, 436–42. Leuven: Peeters, 2001.

Pao, David W., and Eckhard J. Schnabel. "Luke." In *Commentary on the New Testament Use of the Old Testament*, edited by G. K. Beale and D. A. Carson, 251–414. Grand Rapids: Baker Academic, 2007.

Parsons, Mikeal C. *Acts*. Paideia. Grand Rapids: Baker Academic, 2008.

Peterson, David G. *The Acts of the Apostles*. PNTC. Grand Rapids: Eerdmans, 2009.

Pilgrim, Walter E. *Good News to the Poor: Wealth and Poverty in Luke–Acts*. Minneapolis: Ausburg 1981.

Porter, Stanley E. "Further Comments on the Use of the Old Testament in the New Testament." In *The Intertextuality of the Epistles: Explorations of Theory and Practice*, edited by Thomas L. Brodie, Dennis R. MacDonald, and Stanley E. Porter, 98–110. Sheffield: Sheffield Phoenix, 2006.

———. "Scripture Justifies Mission: The Use of the Old Testament in Luke-Acts." In *Hearing the Old Testament in the New Testament*, edited by Stanley E. Porter, 104–26. Grand Rapids: Eerdmans, 2006.

Sanders, James A. "Isaiah in Luke." In *Luke and Scripture*, edited by Craig A. Evans and James A. Sanders, 14–25. Eugene, OR: Wipf & Stock, 2001.

Schottroff, Luise, and Wolfgang Stegemann. *Jesus and the Hope of the Poor*. Translated by Matthew J. O'Connell. Maryknoll, NY: Orbis, 1986.

Sloan, Robert Bryan. *The Favorable Year of the Lord: A Study of Jubilary Theology in the Gospel of Luke*. Austin, TX: Schola, 1977.

Stassen, Glen H., and David P. Gushee. *Kingdom Ethics: Following Jesus in Contemporary Context*. Downers Grove, IL: IVP Academic, 2003.

Stegemann, Wolfgang. *The Gospel and the Poor*. Translated by Dietlinde Elliott. Philadelphia: Fortress, 1984.

Strauss, Mark L. *The Davidic Messiah in Luke-Acts: The Promise and Its Fulfillment in Lukan Christology*. JSNTSup 110. Sheffield: Sheffield Academic, 1995.

Talbert, Charles H. *Reading Luke: A Literary and Theological Commentary on the Third Gospel*. New York: Crossroad, 1982.

Tannehill, Robert C. *The Narrative Unity of Luke–Acts: A Literary Interpretation*. 2 vols. Philadelphia: Fortress, 1986.

Witherington, Ben, III. *The Acts of the Apostles: A Socio-Rhetorical Commentary*. Grand Rapids: Eerdmans, 1998.

Yoder, John H. *The Politics of Jesus: Vicit agnus noster*. Grand Rapids: Eerdmans, 1975.

6

Reframing Social Justice in the Pauline Letters

STANLEY E. PORTER

INTRODUCTION

THE FIRST AND MOST important question that must be asked in discussion of the topic of social justice is this—what is social justice? There is a tendency—and I would say an unhelpful one—to focus social justice upon notions of wealth and poverty. Those topics certainly need to be discussed, but the notion needs to be extended beyond this to include other issues as well. The term "social justice" itself is an unfortunate one, because of its lack of precision—this is an imprecision that allows for the notion to be construed in a variety of ways. I think that it is essential to understand that social justice addresses at least two major issues. The first is the social dimension. By this, I think that we must consider a complex of social relations that were important in the ancient world. Economic issues would have encompassed one of these sets of relations, but in some senses the economic issues were no more important than a number of other issues. As we shall see, in some distinct ways, economic issues are the result of other greater social issues, and thus are secondary social issues. The second dimension is what is meant by justice.[1] Justice is a notoriously complex notion to define, and even worse to try to implement. There are numerous important debates that exist around the notion of justice—what are its origins, what are its bases, what are its warrants, and what are its applications, among many others. I will venture to put forth that human justice is the

1. Justice is a complex notion, widely debated. For an appreciation of the issues within the context of political philosophy, see Ryan, "Political Philosophy," esp. 395–98.

kind of notion that is implied by most references to social justice, because it is related to society, that is, human issues. In other words, social justice is usually an attempt to determine and enshrine in social behavior certain human principles of justice, or ways of treating each other in just ways. This of course still begs the question of what justice is. I realize this, and this is part of the problem. If we wish for justice to be something other than human justice, then referring to it as social justice is probably a misnomer. What we are wanting is not social justice, but some other type of justice. Most of those who would argue for some other kind of justice would want to ground such justice in a kind of ontological or absolute justice. There is some inherent or innate sense of justice they have in mind. This is not the place to argue various theories of ethics,[2] such as pragmatism or situationalism, but I would contend that the only legitimate grounds for understanding justice is to define it in relation to the character and actions of God. However, I would also contend that when this is introduced as the platform for discussion of justice, then it becomes a misformulation of the issue to simply refer to "social justice" as if this is a thing that can stand on its own and be discussed without reference to some of the other characteristics and actions of God. In other words, justice only then makes sense when it is seen within the larger framework of God's actions and dealings with humanity and the world. When this is the perspective, then, I believe, the usual notion of social justice becomes highly problematic, to the point even, in some instances, of distorting the issues that are involved.

In this paper, I wish to examine the notion of social justice in Paul's letters, but I wish to do so in a way that reframes the issue, so as to avoid the shortcomings of the usual definition—by which we are concerned only with some vague notion of human justice in relation to our fellow humans—and endorses the more expansive definition. When this larger definition is taken into account, I think that Paul's letters have a number of comments to make about what we might be tempted to call "social justice," but that are in fact part of a much larger conception of human behavior in relation to God.

If we see issues related to social justice within a larger perspective, I think that we see Paul addressing a number of the major social issues of his time.[3] In order to appreciate how Paul views these, we must first ex-

---

2. See Rachels, *Elements*, for a survey of possible approaches.

3. In the discussion of Paul, I will consider all of the thirteen letters as Pauline. I realize that this introduces some potential problems for the position I am taking, but

amine the Roman socio-economic system, then discuss any Pauline statements that address the appropriate issues, and then formulate a conclusion regarding how they relate to the Pauline worldview.

THE ANCIENT ROMAN ECONOMY AND ITS SOCIAL IMPLICATIONS

Paul lived, wrote, and ministered within the ancient Roman world of the early principate. He was probably born during the time of Augustus and died during the reign of Nero.[4] That is, Paul spanned the lifetime of the Julio-Claudian emperors, who were so significant in establishing and developing the Roman principate, with all of its mighty strengths and calamitous weaknesses.[5] There is much that can be said about each, but that cannot be said here because it would not be germane to the topic. However, one of the important developments of this time was the extension of the Roman political system to encompass areas not previously embraced by Roman law and practice. One of the major results of Roman dominance was the spread of its economic control. The Roman economic system was formulated around socio-economic inequity at virtually all levels. Even under the previous republic, such economic disparity had been firmly entrenched, but it was heightened further under the principate. The Roman social hierarchy was based on and formed around economic strata, inherited order, and relational status.[6] Whereas we equate modern Western society with social progression and the ability to alter each of these to positive effect, such was not the case in the ancient Roman world.

In theory, it was possible to change one's economic stratum. However, the situation that had resulted from the transition from republic to empire

---

believe that the entire traditional corpus is relevant. For reasons to think so, see Porter, *Apostle Paul*, esp. ch. 6.

4. Ibid., ch. 2.

5. This section is dependent upon a number of different sources, including especially, for the historical and social elements, Rostovtzeff, *Social and Economic History*, 1:1–105; as well as Alföldy, *Social History*, 157–85; Carcopino, *Daily Life*, 65–115; Boren, *Roman Society*, 149–63; Taylor, *Roman Society*, 30–37; and MacMullen, *Roman Social Relations*, 88–120 (esp. 96 on economic distribution). For a selection of germane primary texts (in translation), see Shelton, *Sourcebook*, esp. 4–58. Excellent guides to Roman law in all areas of concern to this paper are Nicholas, *Introduction*; and Crook, *Law and Life*, 36–67, 98–205.

6. See Meeks, *First Urban Christians*, 53–55, following Finley, *Ancient Economy*, 35–61, for these categories and their exposition.

had become retrogressive. As a result, there had been a further accumulation of wealth in the hands of the few, so that those in the lower economic strata, such as slaves, servants, and the poor, had increased, and those in the higher strata had become fewer. There were many peasant landowners who willingly sold their property and became servants or even slaves in order to guarantee a sustainable life in the employ or service of an absentee landlord. Only 1 to 3 percent were in the wealthy category, with the rest, including the middle and lower strata, occupying the other 97 percent.[7] For the most part, Roman economics led to the rich getting richer, in particular the principate (or emperor) who became the grand patron of Roman society, keeping those in Rome (especially) satisfied with food and entertainment at his own expense. Further, Roman society had a great divide between the patricians and the plebeians, and one was born to one or the other, where one would always remain.[8] Those in the highest orders, such as the Roman senators and equestrian orders, numbered only in the several hundreds even at the height of the Roman Empire. Relational status is much more difficult to discuss and quantify, but involved relative power, social prestige, occupation, income, accumulated wealth, education, knowledge, religion, family status, ethnic-group status, and local-community status. In light of the other two divisions there was only so much mobility that could occur. There are more than a few instances of the wealthy losing their wealth, but even so, if they were of the upper social orders, they might well endure due to their position. However, there are few instances of the poor achieving significant status or wealth. We know of a few slaves who became freedmen and who, through the patronage of their *potestas*, achieved some social significance, but the vast majority did not and could not have hoped to.

Within this socio-economic situation, I wish to single out three groups for particular note. The first is women.[9] Laws concerning the role of women in Roman society were increasingly complex. The complexity was heightened by Roman marital law, which saw marriage as a social contract (not a religious rite), and with it divorce, in which women had power to divorce on equal terms with men. However, women had essentially no

7. For the latest discussion, see B. Longenecker, *Remember the Poor*, 44–53. Cf. Alföldy, *Social History*, 146, for discussion of the hierarchy of social strata.

8. Boren, *Roman Society*, 14.

9. Besides the sources already noted above, see also Veyne, "Roman Empire," 9–49; Balsdon, *Roman Women*; and the sourcebook, Lefkowitz and Fant, *Women's Life*, 180–203.

legal standing. They were under the power of either their husbands or a guardian. In some instances, they had some financial means on the basis of their family, but their ability to exercise this means was limited. In rare cases, a woman could become independent of her guardian, but usually only when she was older and had already had numerous children to prove her reliability. Whatever the technicalities with regard to women in Roman society, it is fair to say that their relationship was asymmetrical with men. This is in large part because of the Roman notion of the family. The agnate family was headed by the *paterfamilias*, who essentially controlled and even had the rights of life and death over all of the members of his family, including his wife, children, and slaves.[10] Even if some of these powers were mitigated in the first century, the *paterfamilias* remained the overwhelming dominant figure of family life.[11]

The second group is slaves.[12] I have already mentioned the place of slaves in the Roman economy. Slaves were an essential component of the Roman economy. In fact, once the Roman Empire stopped expanding and fewer slaves became available through conquest, which already started occurring in the second century, the Roman economy started to disintegrate, as there were fewer new and cheap workers for a financial system that had come to rely upon cheap labor to satisfy the needs of the wealthy. There is much discussion regarding the social conditions of slaves in ancient Rome, and the fact that manumission was apparently a regularized process by which slaves could be freed, even receive citizenship, and in a number of cases have heightened socio-economic status.[13] However, another noteworthy phenomenon is that there were people who voluntarily put themselves into slavery as a means of economic liberation, so that they could be taken care of by others. Rather than this indicating that slavery was a less horrific institution than we think, I believe that this illustrates that the Romans had a much lower view of the value of human life—a similar perspective evidenced in their view of women. Thus, though essential to the Roman economy, slaves (and with them others of the lowest socio-economic strata) were in a disprivileged position in Roman life.

---

10. This topic is treated in most works. See also Eyben, "Fathers and Sons."

11. There is some discussion of how the law changed in the early years of the empire. See Saller, "Corporal Punishment"; Carcopino, *Daily Life*, 89–93.

12. Besides works above, see Bradley, *Slaves*; Harris, *Slave of Christ*; and Harrill, *Slaves*.

13. See Harris, *Slave of Christ*, 44–45.

The third group that I will mention is foreigners, especially the Jews.[14] In one sense, of course, the Jews were not foreigners to much of the Roman Empire, as they had inhabited various places in it since the days of the republic. Nevertheless, the Romans had an ambivalent view of foreigners. At first, and certainly in the days of the republic, they viewed foreigners as suspect, and being from Rome was a requirement of Roman citizenship and status. However, as the need for a professional army grew, especially as the means of securing and guaranteeing the emperor's position, and the Romans themselves were, on account of their opulent lives, unable to produce the number of people needed for the army, there became a need to recruit and rely upon foreigners. As a result, foreigners became welcome in the empire, especially those who served in the army and became citizens. Those who resisted Rome were subject to the same treatment as other enemies; the Romans attempted to overwhelm them through superior armed force—an approach that worked for over one hundred years. The Jews, however, though they in many ways were a people group who assimilated well to foreign culture (e.g., linguistically and economically), were not well received by the Romans, and there was always residual anti-Semitism throughout the Roman Empire. Thus, foreigners, including Jews, were forced into a position of disadvantaged status.

If I were writing a paper on social justice within the Roman world, I would be compelled to say that there was a widespread asymmetry between the life of Romans and the situation of women, slaves, and Jews and other foreigners. These stand out within the Roman world as those who were particularly disenfranchised by means of their socio-economic stratum, social order, or factors of status—although to be sure there were other factors as well. In other words, most people did not experience what we might reasonably call social justice within the ancient Roman context.

GALATIANS 3:26–29 AND RELATED PASSAGES

In light of this discussion, I think that it is interesting that, in his letter to the Galatians, Paul makes a statement that goes right to the heart of the Roman socio-economic situation. In Gal 3:26–29, he states (translating literalistically): "for all are sons of God through faith in Christ Jesus. For whoever is baptized into Christ, you put on Christ. There is not Jew nor Greek, not slave nor free, not male and female. For all of you are one in

14. See Carcopino, *Daily Life*, 65–69; Alföldy, *Social History*, 113 and *passim*.

Christ Jesus. And if you are of Christ, then you are seed of Abraham, heir on the basis of promise." I wish to concentrate on Gal 3:28: "There is not Jew nor Greek, not slave nor free, not male and female." The three elements that Paul singles out go to the center of the socio-economic imbalance of the Roman world. As a result, Richard Longenecker has chosen this passage as expressing the cultural mandate of the gospel.[15] He may well be right, although noting how this passage addresses Roman socio-economic imbalance is different than establishing the basis of a universal ethic. My task here is not to answer the ethical issues regarding the New Testament, but to examine Paul's letters in light of the topic of social justice. I think that this passage, because it does address the heart of the socio-economic imbalance of the Roman world, offers us prescient insight into Paul's view of social justice.

I do not think that I need to go into exegetical detail regarding Gal 3:26–29, so let me summarize this passage (cf. also 1 Cor 12:13, where the first two of the three negated pairs is given, again in the context of being baptized into the body of Christ). Paul is addressing the (southern or Roman provincial) Galatian believers, that is, Paul is writing to believers located within a Roman provincial governmental area.[16] In that context he recognizes that, through faith in Christ Jesus,[17] the Galatians are sons of God, or adopted into God's family. This is indicated through baptism, which enfolds or engulfs all believers alike—so that there is no such thing as Jew or Greek, slave or free, or male and female. In the sphere of being in relation to Christ Jesus, the Galatian believers are constituted as one, and all participate together as the inheritors of the promises to Abraham.

There are several particularities to note regarding the construction of Gal 3:28. The first is that the first two of the three paired elements are doubly negated, and the third is only singly negated, with the final two items linked by the conjunction "and" (καί). I think that the explanation of this relates to the types of negation used, as well as reference in the third pair to Gen 1:27. Each of the elements has clausal or "nexal" negation, with the first two also having word or "special" negation.[18] To emphasize the construction—Not

---

15. R. Longenecker, *New Testament Social Ethics*.

16. I think this is important to note. See Porter, *Apostle Paul*, ch. 7.

17. I believe that this is phrasing that is functionally equivalent to the so-called objective genitive.

18. On negation, see Moorhouse, *Studies*, esp. 1–7 and 141. The categories of nexal and special are his.

that there is Jew nor Greek, Not that there is slave nor free, Not that there is male and female. The clausal negation negates the entire clause, so that Paul clearly states that such an opposition does not exist. However, whereas race and subservience are exclusive categories—one is either Jew or Greek (according to the Jews) or slave or free, humankind is male and female. Paul does not wish to negate the individual genders themselves, as he does the other categories, but the categorization on the basis of them.

With this statement, Paul attacks the fundamental socio-economic points of distinction within the Roman world. This is not necessarily an ontological statement (it may have the germ of such a statement, but that is not my concern here), but it certainly is a functional statement within the context of the Roman world. As noted above, the Roman world was based upon ethnic or racial distinctions. These cut many different ways, usually to the exclusion of the one who was not Roman, whether that means Roman by birth or incorporation. What Paul is saying here is that such distinctions do not hold when someone is "in Christ Jesus" and one with other believers. Does this mean that Paul does not recognize racial distinctions? Certainly not. Paul's letters are full of statements that show that he clearly recognizes that races are not eliminated. For example, he notes in Romans and Galatians the role of Abraham (Rom 4; Gal 2:6–14) in whose line believers follow; he notes that the Jews had certain benefits from God, in particular that they had received the very words of God (Rom 5:2); he notes that the Gentiles are grafted into the tree that is grounded in ethnic Israel and that they can be just as easily ungrafted (Rom 11:11–24); he grieves for his own people who have not recognized Jesus as God's appointed one (Rom 9:2); and he notes that at some time "all Israel" will be saved (Rom 11:26)—among other places where he notes racial distinctions. Nevertheless, these are theological and, if you will, historical distinctions, which do not pertain to the way that these groups should relate within the group of the baptized. These distinctions do not address the functional relation of those within the "one" group of followers and how they function "in Christ." Here believers function without regard for race. Thus, with the first of Paul's oppositions, he in effect erases the first important Roman socio-economic distinction—that of race—by instructing the Galatians that such a distinction does not functionally exist within the group of followers of Christ Jesus. Some might say that, in some sense, within the first century the Romans had already come to recognize that racial purity was something that they could not maintain. They needed the strength of other ethnic groups to fill their armies, provide their workers, and populate their expanding nation. Even if this is true, they still mandated that those who would attain to significant position would become Romans in the process. Paul believes nothing of the sort—they must be baptized "in Christ."

The second opposition is between the slave and the free person. As with the first opposition, Paul says that such a distinction does not functionally obtain for those who are "in Christ." Paul says that distinctions on the basis of servitude, whether one is a slave or a free person, are not functionally germane to those within the group of followers of Christ. Paul has been criticized by some people for failing to advocate for their conception of social equality. By this, they usually mean a contemporary view of opposition to slavery. In light of the fact that today there are (so I have been told) more people in slavery than were enslaved during the time of slavery in the United States, I am not sure I necessarily want to use a contemporary standard as comparison. Slavery is rampant in North America, especially in the sex trade—it may not be as explicit a form of slavery as in earlier periods, but slavery it is nonetheless. However, I also think that Paul was strongly against slavery, and created the mechanism for its abolition—if we had only read him correctly and acted upon what he said.[19] As noted above, the Roman economy was built upon the backs of slaves. Slaves were vital to the Roman economy, and many people owned slaves, from the poorest tenant farmers, even including some slaves, up to the wealthiest, some of whom owned thousands. There had been a famous slave revolt led by Spartacus, a non-Roman slave trained as a gladiator, who was finally routed in 71 BCE, with six thousand of his surviving followers crucified along the Appian Way (see OCD). Paul would have been foolish to call for a slave revolt, as any type of social unrest put fear and panic into the hearts of Romans—hence the troops kept at the Antonia fortress on the Temple Mount in Jerusalem, in case the Jews acted up. Paul's tactics are much more subtle than calling for outright revolt. These tactics emerge in a number of passages and are consistent with his statement in Gal 3:28 that there is neither slave nor free. One place to see Paul's views on slavery is in his letter to Philemon regarding Onesimus. Paul reformulates the relationship between Philemon and Onesimus from one of stratal hierarchy typical of the Roman world to one of fictive kinship and egalitarian relations. As is usual for Paul, he styles himself at the outset of the letter as one of those oppressed—he is

19. I realize that this position is in opposition to a number of New Testament scholars, but I think that the evidence indicates otherwise than their views.

a "prisoner of Christ Jesus" (v. 1)—while he describes Philemon as a friend and fellow worker, Apphia as a sister, and Archippus as a fellow soldier. He describes Philemon as a partner in the faith and a brother. Even though he is now old and a prisoner, Paul informs Philemon that the once useless Onesimus—useless because he was a troublesome slave, or perhaps because he was not a believer in Christ Jesus—is being returned to Philemon as a useful person and a son of Paul and brother of Philemon. We see that the world has now radically changed. Those in Christ are family—one of the most important institutions in the Roman world, in which the *paterfamilias* controlled the lives and destinies of its members—and Paul is clearly the father, with his now two sons, both brothers in the Lord. He requests that Philemon return Onesimus to him—and how can Philemon refuse? After all, as Paul says, Philemon owes his very life to Paul. In other words, what does slavery now mean in this context, when the slave owner and slave are brothers in Christ, answering directly to their spiritual father?

I think that F. F. Bruce was certainly correct that this letter of emancipation of Onesimus effectively marks what should have been the end of slavery as an institution within the Christian church.[20] This counter-revolutionary tendency is exemplified elsewhere in Paul's writings as well. In the *Haustafeln*, passages reflective of order within the family, Paul, as any good Roman would, refers to the members of the household, including the *paterfamilias*, the wife, the children, and the slaves or servants. In both Colossians (3:22—4:1) and Ephesians (6:5–9), Paul extends the agnate family structure by referring to God or Christ as the ultimate *paterfamilias* (master in heaven). He tells slaves that they are to obey their masters according to the flesh (often translated "earthly masters"), implying that there is another master who is not according to the flesh, in the same way they would obey Christ, as if they were a slave of Christ (note the similarity of the language that Paul uses of himself in a number of his letters, such as Rom 1:1; Phil 1:1; Titus 1:1) and doing God's will, serving the Lord and not humans. Masters are also told that they are to treat their slaves in the same way, that is, in the same way that God and Christ will treat their slaves (followers of Christ), rewarding them for doing good, and reminding masters that—and here is the most important statement—they and their slaves both have the same master in heaven (cf. also 1 Tim 6:1–2, where slaves are expected to glorify

---

20. Bruce, *Paul*, 401. For an even more strongly worded statement, see Petersen, *Rediscovering Paul*, 269, 289–90. See also Porter, "Critical Discourse Analysis," contra Harris, *Slave of Christ*, 57–59.

God with their service, even though they serve their "brothers"). In other words, within God's family, there is only one *paterfamilias*, and those in the faith are all his servants, brothers and sisters in common service, and he demands similar behavior of all. If this did not cause a Roman to go weak in the knees at the very thought of it, I cannot imagine what would have.[21]

The third pair, which is not an opposition, is male and female. Whereas the other two were areas of contention and antagonism, historically, within Roman society, and even possibly within the church, Paul's vision for genders is not either/or but both/and—and he says so in Gal 3:28 in the way he frames the gender opposition in biblical terms. When God created men and women, he created both men and women, not men or women (see Gen 1:26; cf. 1 Cor 11:11, where "in the Lord," men and women are interdependent). This is probably the most highly contentious area of Paul's triad of socio-economic areas today, regardless of its position in the ancient world. The difficulty stems from interpretation of a number of select passages within the Pauline corpus, including especially 1 Cor 14:33–36 and 1 Tim 2:9–15. Responses to such passages are usually framed in one of three ways: to endorse what is often called the "literal" or "plain" sense of the text, to culturally relativize them, or to hermeneutically move beyond them. This is not the place to attempt to explain each difficult passage, but I believe that there is another alternative in many instances. In far too many cases, we have been compelled to respond to the issues on the basis of how they have been framed by others—in this situation by those who have taken restrictive and traditional interpretations of passages that reflect early interpretation by a church that was in many ways unwelcoming to the role of women. Whatever redeeming features theological interpretation of Scripture may have (and they are not as many as some think), one of its serious shortcomings is its tendency to bind us to interpretations or even misinterpretations and (mis)understandings of the past, especially those by church Fathers who, not being inspired but limited by a variety of cultural, historical, and related factors, clearly did not understand important matters such as gender. I suggest that a co-textual and discourse-attentive interpretation of these passages does not indicate the severe limitations upon women that have been argued for by some.

21. Some may raise the question of a passage such as Rom 13:1–7, in which a hierarchical obedience to the state seems (at least in some people's minds) to be taught. I believe that this is a misinterpretation of the passage, on the basis of understanding of Paul's language. Further, the term for "servant" in this passage is not the same as the one for "slave" used in the passages above. See Porter, *Letter to the Romans*, ad loc.

First Corinthians 14:33–36 must be read in the context of emerging expressions of Christian worship, in which women, permitted to engage in corporate worship perhaps in ways that they had never been permitted before, because of their Christian liberation were active participants in such activities as praying and prophesying (1 Cor 11:4), which I believe are emblematic of a range of participative activities. What Paul desires for all Christians is propriety in behavior (e.g., 1 Cor 10:23–33; 14:33, with Westcott and Hort taking the final word group with this verse, not with v. 34; cf. Rom 14:1—15:13). This extends to relations among various social groups, especially when engaged in worship (see 1 Cor 11:1, at the outset of the section on worship). Proper behavior includes the right dress, participation in the Lord's Supper in a proper way, the sharing and demonstration of spiritual gifts, and other elements of worshipful behavior. The tendency has been to take some of the terms, especially those applied to women, in an absolute way that the co-text does not ratify. Thus, the word translated "be silent" in 1 Cor 14 is often interpreted relatively for men and absolutely for women. Paul says that if there is not an interpreter of one speaking in tongues, the person is to be quiet and speak to oneself or to God (1 Cor 14:28), presumably with the idea that this is not an absolute injunction to silence but only one based upon the immediate circumstance. If there are other conditions in effect—such as the appearance of an interpreter—then one need not be silent. Similarly, if while one is prophesying another receives a revelation, then the first is to be silent, again presumably not as an absolute injunction to silence but only one based upon the immediate circumstance. If the second prophet ceases, then the first may presumably begin again. In 1 Cor 14:34, Paul refers to "women" (or possibly wives) with the article. Most would interpret this use of the article as generic. The use of the article, after all these years, is still an enigma to interpreters.[22] I think that in this instance it is invoking (perhaps as a concrete instance) the previous discussion in 1 Cor 11:2–16 concerning the practices within the community. In 1 Cor 14:34–36, Paul is further concerned with a violation of proper behavior in the church. The use of the verb for "be silent" is not absolute, but is apparently used of some kind of speaking other than praying and prophesying and related expressions of spiritual gifts ("speak" must have a particularized meaning here). There is a violation of propriety (that is the law referred to here—not the Old Testament law, but a principle of

22. See Peters, *Greek Article*, for a trenchant critique of previous proposals and a constructive way forward.

proper behavior),[23] probably one in which—in this instance—women are interrupting the service to engage in disruptive enquiry as if they already know the answers, or creating interpretations that are better handled at home in dialogue with their husbands. For it is improper (disgraceful) for a woman to speak in this way in church, as if she knows everything already.

Similarly, 1 Tim 2:9–15 addresses propriety within the Christian community in Ephesus (not necessarily in worship), a community that we know (e.g., Acts 19) was given to religious strife and discord, perhaps related to the cult of Artemis, the goddess of women. All of 1 Tim 1–3 is written with the idea of preserving order and right conduct within God's household (1 Tim 3:15), the church. Paul begins with instructions to Timothy regarding opposing false teachers who threaten the proper order. The purpose of the law (probably any law meant to govern behavior) is to regulate behavior, and apparently some were threatening to be disruptive, just as Paul himself was once a lawbreaker. Paul then offers a progressive and specialized focus upon various aberrations in human behavior, calling violators to return to proper order. He first treats societal order and urges that the societal authorities be prayed for (1 Tim 2:1–7). Then he turns to men and women within the church (1 Tim 2:9–15), before concluding with those who serve within the church (1 Tim 3:1–13).[24] Paul wants men to be orderly in their behavior (he specifically mentions how they pray), just as he wants women to behave properly (he specifically mentions their dress). As he says, he wants them to act in ways that are appropriate or proper for those who claim to worship God (1 Tim 2:10). He further states that a woman (or perhaps a wife) is to learn in quietness. The word translated "quietness" is often taken to mean "silence," even "absolute silence," when it is better understood here, and in other Greek literature, as referring to peace, order, or quietness (see, e.g., Plato, *Rep.* 8.566e). She is also to learn in proper relationship to her situation (not necessarily in the pejorative sense of subjection, but in a proper position, in the Pauline sense).

---

23. On important distinctions regarding law, see Hayek, *New Studies*, 76–80.

24. I am grateful to Holmes, *Text in a Whirlwind*, for discussion of most of these issues and those associated with such positions, especially her use of verbal aspect, even if I take it in a slightly different direction. For the most part, I assume her research on the history of scholarship in what follows below. Because of the constructive proposals she puts forward, many of her predecessors are clearly of limited value in the debate. She is not adequately responded to by Köstenberger and Schreiner, *Women in the Church*, esp. in Schreiner's article, "Interpretation."

In light of this, 1 Tim 2:12—despite its noteworthy and repeated difficulties—becomes clear (at least to me). There are three separate instructions made in this verse. The two elements of teaching and authority are
not linked together into one as a hendiadys, as some have posited. However, one of the neglected elements in this verse is the importance of verbal
aspect. The three elements are related to: teaching—probably here related
to general instruction that occurs within the Christian community (there
is no need to find a restricted or, as a few have, distorted sense of teaching)—the exercise of mastery over another—in terms here of authority (the
idea of abusive authority, to the point of murder, is again unnecessarily
restrictive, and probably linguistically anachronistic)[25]—and orderliness or
quietness. In light of what he has already stated, Paul enjoins, using the
imperfective aspect for the finite in his primary clause, as well as for the two
infinitives, that he does *not* progressively (i.e., in progress, continuously)
or in an ongoing fashion permit (using clausal or nexal negation—this is
crucial) for a woman to be progressively or in an ongoing fashion teaching *nor* (with special or word negation, following the pattern in Hellenistic
Greek) does he permit the progressive or ongoing exercise of mastery over
a man (by a woman).[26] Instead, using the strong disjunction "but," he does
permit (this time the verb is elided—or is another verb understood, such
as "instruct"?) for her to be (using the aspectually vague verb "be," which
is compatible with an imperfective context)[27] or even to continuously be
in order or quietness (note that this is not a command to silence, but an
instruction to order). The issue is not whether a woman ever teaches or has
a position of authority over a man, but whether she does so continuously or
in an ongoing fashion that would be in violation of Paul's desire for orderly
community life. He then explains using the example of Adam and Eve.
Adam was created before Eve, but it was Eve who was deceived and fell into
sin first. This is, according to Paul, simply the way that it happened (and
Genesis seems to say similarly). In the same way, a woman follows orderly
behavior by giving birth to children, that is, she is in spiritual obedience if
she does so, not that she must do so (but she is, by implication, not to not
give birth), when they—both man and woman (the two are implied on the

25. See Wolters, "Semantic Study."

26. Porter, *Verbal Aspect*, 91; Porter, *Idioms*, 29. Cf. Holmes, *Text in a Whirlwind*,
90–95, who has helped my thinking in this area. Schreiner ("Interpretation," 216–17 n
111) apparently misunderstands the role of negation in aspect, and so also misunderstands Holmes.

27. Porter, *Verbal Aspect*, 442–47.

basis of the co-text)—remain in the faith. Just as a man is not to be dominant over a woman, neither is a woman to be dominant over a man. There is a proper order for the Christian community. This is then exemplified in the functional positions of overseer and deacon, positions that, I believe, are not restricted to men on the basis of Paul's formulation, even if he perhaps recognized that in the culture in which he lived many if not most of the positions would be held by men anyway (as evidenced by his reference to a man being the husband of one wife).[28] I believe that what Paul has said, as with his statements regarding slavery, is enough to shake the typical Roman to the bottom of his sandals.

I do not have time here to discuss all of the other passages that bear on this issue of the relation of men and women within the Christian community. Let me note several of relevance, however. The *Haustafeln* similarly transmute Roman social conventions.[29] Since the *paterfamilias* had almost unlimited powers, even those of death in some instances, Paul says that, whereas the idea of an ordered arrangement is not in itself wrong, both husband and wife are to be mutually submissive to one another in fear of Christ (Eph 5:21), who is the ultimate *paterfamilias*. For wives, Paul says, this involves the same kind of submission that would be rendered to Christ as head of the church. So far, this is perhaps not too startling, as it seems to reinforce Roman social order for the sake of ecclesial and family order. Husbands, however, are to love their wives in the same way that Christ loved the church and gave himself for it, to present her in the best possible spiritual light, and to love her in the same way that he loves himself (Eph 5:25–29; cf. Col 3:18–19). Paul here transforms the notion of wife as possession or property into wife as person and equal, one to be loved, cared for, and cherished in the same way that a Roman man would care for himself and his own body—no doubt with thoughts of luxuriating in Roman baths not being too far in the background. Men who attended the baths, engaged in exercise, and pampered themselves in such a way clearly did not hate their own bodies, but were tending to them—in the same way that Christ tends to the church and they were to care for their wives.

An examination of Gal 3:26–29 proves instructive, because, within this passage, especially Gal 3:28, Paul provides in abbreviated form the basis for a complete Roman socio-economic transformation—not a revolution,

---

28. I argue this position more fully in Porter, "Saints and Sinners."

29. Contra Harrill, *Slaves*, 88–89, but who shows that later *Haustafeln* (e.g., *Didache*) do not have the same reciprocity.

because Paul is too wise to confront the entire Roman system that could come crashing down upon the fledgling church—but a radical transformation nonetheless. He addresses the very heart of the Roman socio-economic system—race and ethnicity, servitude, and gender relations—and transforms each one of them from the inside, that is, from the church, out. Paul does not address the situation outside of the church (we will discuss why that is below), but calls upon those within the church, that community of followers of Jesus Christ, to treat each other in new social and economic ways based upon what it means to be baptized "in Christ."

THE CHRISTIAN COMMUNITY

Rather than calling for a slave revolt, which probably would simply have resulted in unnecessary bloodshed and no significant improvement in conditions of servitude, and rather than calling for a radical change in racial views, which probably would simply have resulted in further social ostracization, and rather than calling for a redefinition of the Roman family, which would have struck at the very heart of Roman civilization itself and no doubt resulted in serious backlash, Paul does something much more potentially effective, if subtle. He calls for those who are followers of Jesus Christ to transform their own relationships—to dissolve the boundaries that distinguish one from another on the basis of race, to think of their relations within the bonds of a new family structure in which God or Christ is the *paterfamilias* and we, no matter what the Romans may say we are, are brothers and sisters in Christ, and to think of our wives and husbands as the human individuals that they are, rather than property or possessions without rights.

The basis of Paul's re-evaluation of Roman socio-economic structure is the competing institution of the church, that group of people who are followers of Jesus Christ. All of the major statements that I can find regarding Paul and socio-economic relations are grounded within this framework of what it means to be a follower of Jesus Christ. God is the ultimate *paterfamilias* who has sent his son to be the head (or local *paterfamilias*) of this group of followers, called the church, on the basis of his being its savior through his death and resurrection. One is brought into this "family" by means of faith, as evidenced through baptism and the "putting on" of Christ, like a new garment that signals membership in this new family. This is what it means to be "in Christ."[30]

30. See Porter, *Idioms*, 159.

Membership in this new family, however, comes with its own expectations and obligations. Life in this family is not just the negation of previous divisive distinctions, as noted above, but has socio-economic obligations.

One of these, surprising as it may seem, is the obligation to take care of the other members of the community in appropriate ways. This means service to one another, including taking part in work. Paul himself, even though as the apostle and founder of several churches he was under no obligation to pay his own way, because of his service to Christ and the church, chose to provide for himself (1 Cor 9:1–18; cf. 2 Thess 3:8–9). Therefore, he demanded that others provide for themselves as well. Some of the Thessalonians, probably in anticipation of the return of Christ, had decided not to work (2 Thess 3:6–10; cf. 1 Thess 5:14). Paul stated that when he was with them he told them, "If someone does not wish to work, don't let them eat" (2 Thess 3:10). This statement was particularly addressed to the idle, because Paul believed that it was right and proper that people work (1 Thess 4:11), as he did (2 Thess 3:7–9).

However, what about those who are unable to work? The Roman socio-economic system was particularly harsh on women who did not have means of support, that is, lacked a male provider—being widowed or having no living male relatives including children. Widows were particularly vulnerable if they had no other financial means or family support. This was an apparent problem for the church in Ephesus, which Paul addresses. In 1 Timothy, Paul instructs Timothy in the treatment of people in the church. Note that he reformulates relationships in familial terms—Timothy is not to rebuke older men but address them as he would a father, treat younger men as brothers, older women as mothers, younger women as sisters—all in complete holiness. In other words, as part of the Pauline familial transformation, people are reconfigured within the family of God with their appropriate roles and responsibilities toward each other. However, if a widow has children or grandchildren, she is to turn to them for support. Why? So that the children or grandchildren can learn first to carry out their own religious duties in their own household by repaying their parents (note that the masculine plural form for parents refers to widows), for this is pleasing to God (1 Tim 5:4). Caring for one's relatives and especially for one's own household is a spiritual responsibility, and not doing so is a denial of the faith (1 Tim 5:8).

What about those who are really widows in need with no relatives to help? Their first source of aid is hope in God, as evidenced by continual prayer (1 Tim 5:5). Their second source of aid is a church social welfare system. This is reserved for widows who are over sixty years old (in a culture where the average life expectancy was in the mid-twenties, so these are clearly elderly women), have been faithful to their husbands, and are well known for their good deeds (e.g., child rearing, hospitality, helping others). Younger women should be a part of this system as caregivers to widows related to them, where possible, so that, Paul says, the church can take care of the genuine widows, that is, those with no other means of support (1 Tim 5:16). Younger widows are to be excluded from such a list, because they have the ability to remarry and, note this, the propensity (which Paul knows is part of human nature, as he has already noted to the Thessalonians) for idleness, that is, not having to work to sustain themselves, which results in all sorts of problems, including not only idleness, which is itself an evil, but becoming gossips and busybodies (1 Tim 5:11–14). In fact, he equates such behavior with ultimately turning away to follow Satan (1 Tim 5:15). Paul's statements may seem harsh by today's standards, but there is a clear pragmatic logic to them. There are those who qualify for financial aid due to their poverty, but the standards for qualification are clear—where there are alternative means they are to be taken advantage of—and in fact designed for the beneficiaries' benefit—all within the ambit of the church providing for its own.

OTHER PASSAGES

In a recent study, Bruce Longenecker has made an argument for Paul's concern for the poor.[31] As we have seen above, Paul clearly demonstrates a concern for those who are socio-economically disenfranchised in Roman society—he does not restrict himself to the poor. In fact, Paul goes much deeper and addresses arguably the three most important socio-economic restrictions of Roman society, presenting a solution to them within what it means to be followers of Christ ("in Christ") within his church. The church is, if you will, posited as a counter-institution to Roman society, rectifying the major socio-economic liabilities of the socio-economic structure. Paul specifically confronts the major issues of social justice in his context, and provides counter-remedies to them. (Unfortunately, the church clearly has not followed many if not most of these for many centuries. This is not Paul's fault, but ours.) Nevertheless, many contemporary interpreters, Longenecker apparently included, wish to equate social justice with the issue

31. B. Longenecker, *Remember the Poor*, esp. 135–219.

of poverty, including that outside the church. Specific references to poverty are few in the Pauline letters. Longenecker recognizes this and addresses a number of passages that he believes are about poverty.

Acts 11:29: This passage is Paul's so-called famine visit, when he and Barnabas take aid to Judea. It is beyond the scope of my paper to treat the book of Acts, but I simply note here that Acts says that the gift was for the "brothers" in Judea, that is, the members of the Christian community.

Acts 20:18–35, esp. v. 35: Longenecker interprets Paul's words to the elders at Miletus as endorsing three things: "caring for the poor," concluding his speech by highlighting his "concern for the poor and needy," and embedding his words about "support for the weak" within his "message of God's grace."[32] I am not convinced that this passage is about the poor as Longenecker wishes to argue. I think that instead this passage resonates with 2 Thessalonians above, where Paul distinguishes those who can work from those who will not. Here he means that those who can work must aid those who cannot. Poverty may result, but that is not the main emphasis here. In any case, the context is the Christian community—Paul speaks of his work within the church, along with that of his companions, as examples to others within the church.

2 Corinthians 9:13: Longenecker notes that 2 Cor 9:13 comes at the end of Paul's discussion of the collection for the church in Jerusalem (2 Cor 8–9). He believes that 9:13 should be translated "by the generosity of your contribution for them [i.e., Jerusalem Jesus-followers] and for all [others]."[33] Longenecker is correct that the word translated "contribution" (*koinōnia*) can indicate a gift or contribution (so BDAG), but this is not necessarily a monetary contribution. The one clear place where it does indicate this is Rom 15:26, where the passage says that the Macedonians and Achaians were pleased "to make a certain contribution/gift to the poor of the saints in Jerusalem," with the co-text indicating that the gift or contribution may have been monetary. Therefore, Longenecker is falling victim to a form of illegitimate semantic transfer in reading that into 2 Cor 9:13, where the context does not necessarily indicate a financial contribution. It instead seems to indicate a general "attitude of good will that manifests an interest in a close relationship" (BDAG). Furthermore, the "all others" is not necessarily those outside the Christian community, but probably indicates other believers who have benefited from their generosity. One last idea to

32. Ibid., 152.
33. Ibid., 141.

note is that, rather than this passage indicating an obligation on the wealthy to provide for the poor, Paul characterizes the Macedonian churches who contributed to this gift as giving out of the depth of their own poverty.

Galatians 6:9–10: Paul instructs the Galatians to "work the good" for all people, especially those of the household of faith. Longenecker's only defense that this means giving to the poor outside the church is appeal to the assertions of a number of commentators.[34] It may mean this, but there is nothing that says so, and I think that it is more likely that Paul has in mind all the kinds of good works expected of a Christian.

First Thessalonians 5:12–22, esp. v. 14: In 1 Thess 5:12–22, Paul gives several final warnings, including instruction to warn the idle, encourage the timid, help the weak, and be patient with all. Longenecker takes reference to "weak" as indicating economic vulnerability.[35] This may be so, but in any case the admonitions are given to the Thessalonians (note address of "brothers" in vv. 12 and 14; cf. v. 15, where kindness is extended to others).

Romans 12:13 and 16: Paul says that the Romans are to share in the needs of the saints and associate with the humble or lowly. The first statement is about benefiting the believing community, as probably is the second. Even if it is not, it is a statement regarding social status rather than wealth.

Ephesians 4:28: Paul instructs the one who has been stealing within the community to steal no longer, but to work, so that he may have something to share with those in need. Longenecker cites Best in noting that this verse "provides some evidence for the continuance of communal sharing of possessions among the early Christians,"[36] which is sharing with other Christians rather than with the poor outside the church.

Galatians 2:10: This is the last verse to consider. Longenecker wishes to go against practically all previous interpretation, what he sees as a virtually "'undisputed' consensus,"[37] that this verse refers to giving to the Christians in Jerusalem, and he contends that it refers to giving to the poor in general as a Pauline mission strategy. The passage refers to Paul's visit to Jerusalem, where he was given the hand of fellowship by James, Peter, and John, who encouraged Paul and Barnabas to go to the Gentiles, while they would go to the Jews, with the proviso that Barnabas and he should remember the poor,

34. Ibid., 141–42.

35. Ibid., 143.

36. Ibid., 150 (citing Best, *Ephesians*, 455).

37. B. Longenecker, *Remember the Poor*, 159.

which Paul says he was eager to do. There are a number of difficulties with Longenecker's corrective. The first is that this statement is very little to hang such a large hat on, especially in light of the other Pauline evidence. Second, the other Pauline evidence, where the evidence is clear, endorses an internal support for Christians in need, not a general concern for the poor. The third is that Longenecker does not fully appreciate how Gal 2:1–10 correlates with other elements of Paul's travel itinerary. He is skeptical of the correlation between the visit in Gal 2:1–10 and Acts 11:27–30, but I think unnecessarily so, especially because of the bringing of aid to the believers in Jerusalem. Paul and Barnabas have brought relief to the struggling believers there, and those in Jerusalem ask Paul not to forget them, the poor, in the future. Paul remembered them in the future, by bringing the collection to Jerusalem mentioned above, probably delivered during the visit in Acts 21 (Rom 15:26). Fourth, Longenecker engages in some linguistic legerdemain regarding the tense-forms (invoking various ideas about constative, continual, inceptive, and other meanings) that do nothing to clarify the situation.[38] He wants to make it seem as if Paul had already had remembrance of the poor at heart before the discussion of Gal 2:10, as part of his mission strategy. Fifth, Longenecker wants to see Gal 2:7–9 as not germane to the main argument, but an attempt by Paul to qualify what is said in v. 6. This would connect v. 10 more closely to v. 7 and hence the "targets" of Paul's mission.[39] In other words, Longenecker believes that the major message was that the apostles added nothing to Paul's message except that he should remember the poor. I think that this is special pleading, and neglects other linguistic elements, including the contrastive statement in v. 7 with a perfect tense-form that is used to capture the message that both the apostles and Peter shared.

On the basis of this quick survey, I believe that there is little of substance to endorse the idea that Paul had a vision for social justice that extended beyond the confines of the church, especially if that involved care for the poor at large (or exclusively).

PAULINE ESCHATOLOGY

This discussion raises the question of how it is that Paul would have held to such a position as just summarized. If I am correct in my analysis of Paul's letters on this topic, Paul was a social radical—at least within the confines

38. Ibid., 190–95.
39. Ibid., 196.

of the church. He called for a transformation of fundamental Roman socio-economic structures with regard to race and ethnicity, servitude, and gender, but all within the confines of the church. He must have realized that, even with the best intentions of keeping such actions and attitudes within the church, there would have been obvious spillover into the surrounding culture. There would have been those who would realize that the way that those within the church, including Jews and Greeks, treated each other was very different—there was consideration of the strengths and weaknesses of their character and beliefs, and consideration for each other (e.g., Rom 14:1—15:13, regarding the strong and weak). There was not discrimination on the basis simply of ethnic origin—whereby those born Roman (note the impact of this on the Roman church) would consider themselves superior to others, and Jews would be discriminated against and further ghettoized—when a Roman citizen would gladly open the door and welcome a Jew into his home to be with his family, and when Jewish and Roman and other families would eat together with attention to each other's needs and concerns (1 Cor 11:17–33). There would have been those who would realize that something had gone extravagantly wrong when the master shouldered the burden alongside his slave and offered him a bowl of water rather than the whip on his back; when the slave, rather than trying to steal from his master or take advantage of his situation, would work extra hard and look out for his master's interests; when a master would address his slave as brother and treat his female servant with respect and human dignity, such that it was as much as—and in fact led to—offering them their freedom for nothing in return, and then inviting them to continue to live with his family. There would have been those who would realize that something cataclysmic had happened when a husband put his wife's concerns before his own, and demonstrated love to her that could only be characterized as sacrificial and unselfish, rather than making demands that exerted his legal prerogatives; and when a wife, rather than trying to subtly rebel against oppressive constraints on her activities and even thoughts, showed genuine regard for her husband and they partnered together for the benefit of their entire family. Social justice was intended to become a lived reality—at least within the church for followers of Christ. Alas, such was not to be the case. I do not know what happened, but the church did anything but follow the Pauline model and prescriptions.

If such had happened, however, there are still two possible developments in the ancient world that we might have contemplated. One would be the extension of the socio-economic transformation within the church to outside of the church and to all of society. I think there are a number of reasons that Paul did not consider this option as a viable strategy. One was the revolutionary implications already mentioned above. To promote such a position was to threaten the very existence of the early Christian movement. Another was that Paul perhaps (and rightly) realized that the transformation of the church was a big enough task to accomplish—one that has not yet been realized to our present day. The third was the realization that it would take everything that the church had to be able to sustain such an effort within the church itself.

There is another possible development. Someone once wrote that the reason that people put so much emphasis on social justice today is because they have a poor sense of eschatology.[40] I believe that this is the heart of why Paul confines his statements regarding social justice to the church. For Paul, this life that we now enjoy on earth is not the sum total of life. If this is all there is, then there would be an argument for doing everything possible to redeem all aspects of life and society. (There would, of course, be an argument for exploiting every aspect of life and society as well.) However, that would require a completely different theology than the one I read in Paul. The death and resurrection of Jesus is not about simply the redemption of the earth, but the redemption of individuals who then become participants in a much larger scheme that transcends life as we currently know it. This explains why Paul can comfort the Thessalonians about those who have already died—their death (or sleep, as he refers to it) is not the end. If it were, then there would be reason for extreme sadness at their missing out on the resurrection. But their death is only a temporary state in the larger scheme of things, when the living and the dead are raised together to be in the Lord's presence (1 Thess 4:13–17). Jesus died and rose again as a basis of belief that this is our destiny as his followers as well, and this is meant to be an encouragement, with which we comfort each other (1 Thess 4:14, 18). Second Corinthians 5:1–10 notes that this earthly tent in which we live is destined for destruction, but that this is acceptable in light of our eternal dwelling with God in heaven. While in this tent we are subject to groaning and burdens (perhaps even poverty),[41] but we are confident that

40. This is a paraphrase of the statement as well as I can remember it. I was unable to locate the original source.

41. After all, Jesus said that the poor we would have with us always (Matt 26:11), where he also said that his followers would not always have Jesus; cf. also Matt 5:3 and Luke 6:20, where the poor are commended for their poverty, because it can offer spiritual

THE BIBLE AND SOCIAL JUSTICE

God has provided a means for us to achieve this home (note also that we must appear before the judgment seat of Christ for all that we have done; 2 Cor 5:10).[42] This is grounded in the fact that Jesus' resurrection is a pledge or firstfruit that those who are "in Christ," that is, the community of followers of Jesus, will participate in the resurrection of the dead (1 Cor 15:20–21), which then culminates in the kingdom of God being established, not by humans or their efforts (or even their poverty relief efforts) but by Jesus after he has destroyed all of his enemies, including death itself (1 Cor 15:24–26). I think that there is a compelling internal logic in Paul's approach, in that this winsome way in which believers live would be appealing to others and prompt them to be led to follow Jesus as well. I certainly think that this is to be preferred to an approach that might provide the material (or at least apparent) benefits of the Christian life but without the faith commitment, which I think is all too prevalent today.

I fear that failure to realize that, in Christianity, the end is not the end, but only the beginning, has distorted our vision of the present. We have perhaps focused too closely upon the narrow scope of the present and lost sight of the bigger and broader picture—even of the future. I think that Paul's eschatology enabled him to view the present in the realistic light of God's past, present, and future work, and therefore to establish priorities for God's people in the present time.

CONCLUSION

The perspective that I have presented here may well be different from what one might expect in this day and age. Some may even see it as in contradiction to what they perceive as other clear passages in Scripture that argue to the contrary. I think that Paul was not a haphazard thinker who simply wrote a few words on the basis of the occasion or moment to some of those who were in churches that were connected to him. I think that Paul had a keen insight into both his contemporary socio-economic context and larger theological issues concerning the plan of God and the work of Christ both past and present. This enables Paul to develop a strategy that attacks from within the very heart of the Roman socio-economic system. Rather

---

blessings to those who avail themselves of its advantages.

42. When I presented this paper, one attendee asked whether my view could be construed as letting people off the hook, by not calling for an overt social justice program. This verse answers the question—a proper eschatology shows that no one gets let off the hook. No one.

than avoiding the pressing issues of his day, or focusing upon only one or two particular issues, Paul develops a broad strategy that confronts the structures of the Roman Empire at its very heart, and provides the mechanism for its transformation from within. This mandates those who are "in Christ" to live out in their relations with each other a clear demonstration of what it means for Christ to eliminate the traditional barriers and boundaries of life and develop a new set of standards for what it means to be civil. True civility, according to Paul, can only be achieved within the church, as individuals live with respect, love, and obedience to each other under the guidance of Jesus Christ. I think that Paul had the hope that believers would continue to exemplify this model in their continuing lives together long after he was gone, but in expectation of the return of their Lord and Master, Jesus Christ. I believe that this still provides a good model for believers today. It may, in fact, provide the catalyst for the contemporary church to become much more vibrant and distinctive, and perhaps even provide a compelling and intriguing reason for the surrounding culture to take note of it in a new way—rather than simply benefiting from its generosity on their behalf.

BIBLIOGRAPHY

Alföldy, Geza. *The Social History of Rome*. Translated by David Braund and Frank Pollock. Baltimore: Johns Hopkins University Press, 1988.

Balsdon, J. P. V. D. *Roman Women: Their History and Habits*. New York: Harper & Row, 1962.

Best, Ernest. *Ephesians*. ICC. Edinburgh: T. & T. Clark, 1998.

Boren, Henry C. *Roman Society: A Social, Economic, and Cultural History*. Lexington, MA: Heath, 1977.

Bradley, K. R. *Slaves and Masters in the Roman Empire: A Study in Social Control*. Oxford: Oxford University Press, 1987.

Bruce, F. F. *Paul, Apostle of the Heart Set Free*. Grand Rapids: Eerdmans, 1974.

Carcopino, Jerome. *Daily Life in Ancient Rome*. Translated by E. O. Lorimer. Harmondsworth: Penguin, 1941.

Crook, J. A. *Law and Life of Rome, 90 B.C.–A.D. 212*. Ithaca, NY: Cornell University Press, 1967.

Eyben, Emiel. "Fathers and Sons." In *Marriage, Divorce, and Children in Ancient Rome*, edited by Beryl Rawson, 99–113. Oxford: Clarendon, 1991.

Finley, M. I. *The Ancient Economy*. Sather Classical Lectures. London: Chatto & Windus, 1973.

Harrill, J. Albert. *Slaves in the New Testament: Literary, Social, and Moral Dimensions*. Minneapolis: Fortress, 2006.

Harris, Murray J. *Slave of Christ: A New Testament Metaphor for Total Devotion to Christ*. Downers Grove, IL: InterVarsity, 1999.

Hayek, F. A. *New Studies in Philosophy, Politics, Economics and the History of Ideas.* Chicago: University of Chicago Press, 1978.

Holmes, J. M. *Text in a Whirlwind: A Critique of Four Exegetical Devices at 1 Timothy 2.9–15.* JSNTSup 196. Sheffield: Sheffield Academic, 2000.

Köstenberger, Andreas J., and Thomas R. Schreiner, eds. *Women in the Church: An Analysis and Application of 1 Timothy 2:9–15.* 2nd ed. Grand Rapids: Baker, 2005.

Lefkowitz, Mary R., and Maureen B. Fant, eds. *Women's Life in Greece and Rome: A Source Book in Translation.* Baltimore: Johns Hopkins University Press, 1982.

Longenecker, Bruce W. *Remember the Poor: Paul, Poverty, and the Greco-Roman World.* Grand Rapids: Eerdmans, 2010.

Longenecker, Richard N. *New Testament Social Ethics for Today.* Grand Rapids: Eerdmans, 1984.

MacMullen, Ramsey. *Roman Social Relations: 50 B.C. to A.D. 284.* New Haven: Yale University Press, 1974.

Meeks, Wayne A. *The First Urban Christians: The Social World of the Apostle Paul.* New Haven: Yale University Press, 1983.

Moorhouse, A. C. *Studies in the Greek Negatives.* Cardiff: Wales University Press, 1959.

Nicholas, Barry. *An Introduction to Roman Law.* Oxford: Clarendon, 1962.

Peters, Ronald Dean. *The Greek Article: A Functional Grammar of ὁ-items in the Greek New Testament with Special Emphasis on the Greek Article.* LBS 9. Leiden: Brill, 2014.

Petersen, Norman R. *Rediscovering Paul: Philemon and the Sociology of Paul's Narrative World.* Philadelphia: Fortress, 1985.

Porter, Stanley E. *The Apostle Paul: His Life, Thought, and Letters.* Grand Rapids: Eerdmans, forthcoming.

———. *Idioms of the Greek New Testament.* 2nd ed. London: Continuum, 1994.

———. "Is Critical Discourse Analysis Critical? An Evaluation Using Philemon as a Test Case." In *Discourse Analysis and the New Testament: Approaches and Results*, edited by Stanley E. Porter and Jeffrey T. Reed, 47–70. JSNTSup 70. Sheffield: Sheffield Academic, 1991.

———. *The Letter to the Romans: A Linguistic and Literary Commentary.* NTM 37. Sheffield: Sheffield Phoenix, 2015.

———. "Saints and Sinners: The Church in Paul's Letters." In *The Church, Then and Now*, edited by Stanley E. Porter and Cynthia Long Westfall, 41–67. MNTS. Eugene, OR: Pickwick, 2012.

———. *Verbal Aspect in the Greek of the New Testament with Reference to Tense and Mood.* SBG 1. New York: Peter Lang, 1989.

Rachels, James. *The Elements of Moral Philosophy.* 2nd ed. New York: McGraw-Hill, 1993.

Rostovtzeff, M. *Social and Economic History of the Roman Empire.* 2 vols. Oxford: Clarendon, 1957.

Ryan, Alan. "Political Philosophy." In *Philosophy 2: Further through the Subject*, edited by A. C. Grayling, 351–419. Oxford: Oxford University Press, 1998.

Saller, Richard. "Corporal Punishment, Authority, and Obedience in the Roman Household." In *Marriage, Divorce, and Children in Ancient Rome*, edited by Beryl Rawson, 114–43. Oxford: Clarendon, 1991.

Schreiner, Thomas R. "An Interpretation of 1 Timothy 2:9–15: A Dialogue with Scholarship." In *Women in the Church: An Analysis and Application of 1 Timothy 2:9–15*, edited by Andreas J. Köstenberger and Thomas R. Schreiner, 85–120, 207–29. 2nd ed. Grand Rapids: Baker, 2005.

Shelton, Jo-Ann. *As the Romans Did: A Sourcebook in Roman Social History*. 2nd ed. Oxford: Oxford University Press, 1998.

Taylor, David. *Roman Society*. London: Macmillan, 1980.

Veyne, Paul. "The Roman Empire." In *A History of Private Life*, edited by Paul Veyne, 5–234. Cambridge, MA: Belknap, 1987.

Wolters, Al. "A Semantic Study of αὐθέντης and Its Derivatives." *JGRChJ* 1 (2000) 145–75.

7

Continue to Remember the Poor

Social Justice within the Poor and Powerless Jewish Christian Communities

CYNTHIA LONG WESTFALL

STRONG AND CLEAR STATEMENTS about the roles of the believer and the church in social justice[1] are found in the General Epistles and Hebrews.[2] There is a very good reason for this: they contain letters and homilies of Jewish Christianity that are addressed to the churches. In them we hear

1. The term "social justice" embeds our discussion in a larger ongoing contemporary debate that involves complex theories and competing definitions. The dialogue concerning biblical social justice interfaces with that of political theory, where justice is treated as a fundamental political value. However, political theorists disagree about the analysis and theories of what constitutes justice. See Campbell, *Justice*, for an overview of nine approaches to social justice. The term will be defined below.

2. The position of this chapter is that Hebrews, the General Epistles, Revelation, and the Gospels of Matthew, John, and possibly Mark, are texts associated with Jewish Christianity (otherwise referred to as "Christian Judaism"). As Skarsaune states, "A 'Jewish Christian' is a Jewish believer in Jesus who, as a believer, still maintains a Jewish way of life" ("Jewish Believers in Jesus," 3). Jackson-McCabe points out that "there is not now, nor has there ever been, a generally agreed upon canon of works that constitute definitive examples of Jewish Christianity, Christian Judaisms, or any other such category" ("Introduction," 4). Nevertheless, particularly in the issue of social justice, the placement of these texts powerfully affects their reading. Bauckham asserts: "Most New Testament scholars would now agree that the New Testament writings belong wholly within the Jewish world of their time . . . Even New Testament works authored by and/or addressed to non-Torah-observant Gentile Christians still move within the Jewish world of ideas" (*Jewish World*, 1). The Pauline corpus and Luke–Acts target and accommodate Gentile recipients in cross-cultural communication as part of the mission to the Gentiles, but the rest of the texts are associated with the apostolic mission to the Jews and (even if pseudonymous) place themselves in the Jewish world.

prophetic voices brought forward from the Old Testament.[3] These voices are issued from and directed towards a Jewish worldview in which the Old Testament concepts of social justice already resonate and are considered acutely relevant as interpreted in their new contexts.[4] The varieties of Judaism in the first century were rife with reactions to the domination of the Jewish people and injustices suffered under the Roman Empire.[5] The response of the Jews to the Roman Empire's policies eventually resulted in a series of Jewish rebellions in Palestine as well as innumerable clashes of Jewish Diaspora communities with Roman officials and Gentile communities outside of Palestine.[6] The attitude of the Jews towards the Roman

3. The writers of the Jewish Christian corpus interpret the Old Testament and identify the church as being in continuity with Israel. Though Attridge states that most scholars view Hebrews as "an attempt to prevent a relapse or a failure to move completely out of Judaism" (*Hebrews*, 10), this chapter is part of a growing trend that reads the text in the context of Jewish Christianity and sees that the argument draws heavily from the identification of the readers with the Wilderness Generation and the Jewish models of faith.

4. Grassi argues that Jesus and the New Testament writers were not concerned about the original historical situation of the Old Testament Scriptures, but rather they "followed the traditional Jewish outlook that the Hebrew Bible, especially the Torah and Prophets, was the living, perennial word of God. In reading or listening to it they felt that they were doing so in the same way as the original audience" (*Informing the Future*, 3–4).

5. "Varieties of Judaism" reflects the ongoing discussion of the complexity of first-century Judaism as opposed to the view that first-century Judaism was monolithic or immutable. It has become popular to emphasize the diversity through use of the term "Judaisms" (e.g., Boccaccini, *Middle Judaism*, 18–21; Neusner, *Judaisms and Their Messiahs*, ix–xii), but Bauckham's criticism that the talk of many Judaisms "obscures the distinction between variety and separation or schism" is well-taken (*Jewish World*, 178). See also Skarsaune, *In the Shadow*, 101–8.

6. The indictment of economic and legal injustice in James is recognized as a plausible description of the conditions in Palestine that led to the revolt. The destruction of not only the temple and Jerusalem, but many population centers in Palestine, occurred over a period of seven years under Titus. After the fall of Palestine, the entire Jewish population was subject to social and financial retribution and huge numbers of Jews went into slavery. Outside of Palestine, the treatment of Jewish populations can be illustrated by the severe treatment, overt oppression, and physical attack on the entire Alexandrian Jewish population under Caligula (Gaius) recorded by Philo (Philo, *Flacc.* 1.54–85), as well as the expulsion of the Jews from Rome under Claudius (Suetonius, *Claud.* 25). Jews were also derided for their peculiar monotheism and dietary laws, "mocked as atheists on the one hand and, on the other hand, accused of ignoble idolatry including pig worship and and worshipping an ass's head" (Petronius, *Poems* 24; Plutarch, *Quaest. conv.* 4.5; Josephus, *Ag. Ap.* 2.80; 2.114). The neglect of the existence and influence of Jewish Christianity until recently has resulted in a marked failure by most scholars to "connect the dots" in terms of re-creating these conditions as plausible contexts for the letters that were written by Jewish Christian leaders.

Empire was basically the same as the attitudes of the Israelites towards the oppressive empires found in the Old Testament, particularly towards Babylon.[7] In other words, the identity of a Jew writing to other Jews, or within the Jewish mindset, assumed certain shared values, which included social obligations that provided a foundation upon which certain social practices could be addressed, advocated, or confronted (in contrast with the Pauline Epistles). That is, the social and political framework of the Hebrew Bible was accepted as relevant background and precedent, and had a political and sociological authority even though Jews were no longer in control of their land.[8] What would be strategic discourse from a Jew about social justice/concern within Jewish circles or within the Christian mission to the Hebrews was not the same as what would be strategic outside of Jewish circles—I propose that this statement addresses some of the defining differences between the Jewish Mission and the Gentile Mission (reflected in the Pauline corpus) concerning social justice.[9] However, Jewish ideas of social justice eventually came to be practiced by Gentile Christians to the extent that Gentile churches adopted the Old Testament as authoritative and normative, which is reflected in the known history of social justice practiced in the early church.

In addition, the social and economic experience of Jewish Christianity in the first century entailed a higher degree of marginalization than that of either the non-Christian Jewish communities or the Gentile churches. This group in general was at higher risk of experiencing oppression for economic, racial, or religious reasons. Due to its precarious social position, it was likelier to find itself in need because of disaster, mistreatment, and famine, and more prone to homelessness through being disowned or being a victim of forced migration. Their vulnerability reflected not only their solidarity with the plight of the Jewish people during this time, but also involved various forms of pressure and rejection from the Jewish people themselves. These factors will account for the marked differences between

---

7. We find the Roman Empire blatantly equated to the Babylonian Empire in Jewish Christian literature (1 Pet 5:13; Rev 17–18). In Revelation, Rome is equated with both Babylon and a prostitute, hence the well-known title "the whore of Babylon."

8. The relationship between the people and the land frames the entire Old Testament.

9. Interestingly, Luke–Acts is associated with the Pauline corpus, but has a strong theme of social justice that is in contrast with the interests and focus of the Pauline epistles. An explanation of this contrast in terms of purpose and register could be a focus of further research.

how the Jewish Christian corpus treats social justice issues and the strategies employed in the Pauline epistles to build Christian community in a mission that targeted Gentile recipients who enjoyed the benefits of the *Pax Romana* and who were much more at home in the Roman Empire.[10]

Therefore, in reading the Jewish Christian epistles to identify the thread of social justice, we must also read the texts through the lens of the needy, the oppressed and the marginalized.[11] The writers and recipients of the Jewish Christian corpus are examples of a vulnerable population who are "embedded in the structures of domination."[12] Jewish Christians wrote from the social location of the marginalized and were at risk both within the Roman Empire and within Judaism at that time. The Jewish Christian corpus within the New Testament reflects the practice of social justice in a context where both the authors and recipients belong to needy and oppressed communities.

METHODOLOGY

This chapter is a study of the biblical theology of social justice as practiced in the early Jewish Christian communities, together with an attempt to consider how it may be understood and applied to life in the Western twenty-first-century context. Topics or themes that are related to social justice appear in many guises in Hebrews and the General Epistles. The first task is to compose a working definition of social justice that adequately reflects the elements found in the documents of the early Jewish Christian communities.[13] The following definition and the questions below are informed by

10. For Jewish Christians as "pariahs" in Jewish culture, see Sanders, *Schismatics*, 58–67. For the severe economic conditions in Palestine, see Oakman, *Jesus and the Economic Questions*, 17–80; Moxnes, *Economy of the Kingdom*, 23–35.

11. To successfully accomplish this, we need to be in deliberate dialogue with textual readings from other economic and social perspectives and their interpretations. As Elliott observes, "the exegete himself or herself, no less than the biblical authors, is conditioned by his or her own social and psychological experience." Therefore, "a genuinely sociological exegesis of the Scriptures would seem to require not only the ongoing dialogue of exegetes and sociologists, but also necessary involvement and teamwork of persons from different cultures and strata of society" (*Home for the Homeless*, 12–13). A failure to allow the vulnerable to have a voice and dismissing their interpretations as invalid because they may contain error ensures the continuation of injustice.

12. I am indebted to Schüssler Fiorenza for this description of a vulnerable people group. She uses it to describe "wo/men's lives," but it is applicable to all those who are vulnerable in this way (*Wisdom Ways*, 2).

13. The discussion of social justice in biblical studies reflects various theories and

a preliminary examination of the themes/topics that concern social justice throughout the Jewish Christian corpus and a review of relevant commentaries and literature:

> Social justice in the Jewish Christian texts of the New Testament concerns the provision by the individual believer and the church community of appropriate care for those suffering from need and oppression within sphere of the community's responsibility and influence.

The biblical material determined the content and the boundaries of this definition as far as possible, as opposed to simply starting with a presupposed contemporary definition.[14] Nevertheless, we may position this hopefully biblical definition among contemporary dimensions in the discussions of social justice, which include distributive, commutative, and legal aspects.

Our task is to examine the epistolary part of the Jewish Christian corpus and identify or define:

- What constitutes oppression and need?

- What is appropriate care?

- For whom was the church responsible?

- What was their circle of influence?

We then need to address what our own responsibility and circle of influence is today and how this impacts what we should do.

The definitions and identifications of oppression and need in Hebrews and the General Epistles are guided by the practices and conditions that are condemned in the Old Testament. The theme of oppression is well-developed in the Hebrew Bible/Septuagint and a number of terms and associations are used to describe a range of unjust actions and their effects. The Old Testament condemns degradation, plunder, attack, exploitation, deadly force, crushing domination, and deceit, while it sympathizes with the victim's experiences of harassment, depression, and the longing for justice.[15] People from all ranks of society are vulnerable to oppression given

---

often assumes a current definition through which the text is read. Our focus here is on the description of social justice's underlying theory/theology, and its practice in the first century. The definition and argument of this chapter is derived from the corpus itself, but is clearly informed by or influenced by current approaches.

14. This is not to suggest that this definition was formed in a vacuum apart from the influence of contemporary views of social justice—that would be impossible.

15. The texts are in close dialogue with the Hebrew Bible, the LXX, and the oral

certain circumstances, but the Old Testament had a special concern for those who were consistently at risk: the stranger, the slave, the orphan, and the widow. Those in need were invariably the poor in the land. In addition to the Hebrew Scriptures, the Apocrypha, other literature of Second Temple Judaism, and the oral tradition of the Gospels, Jewish Christianity shared in the experiences of the foundation of the church and its apostolic witness and leadership (Acts 1–12).[16] The radical response of the Jerusalem church to the economic needs of its members in Acts is part of the broader story that frames the Jewish Christian corpus.

Further insight into justice issues is gained through sociological criticism. This places the focus on social interaction, which, among other things, studies race, gender, transactions, relationships, and power in the context of ongoing cultural practices, language, and symbols.[17] Consequently, sociological criticism offers specific help in understanding the relationship between text and context in areas that concern social justice: it probes "the intended and/or actual effect of the document upon the social condition, constitution, and interests of both author(s) and recipients within their larger social and historical contexts."[18] In addition, we may be informed by current social patterns of power and sources of oppression that correspond to certain features in the text. For example, what may be described in the text as the seduction or influence of believers by church authorities in regards to πορνεία (sexual immorality) or μοιχαλίς (adultery) may be related to present-day sexual abuse (including sexual harassment). People who are mastered, entangled, and overcome by depravity in the biblical text may be comparable to those who are vulnerable to addiction or have addictive personalities.[19]

---

traditions of the gospel if not the Gospels themselves. See Tamez, *Bible of the Oppressed*, 8–17, for a fuller description of the vocabulary of oppression.

16. See Porter and Westfall, "Cord of Three Strands," 112–19, and Westfall, "Hebrew Mission," for a general description of Jewish Christianity in Acts and Hebrews, the General Epistles, and Revelation.

17. See Mulholland, "Sociological Criticism." See also Elliott's description of the presuppositions of "sociological exegesis" in *Home for the Homeless*, 8–13.

18. Ibid., 8–9.

19. It may be noted that vulnerability to addiction is a human condition, but some are particularly vulnerable because of certain traits, including family patterns and past experiences such as alcoholism or drug use—such things can characterize both disadvantaged and affluent people groups.

We can also receive insight from people groups that share experiences similar to those found in the Bible and have reflected on them. This includes the modern Jewish experience and its interpretation of its recent history, as well as other individuals and populations/people groups whose experiences parallel those of the Jewish Christian population of the early church. We need to hear the voices of the poor, the homeless, refugees, immigrants, victims of racism, the politically oppressed, and the socially marginalized. We need to be in conversation with global perspectives such as Liberation Theology,[20] Post-colonial Criticism,[21] as well as Feminist/Womanist Criticism.[22] These conversations reflect on the experiences of the poor, the oppressed, and the marginalized, and direct us to consider alternative readings of the Scripture within a context that is closer in certain respects to first-century Judaism than is the Western world. Therefore, while this chapter does not exhaustively engage the voices crying from the margins, it attempts to engage critically with some conversation partners that bring a significantly different social, psychological, and economic perspective to the text. Most biblical studies literature on social justice is written by Catholic theologians who are critically reflecting on the biblical interpretations and arguments of Liberation Theology in the last half of the twentieth century. It is time—rather it is overdue!—for other biblical scholars to join the conversation and responsibly engage their own traditions with this subject.

Finally, the question concerning "circles of influence" is a specific attempt to understand how differences between the context of first-century Jewish Christianity and that of the Western world interact when seeking to apply the models and commands of biblical texts. The first-century Jewish Christian communities practiced forms of social justice even though they were in deep poverty and powerless in their society—they were the victims. Christians and churches in the Western world are comparatively wealthy in terms of material possessions, and often have a measure of social and political influence as well. The final question will explore whether adjustments

20. For an overview of Liberation Theology, see Tombs, "Liberation Theological Interpretation."

21. For Post-Colonial biblical interpretation, see Donaldson, *Postcolonialism and Scriptural Reading*; Segovia, *Decolonizing Biblical Studies*; Sugirtharajah, *Postcolonial Criticism and Biblical Interpretation*.

22. For an overview of Feminist interpretation, see Adams, "Feminist Interpretation." Womanist Theology departs from feminism because it incorporates the perspectives and experiences of women of color. See Mitchem, *Introducing Womanist Theology*.

in our appreciation of the scope of social justice need to be made when the circle of influence changes.

WHAT CONSTITUTES OPPRESSION AND NEED?

The categories of oppression and need in Hebrews and the General Epistles are similar to descriptions in the Old Testament. However, in the Jewish Christian corpus, poverty, victimization, and suffering appear to be the typical condition of believers. Similarly, the communities identify with the difficult experiences of the refugee or resident alien. The experiences of the suffering community fuel the practice of social justice in spite of the fact that there is a lack of resources.

Oppressed groups are particularly in view in the epistles of James and 1 John. They include the generic poor and helpless in society, particularly women.[23] The discussion of the care for orphans and widows in their difficulties as the primary expression of true religion in Jas 1:27 reflects a traditional theme in law codes and inscriptions in the ancient Near East as well the Old Testament.[24] James is particularly concerned with the oppression of day laborers who generally had a subsistence-level existence (Jas 5:4). The oppression of slaves is a concern in 1 Pet 2:18–20.

The plight of victims is addressed in some detail—members of the Christian community or the community as a whole are depicted in the text as victimized, but also the corpus addresses perpetrators of injustice present within the Jewish Christian communities. James particularly speaks of how the church can be guilty of dishonoring the poor (Jas 2:6), but he focuses more on how the poor are victims of the rich and powerful. He addresses hoarding and self-indulgence at the expense of the poor (Jas 5:3, 5), slander (Jas 2:7), abuse of powers such as dragging the poor into court (Jas 2:6c), exploitation (Jas 2:6b), withholding workers' salaries (Jas 5:4),[25] and the condemnation and murder of the innocent (Jas 5:6).[26] The author

23. Widows are mentioned specifically (Jas 1:27), but also the fact that "a brother or a sister (ἤ ἀδελφή)" without daily necessities is given as an example of poverty in Jas 2:15 most likely reflects the greater tendency of women to be below the poverty line. The generic experience of humanity can be represented by the masculine alone (ἀνήρ, ἄνθρωπος, or ἀδελφός) and the occurrence of the feminine is marked (see Tamez, *Scandalous Message*, 20).

24. For the theme of orphans and widows, see Nardoni, *Rise Up, O Judge*, 1–41.

25. The prompt payment of day workers was a particular concern in the Old Testament (Deut 24:14–15; Lev 19:13).

26. Contra Tamez, the just are not necessarily the workers as she assumes (Tamez,

of Hebrews similarly refers to how the recipients' community had suffered economic and social abuse in the past. The recipients themselves shared in the plight of the poor: they experienced great conflict, and suffered insults, persecution, imprisonment, and the seizure of property (Heb 10:32–34). While James is clearly focusing on economic victimization, 1 Peter addresses aspects of social victimization including the disadvantaged social roles of slaves and women, which placed them at risk for insults, physical abuse, and living in a constant state of fear and anxiety (1 Pet 2:18–3:6). First Peter also deals with the abuse and rejection of the Christian community by members of the dominant culture, such as slander and insults (1 Pet 2:23; 3:9–11; 4:14), and various forms of attack (fiery ordeals) that resulted in suffering that was probably characteristic of the Jewish Christian communities (1:6–7; 2:20–21; 4:12–17; 5:8–9).

On the other hand, when Jude and 2 Peter are read together, the concerns of false teachings and unscrupulous ethical practices in Jude lead to 2 Peter's concern for the victims of the perpetrators of these kinds of abuses within the Jewish Christian communities. That is, 2 Peter addresses the topic of spiritual abuse by church leadership or charismatic leaders who take advantage of others. In 2 Peter this can take the form of exploitation (2 Pet 2:3), seduction of the unstable (vulnerable) (2:14), sexual abuse (2:13–14),[27] greed (2:14–15), and the enticement of people with past addictions into alternative habits of depravity (2:18–22).[28] In Jude and 2 Peter, false teaching is not defined so much as the perpetration of non-orthodox propositional heresy or confession, but rather in terms of unethical practice.

The readers themselves are often characterized as needy transients, disenfranchised aliens, or victims of forced migration.[29] This corresponds

---

Scandalous Message, 16–17).

27. The false teachers in 2 Pet 2:14 "have eyes full of adultery." This is "a vivid expression which means that their eyes are always looking for a woman with whom to commit adultery" (Bauckham, *Jude, 2 Peter*, 266). This would be considered sexual harassment at the very least, and when successful in its goal, it would be abuse.

28. The relationship of 2 Pet 2:18–22 to addictive personalities is fairly transparent.

29. Cf. Jas 1:1; 1 Pet 1:1; Heb 11:13 (by relevance to the readers). Tamez argues that "the twelve tribes dispersed abroad" in Jas 1:1 is "a sociological expression and characterizes the position of Christians in Greco-Roman society. These were displaced persons who were currently aliens or were permanently or temporarily residing in Asia Minor. They suffered political, legal, social and religious restrictions." These persons were "deprived of the civil, social, and political rights of the cities or regions in which they lived" (*Scandalous Message*, 19). I would suggest that Tamez is anachronistic in suggesting that James is referring to all Christians. Rather, this is an apt description of Jewish Christians

to contemporary conditions of political and social marginalization and homelessness. First Peter and Hebrews are directly concerned with the social circumstances of their readers, and particularly refer to the resident alien, the sojourner, and the stranger (see Heb 11; 1 Pet 1:1, 17; 2:11).[30] These were roles that were particularly familiar to the Jews at various points in their history, including slavery in Egypt, the Exodus and wilderness experience, the Babylonian captivity, and the Diaspora in the Hellenistic period. As Elliott says, "Dislocation from home, dispossession of the land of promise, life under the conditions of political and religious estrangement were the trying experiences of Israel which shaped the language of religious despair and hope."[31] The Jewish Christians outside of Palestine experienced a compound problem of being Jewish resident aliens, setting them apart from the Gentile majority, as well as experiencing a degree of alienation or separation from the Jewish homeland and its culture. First Peter addresses "the issue of Christian alien residence within the structures of society."[32] It is notable that in 1 Pet 3:3 at least some of the recipients appear to have been Gentiles. However, Peter identifies the readers' experiences of rejection (1 Pet 2:1) and suffering (1 Pet 1:3, 6; 2:12, 18–25; 3:13–18; 4:1, 4, 12–19; 5:1, 7–10) as primary concerns that need to be addressed, and reflects on these concerns from the context of the experiences of Israel, the people of God.[33]

---

during the first century, possibly including those who were forced out of Jerusalem (διεσπάρησαν [Acts 8:1], vs. διασπορᾷ [Jas 1:1]) during the early persecution of the church (Acts 8:1–3).

30. Hebrews 11 provides models of faith that feature marginalization, homelessness, and the theme of death. Furthermore, the readers are compared to the wilderness generation, which suggests that these themes are relevant to the readers' circumstance, whether the recipients already lived in the Diaspora or were facing forced migration from Palestine or Samaria due to the First Jewish Revolt. This is discussed in Westfall and Dyer, "Scared to Death."

31. Elliott, *Home for the Homeless*, 29.

32. Ibid., 13, but he aptly summarizes Goppelt who argues that 1 Peter is the only New Testament document that systematically and thematically addresses the issue of suffering (Goppelt, *Petrusbrief*, 41).

33. I would suggest one of the defining features of the mission to the Hebrews is its orientation towards the Jewish experience in worldview and theology. Gentiles are included in the Hebrew mission, but they primarily relate to the Jewish worldview and community. In contrast, Paul contextualizes his gospel and communities to the Gentile culture, so his work is more intentionally a cross-cultural mission by nature.

WHAT IS APPROPRIATE CARE?

Our next task is to determine what the authors of the Jewish Christian corpus identified as appropriate care. Appropriate care involves a response to need and injustice not only in action, but also through theology and speaking/teaching.

First of all, a caring community is one of welcome and hospitality for the stranger (Heb 11:31; 13:2; Jas 2:25; 3 John 5–8; 1 Pet 4:9),[34] as well as visitation of orphans, widows, the sick, and prisoners (Heb 10:34; 13:3; Jas 1:27; 5:14). The Jewish theme of hospitality for the stranger is based on the history and literature of a people who participated in the plight of slaves, immigrants, refugees, and exiles.[35] In addition to receiving a stranger who arrives on the doorstep or in the town square, the church is to be proactive in visiting or seeking out orphans and widows who historically represent those who "were forsaken for various reasons and who lacked the capacity to sustain themselves in society."[36]

Second, the task of the church is the provision of life's necessities to those who have need.[37] James makes it clear that the church and individual believers should provide for the physical needs of poor believers (2:14–17),

---

34. The references to hospitality in Hebrews and James specifically reference the Old Testament.

35. See, for example, Carroll, *Christians at the Border*, 71–89, who discusses Old Testament ethical teachings from the perspective of Hispanic immigration.

36. Nardoni, *Rise Up, O Judge*, 18.

37. Contra Grassi, who begins his discussion of social justice in the New Testament from the assumption that it entails "the equal and just distribution of economic, social, and cultural resources to all people without discrimination of any kind" (*Informing the Future*, 1). Apart from the model in Acts 2:44, where believers explicitly have everything in common, the New Testament practice of meeting needs should be distinguished from a call to have all things in common. Similarly, contra Tamez who states that the indictment of the rich in James means that the rich "must cease being rich, for the rich for James are those who oppress, who exploit and who blaspheme the name of the Lord" (*Scandalous Message*, 39). James may imply that the rich are in danger (Jas 1:10–11), which is comparable to Jesus' saying about the difficulty of a camel going through the eye of a needle (Matt 19:24//Mark 10:25//Luke 18:25). However, the oppression, exploitation, and blasphemy that James confronts are actual behaviors that a rich person can avoid, and must be distinguished from having possessions alone. Although Jesus asks the rich young ruler to sell all his possessions and distribute the money to the poor in order to be "perfect" (Matt 19:21//Mark 10:21//Luke 18:22), James does not give this as an explicit command to the church. However, it stands as a model in Jesus' teaching with which the readers would undoubtedly be familiar.

with particular concern for orphans and widows.[38] In Jas 2:15–16, James summarizes part of Christian responsibility as providing "what is necessary for life" (τὰ ἐπιτήδεια τοῦ σώματος), which would include clothing, food, and shelter. In 1 John, this practical care is the appropriate expression of loving each other. It is what it really means to lay down our lives for one another: "How does God's love abide in anyone who has the world's goods and sees a brother or sister in need and yet refuses help?" (1 John 3:17). However, the culturally embedded religious practice of caring for the poor, the needy, and the strangers within the Jewish Christian community is understood simply by the expression of "doing good" or "sharing." This is something the Western church and the Western tradition of biblical interpretation sometimes fails to recognize as social justice, due to the radically different environments of Israel and the ancient Near East (Heb 10:24; 13:16).[39] Within the history of Israel and the early Jewish Christian communities, the concept of "sharing" could be radical, and extended beyond the Jewish or faith community. In addition, "doing good" can involve practical care such as building accessible paths for the disabled, both literally and figuratively (Heb 12:12).[40]

Third, social justice is intentionally and consistently treating and speaking of the poor, the disadvantaged, and the vulnerable as equal heirs together with Christ. This is based on the very principle that caused Paul to revolutionize Christianity and accept the Gentiles as equal heirs to the Jews. Paul's application of this principle shatters the entitlement of his fellow Jews in terms of their privileges as the people of God. He extends the same equalization to gender and socio-economic classes (Gal 2:28). In

38. Anyone who wants to be religious must take care of (ἐπισκέπτεσθαι) orphans and widows when they are experiencing hardship. This concept was also appropriately placed under the category of visitation (see above).

39. The hortatory subjunctive command "to do good and to share with others, for with such sacrifices God is pleased" in Heb 13:16 is the paraenetic climax of Hebrews (Westfall, *Discourse Analysis of Hebrews*, 285–86). As such, it combines the theme of drawing near to God as priests (stimulating each other to love and good works) so that sharing and doing good for those in need in the community are sacrifices offered as the believer's priestly service. It is interesting to note that the TNIV study notes on Heb 13:16 cross-reference Phil 4:18, which transforms the sacrifice of "doing good and sharing with others" into stewardship, which is the financial support of church leadership (TNIV, 2071).

40. Granted that Heb 12:12 is a metaphor in the context of a metaphor about running a race, but the metaphors used in such illustrations have a heuristic impact, particularly given the concern for the disabled in the Old Testament: "Do not curse the deaf or put a stumbling block in front of the blind" (Lev 19:14).

Jewish Christianity Peter similarly applies this principle specifically to the slaves and to how husbands treat their wives (as fellow-heirs of the grace of life, ὡς καὶ συγκληρονόμοις χάριτος ζωῆς, 1 Pet 3:7).

Fourth, social justice speaks out prophetically and theologically against practices and teaching that produce injustice. James is notable in the way that he combats the exploitation of the poor by the rich. He speaks against and exposes abuse and pronounces prophetic judgment on the rich. He accuses the rich of oppression, dragging the poor believers into court, and blaspheming the name of Christ. James and 1 John carry forward the theme from the Old Testament that God created humans in his own image, which means that bad treatment of the poor or other believers dishonors God (Jas 3:9–10; 1 John 4:20).[41] James criticizes the arrogance behind business speculation without considering God (Jas 4:13–16). Finally, he pronounces judgment on the rich for living in luxury and self-indulgence while hoarding goods, withholding wages, and committing murder (Jas 5:1–6). While James's language sometimes seems to implicate all the rich in such unjust behavior, it is apparent that a rich believer would be validated if he or she (1) gloried in or embraced his or her ultimate humiliation and lack of status in the church community; and (2) avoided the abuses, and practiced pure and undefiled religion by caring for the poor.[42] In other words, unjust behavior and oppression undeniably collocate with the possession of wealth but are not essential properties of wealth. Nevertheless, Hebrews warns against the love of money and exhorts the community to be content with what they have, motivated by God's presence and ability to help (Heb 13:3–6).

Fifth, within populations that are characterized by poverty and victimization, appropriate care includes forms of intentional and proactive community care that are both practical and theological. The letter of James focuses on the practice of faith or "the living out of religious or philosophical beliefs" in the context of severe poverty and oppression.[43] James relativ-

41. See Gen 1:26–28; Prov 17:5: "Those who mock the poor insult their maker."

42. Contra Tamez, who asserts that the condition for the salvation of the rich is that "they must cease being rich, for the rich for James are those who oppress, who exploit, and who blaspheme the name of the Lord" (*Scandalous Message*, 39). The possession of wealth needs to be differentiated from the unjust practices that are condemned, though the collocation of wealth, power, and abuse is evident. Due to the mere possession of extensive financial resources, the rich will always be at risk of placing wealth before discipleship, as Jesus indicated (Matt 19:24//Mark 10:25//Luke 18:25).

43. Or praxis (ibid., 167). Tamez claims "the content of the letter is concentrated on

izes the status and influence of the rich in the church. They are reduced to humiliation because the wealth that their identity is based on is transitory (Jas 1:10–11).[44] They are not to receive preferential treatment such as special seating in the church—any sense of value that is based on wealth or appearance and entitlement is to be eradicated in the church community (Jas 2:1–4). James reinforces the fact that God opposes the proud but shows favor to the humble and oppressed (Jas 4:6//Prov 3:34). This deconstructs the assumptions and practice of the basic social and political structure of the Roman Empire within the Christian community. The culture's patronage system is stripped of its power, and the associations of honor and shame are flipped.

James illustrates the fact that the elimination of poverty is a fundamental paradigm for the goal of God's salvation in the early church. God acts to reverse the circumstances of the poor, the powerless, the lost, and the helpless. Poverty, helplessness, and oppression are not to be understood as mere metaphors in magnificent statements of this reversal, such as the Magnificat (Luke 1:46–55), the parable of the lost sheep (Matt 18:10–14// Luke 15:4–7), or James's great reversal of the rich and poor (Jas 1:9–11). James emphatically affirms the dignity of the poor when he says that poor believers have a high position in which they can take pride, in contrast to the humiliation of the rich (Jas 1:9). He blasts believers for dishonoring the poor by showing preferential treatment to the rich (2:1–11). Throughout the epistle, James shows solidarity with the poor and indicates that God identifies with the poor.

According to James, the condition of poverty can be transformational. The trials and temptations of the poor and oppressed play a primary role in a process that is meant to bring the believers to a complete maturity

---

this angle" (ibid., 11). She also claims that the focus on praxis has resulted in the neglect or dismissal of the letter in scholarship "due to the privileged place given to abstract thought in our Western societies. The reasonableness of faith is valued more than the practice of faith; the latter is seen as separate from the former, or as a product of faith's reasonableness. That is, ethics, behavior, deeds are considered of secondary importance by our logocentric societies" (ibid., 4).

44. Tamez would have it that "according to James, there is no room for them in the church" (ibid., 21). However, this is a clear contradiction of James who suggests that the welcome of the rich should reflect the principle "You shall love your neighbor as yourself" (Jas 2:8). James does not reject the rich, but he rejects favoritism. This is contra Tamez, who asserts that James resists the addition of the rich to the Christian community, and prefers recruiting the poor: "James insists that the vocation of the church, its mission, is the poor who are rich in faith and the heirs of God's reign (2:5)" (ibid., 26).

in which they lack nothing (Jas 1:2–5). However, for this to happen, the poor believer must rejoice in their position and respond to their difficulties with endurance (1:1–4, 12; 5:7–11), wisdom (1:5–8; 3:13–18), prayer (1:5; 5:13–18), and submission to God (ch. 4).[45] This is why James is able to say, "Hasn't God chosen the poor to be rich in faith?" (2:5). In this scenario, the extreme deprivation of God's people will produce proportionate faith. James's theology projects purpose and hope into the lives of the desperate.

Sixth, 2 Peter demonstrates a theological responsibility for the narrative that frames the life and actions of the Christian community (2 Pet 1:16). This is in direct contrast with the fabricated stories of the false prophets who use their narrative to exploit the community financially: "In their greed, these teachers will exploit you with fabricated stories" (2:3).[46] One of the advances of post-modernism is the recognition of the power of narrative, which has opened up a greater appreciation of the theological importance and interpretation of biblical narrative. It used to be commonly assumed that truth was only propositional, but this notion has been overturned and we understand that even the propositions in Scripture are understood in the context of the narrative in which they are spoken and/ or written. Our lives and our identities are framed by the stories that we tell, whether they be biblical stories, historical/biographical stories about our families, communities, churches, and nations or autobiographical stories of our own experiences. These stories have the ability to build faith and promote love, but they also have the power to dishonor and exploit others. Christians have traditionally paid much more attention to the orthodox propositions that we share than we have to the narrative. While telling stories includes "telling the truth," it can entail consciously defining, framing, and interpreting our lives through the eyes of faith, hope, and love, which encompass biblical ethics. We need to take responsibility for the social structures of isolation, individualization (hoarding), entitlement,

---

45. Again according to liberation theologian Tamez, James "asks of these Christians a praxis in which they show a militant patience, a consistency between words, belief, and deeds, a prayer with power, an effective wisdom and an unconditional sincere love among the members of the community" (ibid., 11). It is agreed that the biblical patience of the believer in response to suffering is proactive and transformative. However, there should be some hesitancy to embrace a "militant" nature if it indicates a warlike opposition, habitual activism, and rejection of the rich and the powerful.

46. Bauckham states, "The meaning is that the false teachers make a good financial profit out of their followers, who are taken in by their teaching and contribute to their support" (*Jude, 2 Peter*, 243).

and oppression that are built into the narratives that reflect our race, class, gender, social status, and national identity.

For Whom Was the Church Responsible?

The term "responsibility of the church" refers to the appropriate target(s) of social justice. When we consider the issue of the responsibility of the Jewish Christian church in the first century, we need to pay attention to the origin of the Jerusalem church and its role in the spread of Christianity, including the mission to the Gentiles. When Paul was writing his letters, the Jewish Christian churches in Judea were models of suffering communities due to persecution, economic stress, and drought/famine (Acts 11:29; 24:17; Rom 15:26; 1 Cor 16:1–4; 2 Cor 8:1–4; Gal 2:10; 1 Thess 2:14). At face value, the authors of the general epistles place themselves within the suffering Jewish Christian churches and communities, which is consistent with their content that deals with social justice issues of suffering, poverty, and exploitation. During the time in which at least part of the New Testament was written, "the disciples" had a close relationship to the church in Jerusalem, and would have been influenced by its practices of social justice.

According to Acts 2:44–47, the needs of all the believers were a concern for the early Jerusalem community. These needs were met by members selling property and possessions. According to Luke, "None of them would say, 'This is mine!' about any of their possessions, but held everything in common" (Acts 4:32). Consequently, "there were no needy persons among them." Those who owned properties or houses would sell them, bring the proceeds from the sales, and place them under the care and authority of the apostles. Then the proceeds were distributed to anyone who was in need" (Acts 4:34–35).[47] Luke indicates that the radical provision for needy believers contributed to the rapid growth of the early church (Acts 2:47).

47. Luke clarifies that yielding private ownership of land and houses was voluntary, as in the case of Barnabas (Acts 4:36–37). In his case, he sold "a field," not necessarily an entire inheritance or a home. The case of Ananias and Sapphira (5:1–11) similarly indicates that private ownership of property/land and money from the sale of property was at the individual believer's discretion (cf. 5:4: "wasn't the money yours to do with whatever you wanted?"). Therefore, the early model of practicing social justice was very radical in voluntarily having the necessities of life in common, but it was not communism where all ownership was erased, or where the church held the land in common. Barrett qualifies that Luke "never suggests, or hints, that church members ought at all times to dispose of their capital assets, and it is clear from the rest of the book that they did not do so" (Barrett, *Acts*, 52). As Nardoni says, the Law "protects the right of the Israelite family to have a home, a parcel of land, and the means to work it" (Nardoni, *Rise Up, O Judge*, 79). In an

At the time that Saul/Paul began his ministry with the Gentile revival in Antioch, the prophet Agabus predicted that a severe famine would spread over the entire Roman world, which happened during the reign of Claudius (41–54 CE). The response of churches in general was to provide aid only to Judea, which they sent through Barnabas and Saul/Paul (Acts 11:27–30). Among other things, this probably indicates that the churches in Judea had no economic cushion to survive a severe famine.[48] At the Jerusalem Council,[49] Paul's policy with the Gentiles was confirmed, and he was acknowledged as the apostle to the Gentiles, with the addendum that he should "continue to remember the poor" (Gal 2:6–10). According to Paul's story, his concern for "the poor" is expressed by his aiding the impoverished Jewish Christian churches in Judea.[50] Possibly the apostles were afraid that Paul would identify with the wealthier Gentile churches and disassociate himself from the concerns and needs of the Jewish Christian churches. Paul was stung or irritated by the addendum, saying that this was "the very thing that I had been eager to do all along" (Gal 2:10). Much of Paul's later work in the third missionary journey involved making a collection for the poor in Jerusalem (1 Cor 16:1–4; 2 Cor 8:1–4; Rom 15:26).[51] He indicated that the Gentile churches owed help to the Jews on the basis

---

agrarian economy, land is the means of ensuring survival, and as James points out, the day laborer is perpetually at risk—this is a condition that the Law attempted to eliminate.

48. Several severe famines hit during Claudius's reign (Suetonius, *Claudius* 18.2; Tacitus, *Ann.* 12.43; Dio Cassius, *Hist. rom.* 40.11). Josephus refers to a famine in Judea (Josephus, *Ant.* 3.15.3; 20.2.5; 20.5.2), and an Asia Minor inscription from this time refers to a worldwide famine (*CIG* 3973.5–6). This is contra Barrett, who suggests that "If the famine was in fact universal no church would have been in a position to send help to any other; it seems best therefore to suppose that in v. 28 . . . Luke has heightened the description of the famine by including the words ἐφ᾽ ὅλην τὴν οἰκουμένην and that originally the Jerusalem prophets (including Agabus, who in 21:20 also comes from Judaea) foretold a famine in Jerusalem, or Judea" (*Acts*, 561).

49. Longenecker (*Galatians*, 53) points out that many have understood the meeting to refer to either the Jerusalem Council or the famine visit (e.g., Zahn, *Galater*, 98; Oepke, *Galater*, 48).

50. "The poor" (τῶν πτωχῶν) refers to the impoverished and the lower classes, but also to a particular kind of Jewish piety and humility as in the Qumran Community (1QH5.1, 21; 18.14; 1QM 14.7; 1QpHab 12.3, 6, 10), so that some have argued that it is a title for the Jerusalem church (e.g., Geyser, "Earliest Name"). However, since the abysmal economic situation in Palestine (cf. James) contributed to the Jewish revolt, there is no reason to suppose that there was not true economic hardship.

51. Ironically, Paul was arrested during the trip in which he delivered the generous gift from the Gentile churches (Acts 21:17–25).

of reciprocity: since the Jews shared spiritual blessings with the Gentiles, the Gentiles should share material blessings with the Jews (Rom 15:27).[52] Therefore, sharing material blessings crossed not only economic lines, but racial, cultural, social, and administrative lines—because the Gentile mission headed by Paul gave support to the Jewish mission headed by Peter. This is comparable to support not only between mission organizations, but across denominational lines and national lines. While Paul appealed to reciprocity as a reason for sharing material blessings in writing to the Romans, the apostle's concern for "the poor" is not be limited to cases of obligation and reciprocity. Rather his concern is defined by need, as is the case in the accounts of sharing in the Jerusalem church.

In James and 1 John, there is a particular focus on the care of brothers and sisters through the use of familial terms for members of the church. In Jas 2:15–17, James mentions the necessity of meeting a fellow believer's urgent physical needs instead of merely wishing them well with words alone. In 1 John there are a number of statements about social justice between members of the community. As in James, love needs to be expressed with words and actions (1 John 4:18). One of the ways that we know that someone is born of God is if they love their brother and sister (3:10). We should love one another because God loved us (4:12). Anyone who hates a brother or sister is a murderer and a liar (3:15; 4:19). If we do not love a believer whom we have seen, we do not love God whom we have not seen (4:20). However, the strongest statements are that we should lay down our lives for one another, and if anyone has material possessions and does not have pity on a brother or sister who is in need, the love of God cannot be in them (4:16–17). Therefore, Jesus' actions on our behalf provide the model for how we should treat each other.

Consequently, the origins of the Jewish Christian church in Jerusalem, Paul's collections for the church in Jerusalem and Judea, and the Jewish Christian texts indicate local and national patterns of social justice that had

---

52. As Dyer observes, acts of charity within the Greco-Roman culture were based on reciprocity ("Good News to the Poor," 119). A gift entailed an obligation in a patron–client relationship for which the patron should receive a benefit or repayment, "the patron providing material gifts or opportunities for advancement, the client contributing to the patron's reputation and power" (DeSilva, *Honor, Patronage*, 99). Paul appeals to the Roman value system in order to motivate the Romans (Rom 15:26–29). However, it should not be assumed that Paul's practice of social justice in human relationships was governed by the principle of reciprocity—he repeatedly indicated otherwise. See, for example, his explicit rejection and subversion of reciprocity in his relationship with the Corinthians in 2 Cor 11:7–9.

pragmatic limitations. The first pragmatic limitation in these passages is that needy Jewish Christian believers were the primary focus of care, rather than the entire city of Jerusalem or the region of Judea. The second pragmatic limitation is that while believers are encouraged to be generous, and giving "beyond what they are able" is commended (2 Cor 8:3), providing the basic necessities of life is in view rather than complete equality of possessions—the possession of private property is not eliminated, and the goal is not complete economic equality. The biblical practice of social justice might legitimately place a ceiling on one's standard of living, but it does not necessarily eliminate property, inheritance, or other bases of income in an agrarian society. On the other hand, the oral traditions and Synoptic Gospels indicate that specific calls to ministry, such as following the itinerant rabbi Jesus, may entail giving everything away to the poor (Matt 19:21// Mark 10:21; Luke 18:22). Regardless, the ideal goal was the elimination of need among believers, rather than the elimination of personal possessions.

In addition, the emphasis on hospitality for the stranger (Heb 11:31; 13:2; Jas 2:25; 3 John 5–8) by definition extends the responsibility beyond the household of faith. The visitation and care of orphans and widows has no specific limitation (Jas 1:27 does not specify only Christian widows and orphans). The extension of care for prisoners and the mistreated was never specifically limited to believers either (Heb 10:34; 13:3). The application of "love your neighbor as yourself" (Jas 2:8//Lev 19:18) would extend beyond the boundaries of the Christian community as it also went beyond the boundaries of race, religion, or ethnicity in the parable of the Good Samaritan (Luke 10:27–37).

In conclusion, within the first-century church, the Jewish Christian community could be taken as synonymous with the "the poor," and yet we find this community most acutely engaged with the issues of poverty and oppression and the practice of social justice. They were the most at risk and the most powerless in the broader church and the Greco-Roman society in their ability to confront overwhelming problems, yet they took responsibility to do what they were able, and even beyond what they were able. The early Jewish Christian community took responsibility for ensuring social justice where they encountered injustice. The most impoverished churches were the most likely to encounter needy people, and furthermore needy people were attracted to the early Jewish Christian community, in part because they cared for each other radically. This was a culture in which the poor and oppressed were understood, welcomed, encouraged, and helped.

The apostle James, the brother of Jesus, was known in Jerusalem as James the Just, which aptly fits the content of the book of James. Legend has it that he was martyred by being thrown down from the walls of the temple.[53] Why was he killed? His sense of justice led him to engage in risky behavior, and he acted and spoke out in a volatile situation. The endurance of suffering and oppression by the Jewish Christian communities in Judea was held up as a model, and they were a primary focus of the concern of all "the disciples." The Pauline churches did not leave the Jerusalem church alone to solve their own problems—Paul urged the Gentile churches to share their material wealth across the boundaries of class, race, and economy.

What Was the Circle of Influence?

The issue of the circle of influence is probably the most central feature of the practice of social justice that we may explore. It is necessary to explain continuities and discontinuities between the practice of social justice in the New Testament, in the Old Testament, and by the church in the Western world. The term "circle of influence" indicates the pragmatic capability and scope that an individual or community possesses to address the issues of the oppressed and the needy.

Most of the Old Testament narratives, the Law, and many of the prophets addressed Israel when it was a sovereign nation that was responsible for executing justice within its boundaries.[54] In contrast, as a religious minority the Jewish Christian population had little power to change policies outside of the confines of the faith community, and had few resources to share other than leadership and their spiritual blessings (Rom 15:27). Within Palestine they experienced oppression from their own people in an occupied country that suffered racism and oppression from the Roman military and political authorities. In the Diaspora, they were resident aliens and strangers who also experienced growing tension with their Jewish compatriots. They represent populations who have little ability to effect any systemic change in society. Yet, the Jewish Christian corpus shows them addressing acute first-hand experiences of poverty and oppression to the

53. James was not killed by his fall from the temple, and was subsequently stoned and beaten with a club (Eusebius, *Hist. eccl.* 2.23.4–20). According to Josephus's less elaborate account, James was killed by stoning at the behest of Ananus the high priest. However, James was highly respected, and influential, and law-abiding Jerusalem Jews petitioned to have Ananus replaced (Josephus, *Ant.* 20.200–203).

54. 2 Chron 36:21 indicates that the Babylonian captivity took place because Israel neglected the Sabbath year.

best of their ability.[55] Peter illustrated both the poverty and the generosity of the Jewish Christian community when he said to the beggar who had been crippled since birth, "I don't have any money, but I will give you what I do have" (Acts 3:6). However, the book of James was dangerously political in the volatile situation of first-century Judaism, particularly if its origin was Palestine. Therefore, one may say that the Jewish Christian community sought to enact social justice beyond what could be reasonably expected.

In contrast with first-century Jewish Christianity, most who read this chapter will have comparatively vast social, economic, and political privileges. We have the advantages of education, we possess a high standard of living, and we have a vote as well as other political privileges, influence, and powers. It is essential that we inventory our capacity and the scope of our circle of influence as individuals, as members of churches, and as members of the larger Christian community. Any privileges, resources, or the possession of power carry commensurate responsibility.[56] Technology raises some interesting issues for our responsibility within our circle of influence—through the media, the internet, and social media we encounter problems and needs to a far greater degree. In addition, we participate in global economic patterns. By definition, the North American church has been involved in globalization from the beginning through colonization and world missions. However, we are now participating in a global community to a greater extent and in a different way. To quote Sam Chaise, the director of Canadian Baptist Ministries, "We are already global consumers. We are already global citizens. The question is whether we will be global followers of Jesus."[57] Our participation involves issues of social justice in terms of patterns and opportunities.

CONCLUSION

We as Christians are called to imitate God in his care for the poor, oppressed, and needy. The terms "oppressed" and "needy" cover the range of

55. Their position corresponds roughly to inner-city churches in the West who are welcoming to the poor in terms of their mission and culture, as well as churches in poor communities and countries in the majority world.

56. "With great power comes great responsibility." Although the writers of the script for "Spiderman" have popularized and been credited with this well-known proverb, it can be traced back to Churchill and ultimately Voltaire (cf. Beuchot and Miger, *Oeuvres de Voltaire*).

57. Sam Chaise, Partner presentation of Canadian Baptist Ministries, CBOQ Assembly 2012, Toronto, 1 June 2012.

the vulnerable and the victims. The care that is deemed appropriate for the needy involves meeting their physical needs as well as defending them and restoring their dignity through practical treatment and corrective theology. We are primarily responsible for other believers, at local and global levels. However, our generosity should not be limited to believers. The Jewish Christian community provides us with models for social justice even though they were poor and powerless. In contrast, we in the industrialized and commercialized West have possessions and social and political power, which we can use in our imitation of God. That would indicate a prophetic stance towards injustice in its various forms and taking righteous action in the areas in which we have any capacity that is relevant to the issues today. We should be committed to radical generosity that fully reflects and utilizes our resources.

BIBLIOGRAPHY

Adams, Sean. "Feminist Interpretation." In *Dictionary of Biblical Criticism and Interpretation*, edited by Stanley E. Porter, 107–8. London: Routledge, 2007.

Attridge, Harold W. *The Epistle to the Hebrews*. Hermeneia. Philadelphia: Fortress, 1989.

Barrett, C. K. *Acts 1–14*. ICC. London: T. & T. Clark, 1994.

Bauckham, Richard. *The Jewish World around the New Testament*. Grand Rapids: Baker Academic, 2008.

———. *Jude, 2 Peter*. WBC 50. Waco, TX: Word, 1983.

Beuchot, A. J. Q., and P.-A.-M. Miger, eds. *Oeuvres de Voltaire*. Vol. 48. Paris: Lefèvre, 1832.

Boccaccini, G. *Middle Judaism: Jewish Thought 300 B.C.E. to 200 C.E.* Minneapolis: Fortress, 1991.

Campbell, Tom. *Justice*. 3rd ed. London: Palgrave MacMillan, 2010.

Carroll R., M. Daniel. *Christians at the Border: Immigration, the Church, and the Bible*. Grand Rapids: Baker Academic, 2008.

DeSilva, D. A. *Honor, Patronage, Kinship and Purity: Unlocking New Testament Culture*. Downers Grove, IL: InterVarsity, 2006.

Donaldson, Laura, ed. *Postcolonialism and Scriptural Reading*. Semeia 75. Atlanta: Scholars, 1996.

Dyer, Bryan R. "Good News to the Poor: Social Upheaval, Strong Warnings, and Sincere Giving in Luke–Acts." In *The Bible and Social Justice: Old Testament and New Testament Foundations for the Church's Urgent Call*, edited by Cynthia Long Westfall and Bryan R. Dyer, 102–24. Eugene, OR: Pickwick, 2016.

Elliott, John H. *A Home for the Homeless: A Sociological Exegesis of 1 Peter, Its Situation and Strategy*. Philadelphia: Fortress, 1981.

Geyser, A. S. "The Earliest Name of the Earliest Church." In *De fructu oris sui*, edited by F. S. A. van Selms et al., 58–66. Leiden: Brill, 1971.

Goppelt, Leonhard. *Der erste Petrusbrief*. Meyer K. Göttingen: Vandenhoeck & Ruprecht, 1978.

Grassi, Joseph A. *Informing the Future: Social Justice in the New Testament*. New York: Paulist, 2003.

Jackson-McCabe, Matt. "Introduction." In *Jewish Christianity Reconsidered: Rethinking Ancient Groups and Texts*, edited by Matt Jackson-McCabe, 1–6. Minneapolis: Fortress, 2007.

Longenecker, Richard N. *Galatians*. WBC. Waco, TX: Word, 1990.

Mitchem, Stephany Y. *Introducing Womanist Theology*. Maryknoll, NY: Orbis, 2002.

Moxnes, Halvor. *Economy of the Kingdom: Social Conflict and Economic Relations in Luke's Gospel*. Minneapolis: Fortress, 1988.

Mulholland, M. Robert, Jr. "Sociological Criticism." In *Interpreting the New Testament: Essays on Methods and Issues*, edited by David Aland Black and David S. Dockery, 170–86. Nashville, TN: Broadman & Holman, 2001.

Nardoni, Enrique. *Rise Up, O Judge: A Study of Justice in the Biblical World*. Translated by Seán Charles Martin. Peabody, MA: Hendrickson, 2004.

Neusner, J., W. S. Green, and E. Frerichs. *Judaisms and Their Messiahs at the Turn of the Christian Era*. Cambridge: Cambridge University Press, 1987.

Oakman, Douglas E. *Jesus and the Economic Questions of His Day*. Lewiston: Edwin Mellen, 1986.

Oepke, A. *Der Brief des Paulus an die Galater*. 3rd ed. THKNT. Berlin: Evangelische Verlagsanstalt, 1973.

Porter, Stanley E., and Cynthia Long Westfall. "A Cord of Three Strands: Mission in Acts." In *Christian Mission: Old Testament Foundations and New Testament Developments*, edited by Stanley E. Porter and Cynthia Long Westfall, 108–34. Eugene, OR: Pickwick, 2010.

Sanders, Jack T. *Schismatics, Sectarians, Dissidents, Deviants: The First One Hundred Years of Jewish–Christian Relations*. Valley Forge: Trinity, 1993.

Schüssler Fiorenza, Elizabeth. *Wisdom Ways: Introducing Feminist Biblical Interpretation*. Maryknoll, NY: Orbis, 2001.

Segovia, Fernando. *Decolonizing Biblical Studies: A View from the Margins*. Maryknoll, NY: Orbis, 2000.

Skarsaune, Oskar. *In the Shadow of the Temple: Jewish Influences on Early Christianity*. Downers Grove, IL: InterVarsity, 2002.

———. "Jewish Believers in Jesus in Antiquity—Problems of Definition, Method, and Sources." In *Jewish Believers in Jesus: The Early Centuries*, edited by Oskar Skarsaune and Reidar Hvalvik, 3–21. Peabody, MA: Hendrickson, 2007.

Sugirtharajah, Rasiah. *Postcolonial Criticism and Biblical Interpretation*. Oxford: Oxford University Press, 2002.

Tamez, Elsa. *Bible of the Oppressed*. Translated by Matthew J. O'Connell. Maryknoll, NY: Orbis, 1982.

———. *The Scandalous Message of James: Faith without Works Is Dead*. New York: Crossword, 1990.

Tombs, David. "Liberation Theological Interpretation (Latin America)." In *Dictionary of Biblical Criticism and Interpretation*, edited by Stanley E. Porter, 197–98. London: Routledge, 2007.

Westfall, Cynthia Long. *A Discourse Analysis of the Book of Hebrews: The Relationship between Form and Meaning*. London: T. & T. Clark, 2006.

————. "The Hebrew Mission: Voices from the Margin?" In *Christian Mission: Old Testament Foundations and New Testament Developments*, edited by Stanley E. Porter and Cynthia Long Westfall, 187–207. Eugene, OR: Pickwick, 2010.

Westfall, Cynthia Long, and Bryan R. Dyer. "Scared to Death: Clues to the Circumstance of the First Readers of the Book of Hebrews." Unpublished paper delivered July 6, 2011, at the Society of Biblical Literature International Meeting 2011, London.

Zahn, T. *Der Brief des Paulus an die Galater*. 3rd ed. Kommentar zum Neuen Testament. Leipzig: Deichert, 1922.

8

Social Justice in the Book of Revelation

Reading Revelation from Above

DAVID L. MATHEWSON

INTRODUCTION

THAT THE BOOK OF Revelation is interested in social justice might seem to be a foregone conclusion. With Revelation's ostensible historical backdrop being an imperial system that is bent on wealth, exploiting the nations, and oppressing God's people, issues of social justice would seem to emerge from the text quite naturally. Furthermore, given the fact that Revelation is intertextually linked with the Old Testament prophetic tradition, which frequently railed against social and economic injustices, it would seem that Revelation would clearly address issues of social justice.[1]

However, this conclusion has been strongly contested by some. Paul Duff has recently argued that Revelation includes no interest in issues of social justice, since there is no evidence that the poor resented Rome. "So if the lower class felt exploited by Rome, they did not voice it."[2] Thus, Revelation does not directly condemn Rome for exploiting the poor. Moreover,

---

1. Thus, from a liberationist perspective, Schüssler Fiorenza concludes that "the imagery of chapters 13 and 17–18 as well as chapters 21–22 is very popular with the peasants and poor of Central and South America who are reading the Bible in Christian-base communities. Since Revelation depicts the exploitation of the poor and the concentration of wealth in the hands of the powerful, the injustices perpetrated by the colonialist state, and a society that has grown obscene by perpetrating stark contrasts between the rich and poor, they can read it as speaking to their own situation of poverty and oppression" (*Revelation*, 11).

2. Duff, *Who Rides the Beast*, 64.

in the grouping of kings, merchants, and sailors in Revelation 18, only the first group was considered elite and they would have despised anyone who worked for a living.[3] "John does not seem particularly concerned with the exploitation of the poor, and he is hardly interested in condemning wealth."[4] Rather, what John opposes in Revelation 18 is being too involved in the general, including religious, culture of Rome through commerce.

In even more detail, Robert Royalty also draws attention to the lack of interest in social justice in Revelation. First, although John draws much of his language, especially about wealth, from Old Testament prophetic texts, he does not reflect their concern for an important prophetic theme—"concern for social and economic justice and care for the poor, the widowed, and the orphaned."[5] According to Royalty, one of the notable features of Second Temple and Old Testament texts is that they include a strong concern for the poor (cf. Isa 60–62).[6] "But nowhere in the Apocalypse is there a strong concern for social justice or the oppression of the poor, the widowed, or the orphaned. Babylon is condemned for her wealth and love of luxury, but not for her oppression of the poor."[7] Again, "The concern for social justice in the Jewish tradition [is] a concern totally absent in Revelation."[8] John shows "a complete disregard for issues of social justice."[9] Second, "in the narrative world of the Apocalypse, God shows no partiality to the poor or oppressed when sending disasters from heaven . . . While this does not necessarily mean that God, in the Apocalypse, has a bias *against* the poor, God shows no special concern for economic justice either."[10]

If Duff and Royalty are correct, this chapter could conclude right here. It is, of course, true that John does not voice the concerns of the Old Testament prophets for the poor and oppressed, nor does he say anything that

3. Ibid., 65.

4. Ibid.

5. Royalty, *Streets of Heaven*, 40.

6. Ibid., 78: "The more one reads Jewish literature with an eye for passages about wealth and trade, the more striking it is that nowhere in the Apocalypse is there any strong concern for social justice, the poor, the widowed, or the orphaned." Much of Royalty's argument in relationship to John's connection to prophetic literature depends on his overall view of John's use of the Old Testament. Royalty doubts that John's readers would have picked up on all of his subtle usages of the Old Testament.

7. Ibid., 71.

8. Ibid.

9. Ibid., 154.

10. Ibid., 183.

resembles, for example, James's "Has not God chosen the poor in the world to be rich in faith and heirs of the kingdom," or his concern for visiting "orphans and widows in their distress."[11] However, to require that Revelation voices explicit concern for the poor is to cast the net too narrowly and to limit the scope of social justice. What this paper will argue is that John in Revelation is concerned with social justice, but he goes about speaking against injustice by exposing and undermining the ideology that lies behind it. Revelation engenders resistance against the dominant empire that perpetrates such injustices and exposes the evil behind it. At the same time, there are occasions where Revelation addresses the effects of empire in terms of economic injustices.

Before looking explicitly at social justice in Revelation, it is necessary to locate my discussion in relation to broader issues of date, authorship, and background. Though the conclusions of this paper do not ultimately rest on a specific dating for Revelation, I accept the common dating in the last half of the last decade of the first century CE when Rome was under the emperorship of Domitian. Furthermore, although a case can be made for the apostolic authorship of Revelation, the author clearly claims the authority of a prophet who stands and writes at the climax of the Old Testament prophetic tradition.[12] The primary issues that John appears to address affecting the churches in Asia Minor are a cluster of problems related to imperial Roman domination, especially issues related to the imperial cult.[13] I also follow those commentators who see the primary issue faced by the readers of Revelation as not predominantly persecution, though this no doubt took place at different levels, but compromise and accommodation by the churches of Asia Minor with imperial Rome.[14] This means that, for much of the readership, John's Apocalypse functioned more as a prophetic warning than an encouragement. However, while it is unnecessary to think that John was only responding to a perceived crisis, for many of John's readers, Revelation would have functioned to awaken them to a real crisis that they did not correctly perceive.

11. Cf. Jas 2:5 and 1:27 respectively.

12. See Bauckham, *Theology of Revelation*, 5.

13. On this, see the helpful and readable summary in Howard-Brook and Gwyther, *Unveiling Empire*, 87–119.

14. This observation is based on examination of the messages to the seven churches in Rev 2–3. Only two of the churches are faithful in their witness and are, incidentally, suffering persecution at some level; they receive no censure (2:8–11; 3:7–13). However, the other five are compromising their witness.

IDOLATRY, ARROGANCE, AND VIOLENCE: THE HEART OF JOHN'S CRITIQUE

As mentioned above, there is widespread agreement that John writes what is nothing less than a thoroughgoing critique of first-century imperial Rome and the system of imperial worship within the Roman provinces. As an "Apocalypse," John's book unveils and exposes the true nature of the dominant imperial system of the day, even if John's voice is a deviant and minority one.[15] That is, Revelation is an ideological critique of Roman power and religion. John's critique actually begins quite early in his book with the various epithets that are applied to God and his Messiah in the first chapter. To consider only the introductory section in Rev 1:1–8, God is described as ὁ ὢν καὶ ὁ ἦν καὶ ὁ ἐρχόμενος ("the one who is and who was and who is to come," 1:4),[16] which points to God's eternity and sovereignty over all things. Furthermore, he is already given a throne in this verse. God is also depicted as the one who is the source of peace (εἰρήνη). Together, these descriptions would have constituted an affront to the claims of imperial Rome and its system of emperor worship. It is God who is the one who is eternal, not Rome, and God is sovereign over all things, not Caesar. And giving God a throne would be a direct challenge to the sovereignty and authority of the emperor. Moreover, the fact that God is the source of peace would perhaps be heard as a contradiction to the myth of *Pax Romana*. Furthermore, God's Messiah, Jesus, is the faithful and true witness, the firstborn from the dead, but is also ὁ ἄρχων τῶν βασιλέων τῆς γῆς ("the ruler of the kings of the earth," 1:5). By his act of redemption accomplished by his death on the cross, Jesus has established an alternative kingdom to imperial Roman rule (1:5–6). "Where Rome is concerned, any such reign is unauthorized ... [and] is by definition a counterreign and a political provocation."[17]

Furthermore, in v. 8 God is the "alpha and omega" (τὸ ἄλφα καὶ τὸ ὦ), once again indicating his eternity and sovereignty over all things. The description of God ends with the title "almighty" (παντοκράτωρ), another reference to God's absolute sovereignty.[18] Already at the outset of the Apocalypse, then, the author has established the primary point of contention:

15. Ruiz, "Taking a Stand," 126–30.

16. My English Bible quotations are from the NRSV.

17. Blount, *Revelation*, 37.

18. This designation occurs seven times in Revelation: 1:8; 4:8; 11:17; 15:3; 16:7; 19:6; 21:22.

Rome has arrogated divine authority and rule for itself and poses a challenge to the exclusive rule of God and his Messiah on earth.

It is in chs. 4–5 where John tackles the claims of imperial Rome head on. Here, the vision proper of the Apocalypse commences with a vision of the heavenly reality that lies behind all earthly realities. The focal point of the vision is the "throne," and the "one seated on the throne." The word θρόνος occurs seventeen times in these two chapters with reference to God's (and the Lamb's) throne.[19] The throne indicates the central theological significance of God's sovereignty for the entire book. Yet it also indicates what is at stake in John's vision: who is the Lord of the universe? In this sense John's vision of a throne in heaven would have been a direct challenge to the right of Caesar to rule (or Caesar is a challenge to God in his right to rule!). The true throne stands in heaven, and Caesar's throne is but a gross parody. The throne blends both cultic and political meanings.[20] Heaven is the temple of God where heavenly beings worship God in unending liturgy. However, the throne of God, especially in the context of imperial Roman rule, connotes God's dominion over the entire universe.[21] As Richard Bauckham notes, this dual emphasis of the religious and political corresponds to the religio-political context of imperial Rome:

> The Roman Empire, like most political powers in the ancient world, represented and propagated its power in religious terms. Its state religion, featuring the worship both of deified emperors and of traditional gods of Rome, expressed political loyalty through religious worship. In this way it absolutized its power, claiming for itself the ultimate, divine sovereignty over the world.[22]

This perspective is even further bolstered by the observation that Rev 4–5 parodies the Roman imperial court (or is it the other way around?). The throne, brilliant display of jewels, the courtiers shouting acclamations of praise, the crowns and other features have parallels in early Roman court ceremonies.[23] However, in John's depiction it is God and the Lamb, not the

---

19. θρόνος occurs twice with reference to the thrones of the twenty-four elders (4:4; 11:16).

20. For this mixture of the cultic and political in chs. 4–5, see Bauckham, *Theology of Revelation*, 33–35.

21. Beale, *Revelation*, 320.

22. Bauckham, *Theology of Revelation*, 34.

23. Cf. Aune, "Roman Court Ceremonial." In greater detail see Gill, "Revelation and Rome."

emperor, who sit at the center of heavenly celebration. Rome is guilty of arrogating to itself divine power and authority, expressed in worship of Rome and its emperors. Rome is a system of idolatrous worship that contests on earth the true worship that belongs only to God and the Lamb.[24]

Rome's arrogance and idolatry are highlighted elsewhere in Revelation. In 13:4 John gives voice to the dominant discourse concerning the Roman Empire: "Who is like the beast, and who can fight against it?" proclaiming in words that usurp what belongs only to God (Exod 15:11; Pss 35:10; 71:19; 113:5; Isa 44:7). The beast exercises authority over the entire earth (13:7), blasphemes God and his heavenly dwelling (13:6), and is the object of universal worship (13:8). Moreover, 18:7 provides one of the reasons for the ultimate judgment and destruction of Rome: she exalts herself (ἐδόξασεν αὐτήν) as queen seated (κάθημαι βασίλισσα) on her throne, arrogantly boasting about her security. This reference is to be read in deliberate contrast to the worship of the one seated on the throne in chs. 4–5, and to other sections where "glory" and "glorify" are used in relation to God and the Lamb.[25] As Barbara Rossing claims, 18:7 is nothing less than "an arrogant provocation against God."[26] Or as J. Nelson Kraybill concludes, "The great offense of Rome was taking the glory that belonged to God, the 'King of the nations,' and claiming it for itself."[27]

Thus, the counter-discourse of Revelation exposes the true nature of imperial Roman rule. It has arrogantly set itself up as God and illegitimately demands the worship of its subjects. It has absolutized its power here on earth, an affront to the true authority and worship that belong only to God. John's critique, then, is an ideological one that gets to the heart of what is wrong with the Roman Empire.

Furthermore, John not only condemns Rome for its arrogance and its idolatry, he also portrays Rome as maintaining its status through violence and bloodshed. Rather than the provider of peace (*Pax Romana*), Rome is depicted in Revelation as a perpetrator of murder and as imposing its imperial will by violence. Rome is portrayed as bent on violence and warfare in the form of the first two seals (6:1–4), which are "a sociopolitical critique of imperial rule."[28] At several junctures throughout the Apocalypse, Rome is

---

24. Bauckham, *Theology of Revelation*, 35.

25. Thompson, *Revelation*, 169.

26. Rossing, *Choice between Two Cities*, 125.

27. Kraybill, *Imperial Cult*, 159.

28. Schüssler Fiorenza, *Revelation*, 63.

depicted as a violent perpetrator that maintains peace and power through violence.[29] The fifth seal contains a vision of the souls of the martyrs under the altar who have been slain because of the word of God (6:9). These God will vindicate. In ch. 13 the beast is allowed to make war with the saints and to put to death those who do not worship the image of the beast (13:15). It also enforces its will through economic sanctions (13:16–17). Furthermore, Rome is portrayed as drunk with the blood of the saints because of their witness (17:6). While most of these could be limited to Rome's mistreatment of God's people, in 18:24 Rome's murderous and violent acts are universalized to include anyone who did not acknowledge its sovereignty: "And in you was found the blood of prophets and of saints, and of *all who have been slaughtered on the earth*" (emphasis mine). Therefore, "Revelation portrays the Roman Empire as a system of violent oppression, founded on conquest, maintained by violence and oppression."[30] Victory and *Pax* came at the cost of military violence and bloodshed throughout the entire earth. The reason for this is that no society can absolutize its power without victims; those who stand in the way or contest its power must be eliminated.

John responds to the dominant discourse about Rome with his own counter-discourse. John exposes Rome's true colors as an empire that secures its rule here on earth by arrogantly setting itself up over God, expressed in idolatrous worship and maintained through violence. Though Revelation does not explicitly call for God's people to champion the cause of the destitute, the poor, and the widows (Jas 1:26–27), as other prophets had done in the past (Isa 1:17), John renders a powerful ideological critique of the root of social injustices: arrogation of divine power, control, idolatry, and violence. John shares God's concern for God's people (the prophets and saints, and Jesus himself), victims of the empire who have suffered or will suffer violent death at the hands of Rome.

ECONOMIC INJUSTICE IN REVELATION

In the midst of John's powerful ideological critique of empire, issues of injustice and exploitation do surface from time to time. This section will examine three passages in Revelation that appear to address problems of economic and social justice: chs. 6, 17–18, and 21–22. In these passages

29. Howard-Brook and Gwyther, *Unveiling Empire*, 170.

30. Bauckham, *Theology of Revelation*, 35. As Howard-Brook and Gwyther have shown, Revelation "deconstructs" several imperial myths: Empire, Roman *Pax*, *Victoria*, Faith, and Eternity (*Unveiling Empire*, 223–35).

John portrays the Roman Empire as exploitative and unjust in its economic practices (chs. 6, 17–18), while the counter vision of the New Jerusalem envisions the ideal just and perfect society (chs. 21–22).

Revelation 6:5–6

As noted above, in the seal sequence in Revelation 6, "the first four seals . . . reveal and highlight the true nature of Roman power and rule."[31] Roman rule is sustained through violence (seal 1). Specifically, the third seal is a commentary on the economic situation engendered by Roman rule. This becomes clear with the scale that is supported in the hand of the rider of the third horse. The scale was often emblematic in the Old Testament of economic equity (cf. Prov 6:11).[32] But the voice that accompanies only this rider indicates that something has gone awry: a quart of wheat, enough to feed one person for a day, costs a day's wage; three quarts of barley, enough to feed a small family, though less desirable, was also a day's wage. And the wine and oil are not to be touched.

There has been considerable debate as to how we should understand the words of this voice. Most would agree that extreme famine could be envisioned here, reflected in the inflated prices. A common misunderstanding is that the oil and wine were luxuries to be enjoyed only by the wealthy.[33] However, oil and wine would also have been staples, so not necessarily limited to consumption by the wealthy. More likely, the picture is of the scarcity of staples such as wheat and barley, but a surplus of oil and wine. This voice probably reflects the situation in the provinces where much land was used for vineyards and orchards for producing oil and wine, because these were the most profitable for export, especially to Rome (see the list in Rev 18:13). Large estates would have been owned by the wealthy, with vines being planted and cultivated at the expense of food grains, since the former would have been more profitable for trade.[34] Given the large volume of grain that it would have taken to support Rome, much of the grain would have been imported from the provinces, and Rome would have had first dibs on grain imported from Egypt. This would have been disastrous, especially in times of famine: lack of staple foods in the provinces and inflated prices

31. Schüssler Fiorenza, *Revelation*, 63.

32. Osborne, *Revelation*, 280; Boxall, *Revelation*, 110. Boxall also lists Lev 19:36; Ezek 45:10; Amos 8:5; Hos 12:8; Prov 11:1; 20:23.

33. Boesak, *Comfort and Protest*, 64. Cf. also Richard, *Apocalypse*, 69.

34. Howard-Brook and Gwyther, *Unveiling Empire*, 98.

for the grain that was available, yet a surplus of less necessary oil and wine. Rome's economic monopoly meant that, particularly in times of famine, the staple foods were so exorbitantly priced in the provinces that the poor could scarcely survive. Ironically, there was a surplus of those things that were less important and not as necessary for sustaining life—oil and wine.[35] As Bauckham concludes, "the general population of Rome survived only at the expense of the rest of the empire."[36] Economically, Rome survived by exploiting the provinces for its own gain.[37] Moreover, it would have done so particularly to the detriment of the poor, who could not even afford the food staples.

Revelation 17–18

The economic and religious critique of Rome is taken up in even more poignant fashion in chs. 17–18.[38] The space given to the critique of Rome's economic practices in ch. 18 demonstrates its importance. It is crucial to remember at the outset how intertwined Rome's political and economic systems were with religious practices. Kraybill and others have shown the religious character of the trade and commerce through the influence of pagan religions and emperor worship.[39] As Leonard Thompson summarizes, "the seer wrote in a period of time when imperial Rome offered Asians a coherent, ordered structure of reality which unified religious, social, economic, political and aesthetic aspects of the world."[40] Thus the religious, economic, political, and social aspects of the Roman Empire were all integrated "within a web of imperial power."[41] Consequently, John's critique of Roman power encompasses its religious, political, and economic dimensions.

In Revelation 17 the Seer begins to expose Rome for what it truly is. The dominant image used to portray Rome in this section of the discourse is

---

35. Giesen, *Johannesapokalypse*, 279, who concludes that oil and wine are not for sustaining life, since no one can live off of them alone ("Mit ihnen allein kann niemand seinen Hunger stillen").

36. Bauckham, *Climax*, 363.

37. See also Richard, *Apocalypse*, 68.

38. Here I am assuming that Babylon is a cipher for the city of Rome.

39. Kraybill, *Imperial Cult*, 110–41. Cf. Howard-Brook and Gwyther, *Unveiling Empire*, 87–119.

40. Thompson, "Sociological Analysis," 159; also, Malina and Pilch, *Revelation*, 221.

41. Howard-Brook and Gwyther, *Unveiling Empire*, 89.

a "harlot" (πόρνη), an image that has significant Old Testament antecedents. This image is coupled with the lurid images of "fornication" (ἐπόρνευσαν) and "intoxication" (ἐμεθύσθησαν) in vv. 1–4. While in the Old Testament the image of a "whore" or "prostitute" was frequently applied to God's people, Israel, due to their spiritual unfaithfulness, it could also be applied to other cities. In Nah 3:1–4, the city of Nineveh is castigated for its violence (3:1–3) and its seduction and enslavement of other nations (3:4). The primary intertextual background for Rev 17:1–2 is Isa 23:17, where Tyre, which forms an important model for John's portrayal of Babylon/Rome, is depicted as a harlot who enters into commercial alliance with other nations, its lovers (Isa 23:14–18).[42] The image of a whore indicates allurement, seduction, and power.[43] Rome, then, plays the role of the harlot by seducing other nations into political and economic alliances with it ("with whom [the harlot, Rome] the kings of the earth have fornicated" [17:3a]). Moreover, the metaphor of "intoxication" further suggests, then, "the victimization of the people of the world by Rome."[44] Therefore, as a whore Rome seduces and leads the world into fornication through political and economic alliance and control. Bauckham in particular has noted the commercial and economic associations of the harlot imagery.[45] As deSilva summarizes,

> The wealth to be enjoyed by participating in the larger global economy was, as far as John was concerned, a dangerous lure to sharing in the violence and political injustice that created the sociopolitical context that maintained such an economy, as well as sharing in the economic injustice that allowed the resources to be siphoned off to satisfy the immoderate cravings of Rome's inhabitants and worldwide elite.[46]

Yet participation in Rome's economic system would have also entailed participation in its idolatrous religion.[47] Therefore, idolatrous connotations of "harlot" and "fornication" were also in the author's mind.

---

42. See Fekkes, *Isaiah and Prophetic Traditions*, 211–12. Cf. Kuhn, "Βαβυλών," 515 n 11; Hauck and Schultz, "πόρνη κτλ," 587. John's ἐπόρνευσαν translates the Hebrew זנה (the LXX has ἔσται ἐμπόριον) which is used figuratively in Isa 23:17 as it is in Rev 17:2.

43. Goodfriend, "Prostitute," 509.

44. Aune, *Revelation 17–22*, 932.

45. Bauckham, *Climax*, 343–50.

46. deSilva, *Seeing Things John's Way*, 47.

47. Ibid.; Fekkes, *Isaiah and Prophetic Traditions*, 211–12; Hauck and Schultz, "πόρνη κτλ," 594–95; Beale, *Revelation*, 895.

As already noted above, the system of imperial power would have united political, economic, cultural, and religious aspects. As Kraybill and others have demonstrated, participation in the economic system of Rome in the form of trade guilds, or even the shipping industry, would have involved one with pagan deities and, more importantly, emperor worship, so that alliance with Rome had economic and religious implications.[48] But much more than just the integration of commerce with pagan religious observance and the emperor cult is intended here. As already observed, Rome is guilty of excessive pride and arrogance, which claims for itself the glory that belongs only to God (18:7; cf. chs. 4–5). It is guilty of idolatry by absolutizing its power and usurping the kingship that belongs only to God.[49] Yet, it also boasts in its own prosperity and economic security and seduces others into the same self-reliance. In addition to the imperial cult, John may also have in mind here the worship of goddess Roma.[50] Therefore, Rome has deified its own power, prosperity, and violence, legitimized and mediated through the imperial cult, evoking John's critique of the empire as an idolatrous system. In this way the nations also fornicate with Rome through their economic cooperation with Rome's idolatrous system.[51] Moreover, the choice of prostitution and fornication imagery may also function as a reminder to John's churches of what they would be guilty of as God's people if they should traffic with her.

The description of the harlot Rome is continued in v. 4, where she is described as a courtesan who is dressed in gaudy dress and jewelry, again highlighting her seductive nature. Further, the fact that all the features of her dress here in 17:4 (περιβεβλημένη πορφυροῦν καὶ κόκκινον καὶ κεχρυσωμένη χρυσίῳ καὶ λίθῳ τιμίῳ καὶ μαργαρίταις)[52] appear later on in the list of cargo extracted from the nations for Rome's benefit in 18:12 (γόμον χρυσοῦ . . . καὶ λίθου τιμίου καὶ μαργαριτῶν . . . καὶ πορφύρας . . . καὶ κοκκίνου)[53] suggests that the dress of the courtesan here has been extracted from her

48. Aune, *Revelation 17–22*, 931; Beale, *Revelation*, 848–49. As Beale suggests, fornication involves "acceptance of the religious and idolatrous demands of the ungodly earthly order" (848). Cf. also Siitonen, "Merchants and Commerce," 157.

49. See Smalley, *Revelation*, 429.

50. Court, *Myth and History*, 148–53; Witherington, *Revelation*, 218; deSilva, *Seeing Things John's Way*, 40–41.

51. Cf. Blount, *Revelation*, 326.

52. NRSV: "The woman was clothed in purple and scarlet, and adorned with gold and jewels and pearls . . ."

53. NRSV: "cargo of gold . . . jewels and pearls . . . purple . . . scarlet . . ."

lovers.[54] In Bauckham's words, "she is a rich courtesan, whose expensive clothes and jewelry (14:4) indicate the luxurious lifestyle she maintains at her lover's expense."[55] As a prostitute, Rome is not a victim, but victimizes those who would traffic with her. The final important feature in the harlot's description is that she sits on many waters (17:1). In 17:15 the waters upon which the harlot was seen sitting are identified as "people and multitudes and nations and tongues," which also demonstrates her control over the nations.

Thus, John's depiction of Rome as a harlot suggests her power and control over other people and nations through economic associations by means of seduction and deception. Furthermore, the harlot imagery indicates her idolatrous religious practices. By deifying her power and financial security, expressed through and legitimized by the emperor cult, she has become a "divine and absolute subject."[56] The entire economic system of Rome is corrupt, as it is associated with its idolatrous religious system and claims, and Rome is guilty of seducing other nations to participate in its idolatrous ways.

Chapter 18 builds on the economic-religious critique already begun in 17:1–4. Though slightly overstating, Christopher R. Smith calls this chapter "one of the most explicit social justice passages."[57] Here John draws heavily on Ezekiel's oracles against Tyre (Ezek 26–28), where it is condemned for its idolatrous pride and greed (28:1–3). The most revealing section in John's critique is the list of imports found in vv. 12–13. Bauckham and Aune have provided an extensive discussion of the description, importance, source, and value of the various cargoes.[58] More important is what this list says about Rome's economic activities. First, the list of cargoes depicts extravagant and luxury goods that would have primarily benefited the wealthy elite in Rome.[59] John accuses Rome of excessive luxury (18:7). According to Aune, "this list is limited to luxury trade goods primarily for

---

54. Aune, *Revelation 17–22*, 935. "Placing the name upon the forehead (probably upon a headband) appears to have been a custom of Roman courtesans" (Mounce, *Revelation*, 310).

55. Bauckham, *Climax*, 347.

56. Richard, *Apocalypse*, 129.

57. Smith, "Reclaiming the Social Justice Message," 28.

58. Bauckham, *Climax*, 350–66; Aune, *Revelation 17–22*, 998–1003.

59. Aune, *Revelation 17–22*, 998; Osborne, *Revelation*, 647; Boxall, *Revelation*, 261; Bauckham, *Climax*, 350–71.

the consumption of the very wealthy."[60] The list gives the impression of the enormous trade that flowed into the city and enabled Rome to "live luxuriously as the mistress of the world,"[61] as well as benefiting some who traded with Rome. But second, there is some debate over whether John is critiquing Rome's economy for its exploitation of its subjects.[62] It is true that John does not explicitly condemn Rome for its exploitative economy. Rather, his critique is directed at the idolatry, arrogance, and greed that accompany its pursuit of wealth.[63] However, it appears that John does subtly critique Rome as unjustly exploiting the provinces and other nations for its own benefit. The list mentions wine, oil, and wheat (v. 13), which would have been staples, parasitically extracted from the provinces themselves, for the sole purpose of satisfying all of Rome. We have already seen that in 6:5–6 John appears to expose the effects of Rome's economic practices on the provinces: a scarcity of grain that makes it unaffordable to the poor in the provinces, while the commodities less important for survival, oil and wine, are in surplus since they are of more importance for trade. Furthermore, the link between the portrayal of Rome as a courtesan in 17:2 (cf. 18:16) dressed in the very jewels and apparel that appear in the list of imports in 18:12–13, as well as John's critique of the city's wealth in 18:6–7, suggest that, though some benefit from Rome's economy (kings of the earth, merchants, those at sea in ch. 18), Rome's wealth comes at the expense of the provinces and the rest of the world.[64] This would also seem to be consistent with the portrayal of Rome as a prostitute (17:1–3) who seduces the nations and even intoxicates them. Thus, the exploitative nature of Rome's

60. Aune, *Revelation 17–22*, 998.

61. Mounce, *Revelation*, 329.

62. For assessment that sees exploitation as John's concern, see Bauckham, *Climax*, 343–71; Kraybill, *Imperial Cult;* Howard-Brook and Gwyther, *Unveiling Empire*, 116; Osborne, *Revelation*, 650; Boxall, *Revelation*, 261; Richard, *Apocalypse*, 130; deSilva, *Seeing Things John's Way*, 74. But cf. Provan, "Foul Spirits," 86–87; Aune, *Revelation 17–22*, 990: "In fact, Rev 18 does not deal with the issue of economic exploitation at all." Smith provides a discussion of ways that Rome may have oppressed and exploited its subjects economically ("Reclaiming the Social Justice Message," 30–31), though it is difficult to know how much of this John intended and his readers would have grasped since he does not inscribe it in his discourse.

63. See Provan, "Foul Spirits," 88; Kraybill, *Imperial Cult*, 102.

64. It is difficult to see why Aune denies that John deals with the issue of exploitation, when he concludes that John portrays Rome as a courtesan in v. 4, where her ostentatious dress and gaudy jewelry have been extracted from her lovers (*Revelation 17–22*, 935).

economy, while not the primary object of John's invective, is nevertheless an implicit aspect of John's critique. John portrays Roman imperial economy as "structured chiefly to benefit Rome."[65] The riches of the world flow toward the geopolitical center, Rome.[66]

Even more telling is the feature that occurs at the climax of the list. One of the commodities extracted from Rome's subjects is slaves (v. 13): "slaves (σωμάτων), that is, human souls."[67] Most commentators draw attention to the fact that this feature occurs at the end of the list, giving it some emphasis.[68] Moreover, it comes right on the heels of the mention of livestock as part of Rome's trade. By ending the list with ψυχὰς ἀνθρώπων ("human souls"), John is pointing out that slaves are not property, like livestock, but are in fact human lives.[69] "By putting slaves at the end of the list of commodities, the author of *Revelation* 'signifies' on Rome's devastating and dehumanizing treatment of slaves for profit."[70] Asia Minor was one of the areas most heavily exploited for slaves, evoking a polemic by John, which Clarice Martin labels an "indictment of the pervasive and baleful commodification and trafficking of human beings throughout the Roman Empire."[71]

By way of summary, John's critique of Rome in chs. 17–18 reveals the closely intertwined features of Rome's religious, economic, and political life. John condemns Rome for its religious and economic idolatry, arrogance, violence (murder of victims) and greed, and for seducing other nations to associate with its empire through participation in its idolatrous economic system.[72] In addition, Rome has satisfied its craving for wealth at the expense of its provinces and other nations whom she controls. Its economy is exploitative. It is also guilty of the abuse of human life through its slave trade. In this way, these chapters are "a clarion call for Christians

---

65. deSilva, *Seeing Things John's Way*, 208.

66. González, "Clarity and Ambivalence," 55–56.

67. For evidence that σωμάτων refers to slaves, see Aune, *Revelation 17–22*, 1002; Smalley, *Revelation*, 455–56.

68. Boxall, *Revelation*, 261, calls it "shocking."

69. Bauckham, *Climax*, 370–71.

70. Martin, "Polishing the Unclouded Mirror," 100.

71. Ibid., 86.

72. Collins, "Revelation 18," 203, who sees the following reasons for Rome's judgment: (1) idolatrous and blasphemous worship; (2) violence; (3) arrogance and self-glorification; (4) wealth.

to sever all economic and political ties with an Empire that had sold out to injustice, idolatry, and greed."[73]

Revelation 21–22

The final text that can be seen to address issues of social justice is the climactic visionary segment in 21:1—22:5. Structurally, 21:1—22:5 plays a significant role as a contrastive image to the prostitute/Babylon.[74] Here we are introduced to the bride/New Jerusalem, which stands as the reward for those who will disassociate from Babylon: "Come out of her, my people" (18:4). Further, the bride/New Jerusalem is an antithesis to all that is wrong with the prostitute/Babylon. Thus, it provides the counterpart to the idolatry, arrogance, violence, greed, and injustice that characterized Rome.[75]

The New Jerusalem, therefore, reflects God's glory (21:11, ἔχουσαν τὴν δόξαν τοῦ θεοῦ) in contrast to the arrogation of divine worship in Babylon, which glorifies itself (18:7, ἐδόξασεν αὐτήν). At the center of the New Jerusalem is the throne of God, the symbol of sovereignty, which now functions to give life and healing (22:1–2), a stark contrast with the murderous activity and violence by which the abusive power of Rome was maintained, as well as the lack of sustenance for some that resulted from Rome's exploitative economy (6:5–6). Perhaps the strong decreation language in chs. 20–21, where the first heaven and earth flee on the day of judgment so that no place is found for them (20:11) and are now replaced by a new heaven and earth (γῆν) (21:1), is to be understood not only in physical but in political terms as the complete reversal of the exploitation, destruction, and violence done by the ungodly empire on this earth.[76] "Earth is the perspective of Empire."[77] The former state of things, under the rule of Babylon/Rome, has been banished to make way for an entirely new state of affairs, where the suffering,

---

73. Kraybill, *Imperial Cult*, 16. There is no need to deny that John critiques both Roman ideology and those in the churches (cf. 2:20–22) who would engage in commerce with it. See Siitonen, "Merchants and Commerce," 160.

74. See esp. Deutsch, "Transformation of Symbols"; Rossing, *Choice between Two Cities*.

75. This is not to downplay the stark redemptive-theological themes in Rev 21–22. Rather, it is to draw attention to the historical-religious-political background against which these themes are to be read. On this entire section and its Old Testament background, see Mathewson, *New Heaven and New Earth*.

76. Boesak, *Comfort and Protest*, 126: "This earth, raped, robbed, torn, filled with anger and revenge, with hurt and pain, cannot and should not remain."

77. Howard-Brook and Gwyther, *Unveiling Empire*, 128.

pain, death, oppression, and corruption that characterized Rome's earthly empire is "no more" (21:4, οὐκ ἔσται ἔτι). In fact, the dominant intertext for John's new creation and New Jerusalem imagery is Isa 65:17–18. This text itself resonates with concern for creational and social justice. In contrast to the old created order, in the new creation made for God's people, "no longer will they build houses and others live in them, or plant and others eat" (Isa 65:22). The new creation will be a complete reversal of the present state of affairs, where land is confiscated by the wealthy or foreign invaders. Revelation 21 exemplifies the same concern for the liberation of creation from the destructive, oppressive rule of empire in a new creative act by God.

In the New Jerusalem, all peoples are kings and priests who rule forever (22:5). As Richard says, in contrast to Babylon, "In the New Jerusalem all are priests, all see God, and all reign. There are no hierarchies, no differentiations, no power elites, and no oppressed."[78] The same wealth terminology that characterized Babylon/Rome now features in the New Jerusalem (gold, precious stone and pearls, fine linen; 17:3, 8; and 19:8; 21:11–21). The wealth that the New Jerusalem has to offer more than compensates for what the readers might have sacrificed in the Roman imperial economy. They now have access to true eternal wealth. Moreover, it is given as a gift, an inheritance (21:5–7) to be enjoyed by all, rather than by a wealthy, elite few. It has lost all associations with greed, arrogance, and exploitation. Further, there are two other possible pointed critiques of Roman economy. First, those who are faithful and enter the New Jerusalem are promised the water of life "without payment" (δωρεάν) in 21:6.[79] According to Rossing, this should be understood politically and economically, so that "The water given without money becomes a pointed critique of Babylon/Rome's exploitative economy."[80] Second, the kings of the earth now bring their glory (δόξαν) into the New Jerusalem (21:24b). In contrast to their allegiance to idolatrous Rome, and rather than feeding the greedy self-indulgance of seductive empire, the nations now "will freely bring their glory to the Holy City ... Abundance provided by God overflows on all without hoarding or greed."[81] The Old Testament text from which much of John's language

78. Richard, *Apocalypse*, 166.

79. This is an allusion to Isa 55:1. Cf. Sir 51:25.

80. Rossing, *Choice between Two Cities*, 152. See also Howard-Brook and Gwyther, *Unveiling Empire*, 190: "In New Jerusalem, the water freely given by God prevails over the imperial economy of exploitation and debt"; Boxall, *Revelation*, 296; Maier, "Coming Out of Babylon," 76–77.

81. Howard-Brook and Gwyther, *Unveiling Empire*, 191–92. Cf. Bauckham, *Climax*,

is drawn in this section (21:22–26) is Isa 60, where those who formerly oppressed Jerusalem will now bow down (Isa 60:14), and the violence and ruin experienced by the Holy City will be banished (60:18). This concern for justice carries over into John's use of the motif of the entrance into the city by the nations that formerly served Babylon/Rome to now contribute to the Holy City. In these ways the New Jerusalem/bride is portrayed in Revelation as the antithesis to the idolatry, arrogance, violence, greed, and injustice of Rome. The New Jerusalem is a godly, peaceful, just city where all have access freely to the abundance of the city, and all serve as kings and priests.

Here Revelation implicity comes closest to the explicit concerns of Jas 1:26–27 or Isa 1:17 for social justice. In that John's readers already consti-tute a kingdom and priests (Rev 1:6: ἐποίησεν ἡμᾶς βασιλείαν, ἱερεῖς τῷ θεῷ καὶ πατρὶ αὐτοῦ, "[Jesus] made us to be a kingdom, priests serving his God and Father"), they are to witness to the ideals of the New Jerusalem within a dominant culture built on idolatry, violence, oppression, and injustice. The New Jerusalem calls God's people to pursue practices that extend the peace, healing, equality, and resources of the New Jerusalem to those who suffer at the hands of empire. John's community should already witness to and model a just community that stands in antithesis to the dominant imperial culture, however anticipatory and imperfect their community might be in advance of its consummation in Rev 21–22.

CONCLUSION

We have seen that Revelation is indeed concerned with social justice. However, we cannot cast the net too narrowly. John does not show explicit concern for caring for the poor, widows, and others who are in need (cf. Jas 1:26–27; 2:5). Instead, John exposes the true nature of Rome—an empire that arrogantly sets itself up as God, deifying its political and economic power and maintaining its power through violence. As Kraybill notes, "While John occasionally addresses specific social and economic injustices, his primary focus remains on broader issues of power and idolatry."[82] My conclusions are consistent with this observation. John's Apocalypse is just that, an uncovering or unveiling of the true nature of things, including im-perial Roman rule. John's critique of Rome is an ideological one. Through

---

315.

82. Kraybill, *Imperial Cult*, 148.

his use of familiar images the author's "anti-imperialistic counterdiscourse"[83] exposes Rome's idolatry, arrogance, violence, and greed, for which she will be judged. These are all concerns of social justice. And these concerns are precisely Revelation's contribution to the issue of social justice. It is this ideology that causes dominant powers to control, exploit, dehumanize, oppress, and even eliminate those who stand in the way of its progress. John speaks out against the violence against God's people; God's own commitment to justice can be seen in his commitment to vindicate the innocent victims of the oppressive empire. John also speaks out against an economy that is exploitative in that it ravages the rest of the world to satisfy its own opulent tastes. John is further concerned with the dehumanization of life, exemplified by the abuse perpetrated in slave trade. And John envisions a new society where peace, inclusion, equality, justice, and human dignity are paramount. John's primary contribution to social justice is to expose the ideology (arrogance, idolatry, violence) that engenders such injustices and to call on God's people to resist it.

Though Revelation is read often from the margins, from the perspective of the oppressed and suffering (a reading from below) as has been done in liberationist readings and more recently in cultural readings of Revelation,[84] not all were victims of Rome's oppression and exploitation. Many were affluent and compromising with Roman rule. I would advocate the need also for a complementary reading of Revelation from "above," that is, from a position of relative wealth and high social standing, which is the perspective from which at least one church, the Laodicean church in Rev 3:14–22, would have read it. From a perspective from "above," the book of Revelation calls on the reader to respond in at least two ways in light of its concern for social justice. First, the reader must actively confront and resist empire and its idolatrous, unjust, and exploitative practices. Yet Revelation makes it clear that God's people accomplish this through their faithful witness. This takes place when God's people refuse to associate with and support the dominant empire and its idolatrous, godless, violent, and unjust values and practices, and as God's kings and priests (1:6) they seek to witness to the truth and reality of God's just counterreign in their speech and practice.[85] As Harry O. Maier correctly observes, "Readers will misun-

83. Ruiz, "Taking a Stand," 126.

84. Cf. Boesak, *Comfort and Protest*; Rhoads, *From Every People and Nation*.

85. deSilva, *Seeing Things John's Way*, 347. See the helpful suggestions in Bauckham, *Theology of Revelation*, 159–64. The book of Revelation is bracketed by a blessing for

derstand these visions if they read them only as descriptions of the fate of the persecutors of the seven churches."[86] Revelation's visions of judgment function as a mirror for those who refuse to disentangle from the dominant imperial culture. In this case, chs. 17–18 will function as a warning to readers who fail to disassociate from Rome, lest they remain part of the dominant culture, completely neutralizing the force of their witness, and are implicated in Babylon's judgment for refusal to repent (ch. 18). "Long before the prophets of postcolonialism, John understood that a person cannot share in the profits of domination without also sharing in its crimes."[87] Revelation is a call to disassociate from empire and to witness in word and deed to God's kingdom, to model an alternative society (chs. 21–22) and resist any ideology opposed to it.

Second, through this refusal to participate, God's people identify with the oppressed and victims of empire and become victims themselves—a move already modeled by the slain Lamb.[88] John calls on his readers to "come out" of Bablyon (18:4) by disentangling themselves from her idolatrous, unjust, exploitative economic system and its practices.[89] This would have meant to risk being cut off from the benefits of the dominant world power and experiencing deprivation and marginalization, and even death, thus siding with the victims of the oppressive empire.[90] This is nothing less than a reflection of God's own commitment to justice reflected in his vindication of the slain Lamb and his commitment to vindicate other innocent victims of empire (6:9–10). It is possible that John himself exemplifies such a move. In 1:9 John describes his situation as being on the island of Patmos "because of the word of God and the testimony of Jesus." If John is there as a disciplinary measure for his prophetic activity, Howard-Brook and Gwyther have suggested that this exile would be an indication of John's relatively high social status, since crucifixion would have been the lot of the lower classes.[91] Furthermore, John chooses to identify with his read-

---

obedience (1:3) and a curse for refusal to obey (22:18–19).

86. Maier, "Coming Out of Babylon," 71.

87. deSilva, Seeing Things John's Way, 47.

88. Bauckham, Climax, 378.

89. Ruiz, "Taking a Stand," 133.

90. Contra Siitonen, "Merchants and Commerce," 160, who is uncertain exactly what John is demanding of his readers.

91. Howard-Brook and Gwyther, Unveiling Empire, 117. See also deSilva, Seeing Things John's Way, 33–34.

ers in their "tribulations" (1:9, συγκοινωνὸς ἐν τῇ θλίψει). Therefore, "John's willingness to trade his privileged social location in Roman society for life among the struggling *ekklēsiai* represents John's 'coming out' of the 'great city Babylon.'"[92] Revelation calls all, especially the wealthy and self-satisfied, to forsake associations with empire and to take a position of solidarity with its victims by suffering the consequences of such a refusal to associate with empire. To read Revelation from this perspective may be discomforting for those of us who read it "from above." Yet a book that claims to be an "unveiling" may function to unveil our own commitments. As Maier reminds us, "To read *Revelation* in the contemporary first-world comfort of the middle class . . . is to risk coming away with the sinking sense that one is a Laodicean."[93]

BIBLIOGRAPHY

Aune, David E. "The Influence of Roman Imperial Court Ceremonial on the Apocalpyse of John." *Biblical Research* 28 (1983) 5–26.

———. *Revelation 17–22.* WBC. Nashville: Thomas Nelson, 1998.

Bauckham, Richard J. *The Climax of Prophecy: Studies in the Book of Revelation.* Edinburgh: T. & T. Clark, 1993.

———. *The Theology of the Book of Revelation.* Cambridge: Cambridge University Press, 1993.

Beale, Gregory K. *The Book of Revelation.* NIGTC. Grand Rapids: Eerdmans, 1999.

Blount, Brian K. *Revelation.* NTL. Louisville, KY: Westminster John Knox, 2009.

Boesak, Allan A. *Comfort and Protest: The Apocalypse from a South African Perspective.* Philadelphia: Westminster John Knox, 1987.

Boxall, Ian. *The Revelation of Saint John.* Black's New Testament Commentary. Peabody, MA: Hendrickson, 2006.

Collins, Adela Yarbro. "Revelation 18: Taunt Song or Dirge?" In *L'Apocalyptique johannique et l'apocalyptique dans le Nouveau Testament,* edited by J. Lambrecht, 185–204. BETL 53. Gembloux: Duculot/Leuven University Press, 1980.

Court, John M. *Myth and History in the Book of Revelation.* Atlanta: John Knox, 1979.

deSilva, David A. *Seeing Things John's Way: The Rhetoric of the Book of Revelation.* Louisville, KY: Westminster John Knox, 2009.

Deutsch, Celia. "Transformation of Symbols: The New Jerusalem in Rv 21.1—22.5." *ZNW* 78 (1987) 106–26.

Duff, Paul B. *Who Rides the Beast: Prophetic Rivalry and the Rhetoric of Crisis in the Churches of the Apocalypse.* Oxford: Oxford University Press, 2001.

Fekkes, Jan. *Isaiah and Prophetic Traditions in the Book of Revelation: Visionary Antecedents and Their Development.* JSNTSSup 93. Sheffield: Sheffield Academic, 1994.

Giesen, Heinz. *Studien zur Johannesapokalypse.* Stuttgart: Katholisches Bibelwerk, 2000.

92. Howard-Brook and Gwyther, *Unveiling Empire,* xxvii.

93. Maier, "Coming Out of Babylon," 78.

Gill, Emily L. "Revelation and Rome: A War of Thrones: Roman Imperial Ceremonial in John's Heavenly Throne Room Vision." Unpublished MA thesis, Denver Seminary, 2012.

González, Justo L. "Revelation: Clarity and Ambivalence: A Hispanic/Cuban American Perspective." In *From Every People and Nation: The Book of Revelation in Intercultural Perspective*, edited by David Rhoads, 47–61. Minneapolis: Fortress, 2005.

Goodfriend, Elaine. "Prostitute." In *ABD* 5:505–10.

Hauck, F., and S. Schultz. "πόρνη κτλ." In *TDNT* 6:579–95.

Howard-Brook, Wes, and Anthony Gwyther. *Unveiling Empire: Reading Revelation Then and Now.* New York: Orbis, 2000.

Kraybill, J. Nelson. *Imperial Cult and Commerce in John's Apocalypse.* JSNTSSup 132. Sheffield: Sheffield Academic, 1996.

Kuhn, K. "Βαβυλών." In *TDNT* 1:514–17.

Maier, Harry O. "Coming Out of Babylon: A First-World Reading of Revelation among Immigrants." In *From Every People and Nation: Reading Revelation in Intercultural Perspective*, edited by David Rhoads, 62–81. Minneapolis: Fortress, 2005.

Malina, Bruce J., and John J. Pilch. *Socio-Science Commentary on the Book of Revelation.* Minneapolis, Fortress, 2000.

Martin, Clarice J. "Polishing the Unclouded Mirror: A Womanist Reading of Revelation 18:13." In *From Every People and Nation: The Book of Revelation in Intercultural Perspective*, edited by David Rhoads, 82–109. Minneapolis: Fortress, 2005.

Mathewson, David. *A New Heaven and a New Earth: The Meaning and Function of the Old Testament in Revelation 21.1—22.5.* JSNTSSup 238. Sheffield: Sheffield Academic, 2003.

Mounce, Robert H. *The Book of Revelation.* NICNT. Grand Rapids: Eerdmans, 1977.

Osborne, Grant R. *Revelation.* BECNT. Grand Rapids: Baker, 2002.

Provan, Ian. "Foul Spirits, Fornication and Finance: Revelation 18 from an Old Testament Perspective." *JSNT* 64 (1996) 81–100.

Rhoads, David, ed. *From Every People and Nation: Reading Revelation in Intercultural Perspective.* Minneapolis: Fortress, 2005.

Richard, Pablo. *Apocalpyse: A People's Commentary on the Book of Revelation.* Marknoll, NY: Orbis, 1995.

Rossing, Barbara R. *The Choice between Two Cities: Whore, Bride and Empire in the Apocalypse.* Harrisburg, PA: Trinity, 1999.

Royalty, Robert M., Jr. *The Streets of Heaven: The Ideology of Wealth in the Apocalypse of John.* Macon, GA: Mercer University Press, 1998.

Ruiz, Jean-Pierre. "Taking a Stand on the Sand of the Seashore: A Postcolonial Exploration of Revelation 13." In *Reading the Book of Revelation*, edited by David L. Barr, 119–35. Atlanta: SBL, 2003.

Schüssler Fiorenza, Elisabeth. *Revelation: Vision of a Just World.* Minneapolis: Fortress, 1991.

Siitonen, Kirsi. "Merchants and Commerce in the Book of Revelation." In *Imagery in the Book of Revlation*, edited by Michael Labahn and Outi Lehtipuu, 145–60. Leuven: Peters, 2011.

Smalley, Stephen S. *The Revelation to John: A Commentary on the Greek Text of the Apocalypse.* Downers Grove, IL: InterVarsity, 2005.

Smith, Christopher R. "Reclaiming the Social Justice Message of Revelation: Materialism, Imperialism and Divine Judgment in Revelation 18." *Transformation* 7, no. 4 (1990) 28–33.

Thompson, Leonard. *Revelation.* Nashville: Abingdon, 1998.

———. "A Sociological Analysis of Tribulation in the Apocalypse of John." *Semeia* 36 (1986) 147–74.

Witherington, Ben, III. *Revelation.* Cambridge: Cambridge University Press, 2003.

Index of Authors

Index of Authors

Dempsey, Carol J., 68
deSilva, David A., 169, 185, 186, 188, 189, 193, 194
Deutsch, Celia, 190
Dever, William G., 66
Domeris, William Robert, 66
Donaldson, Laura, 158
Dorsey, D. A., 67
Drewes, Barend F., 59
Duff, Paul B., 176, 177
Dunn, James D. G., 112
Dyer, Bryan R., xx, xxi, 161, 169

Eckstein, Hans-Joachim, 94
Eichler, Barry Lee, 15
Eissfeldt, O., 97
Ellacuría, Ignacio, 65
Elliott, John H., 155, 157, 161
Eph'al, Israel, 68
Estes, Daniel J., 51–52,
Evans, Craig A., xx, 91, 102, 108, 113
Evans, Paul S., xviii
Eyben, Emiel, 129

Fant, Maureen B., 128
Fekkes, Jan, 185
Fendler, Marlene, 67
Fensham, F. Charles, 4, 68
Finkelstein, J. J., 4
Finley, M. I., 127
Fitzmyer, Joseph A., 103, 106, 108, 109, 114, 115
Fleischer, Gunther, 67
France, R. T., 93
Fredericks, Daniel C., 51, 52,
Fretheim, Terence E., 5, 69, 70, 79, 105

Garland, David E., 43, 47
Garlington, Don, 94
Garrett, Duane A., 46
Geyser, A. S., 168
Giesen, Heinz, 184
Gill, Emily L., 180
Girard, René, 56
Goldingay, John, 5, 6, 8, 9, 24, 28–31
González, Justo L., 189
Goodfriend, Elaine, 185
Goppelt, Leonhard, 161

Gowan, Donald E., 105, 106
Grassi, Joseph A., 91, 153, 162
Green, Joel B., 106, 107, 109, 110, 114, 117, 119
Greenberg, Moshe, 9, 14, 57
Greengus, Samuel, 5, 6, 7, 8
Gushee, David O., 80, 113
Gutiérrez, Gustavo, 59–60, 65
Gwyther, Anthony, 178, 182, 183–85, 188, 190, 191, 194, 195

Haas, Peter J., 7
Habel, Norman C., 54, 55, 57
Hagner, Donald A., 91, 97
Hamborg, Graham R., 72
Hanson, Paul D., 9, 23
Harrill, J. Albert, 129, 139
Harris, Murray J., 129, 134
Hatton, Peter T. H., 41–42
Hauk, F., 185
Havice, Harriet Katherine, 4
Hayek, F. A., 137
Hayes, E. R., 86
Hays, Christopher M., 102, 110
Hays, J. Daniel, 104, 105, 115
Heschel, Abraham, 69, 70
Holmes, J. M., 137, 138
Houston, Walter J., 36–38, 48, 49, 53, 54, 58, 59, 66, 71, 72
Howard-Brook, Wes, 178, 182, 183–85, 188, 190, 191, 194, 195
Hume, Douglas A., 118
Huwiler, Elizabeth, 38, 40, 42, 47, 49

Jackson-McCabe, Matt, 152
Jackson, B. S., 86
Jaramillo Rivas, Pedro, 78
Johnson, B., 77
Johnson, Luke Timothy, 102, 106, 118, 119

Kampen, J., 91
Keener, Craig S., 120
Kim, Kyoung-Jin, 102
Knight, Douglas A., 66
Koestenberger, Andreas J., 137
Koet, Bart J., 108
Koptak, Paul E., 40

Index of Authors

Index of Authors

Index of Ancient Documents

CPSIA information can be obtained
at www.ICGtesting.com
Printed in the USA
LVHW021727090323
741285LV00001B/121